WONDER
is My Compass

is My Compass

Preparing your child to
navigate a science-rich future

JAYME M. CELLITIOCI

ISBN 978-0-9997459-0-8

Visit jaymecellitioci.com

Edited by
Paul Reali
Julia Figliotti
Diana Rangaves
Jay Blackstone
Joelle B. Burnette

Cover and interior design by
Joelle B. Burnette

Illustrations by
Reed Cellitioci

Author photos by
Emily Payne

This book is dedicated to Reed
who inspires me to use
Wonder as My Compass
every single day

Contents

Foreword by Dr. Richard Pyle

WE WERE THIRTEEN minutes into our thirteenth dive nearly four hundred feet deep off Sodwana Bay, South Africa, and we were once again going to come up empty. I could have blamed our bad luck on the number thirteen, but as a scientist, I knew not to succumb to such superstitions. Besides, our luck on the previous twelve dives along the exact same rocky ledge had been equally bad. And the thirteen-minute marker had been pre-determined at the start of our expedition as the maximum time we should spend on the bottom. When diving to such depths, well beyond the limits of normal scuba (self-contained underwater breathing apparatus), every minute we spend on the bottom comes with a time penalty that must be paid while making our way back to the surface. In this case, thirteen minutes on the bottom would require us to spend nearly two and a half hours slowly ascending back to the surface. If we skipped this required decompression time, we would experience decompression sickness, or the "bends," leaving us paralyzed or worse. Our special computer-controlled, mixed-gas rebreathers allow us to make much longer dives (eight hours or more), but at this particular spot off Sodwana Bay, the currents would have pushed us out into treacherous water if we extended our decompression any longer than two and a half hours. Thus, thirteen minutes is all we allowed ourselves on the bottom.

Having reached the thirteen-minute mark on that thirteenth dive, I reluctantly turned to my diving partner Rob and signaled that we should start heading up, and he signaled back that he agreed. I glanced down the slope and could see bubbles coming from over the edge of the drop-off below. Our guide, Peter, and the National Geographic cameraman who was there to film us, Dan, were still below us, out of sight over the edge of the drop-off. It was comforting to see the bubbles confirming they were OK. No doubt they would come up to join us in a moment, and we would all begin our long ascent towards the surface, for the thirteenth time. While I waited, I used my underwater camera to capture video of some interesting fish that were swimming about nearby. After glancing at my computer and seeing we were now well into minute fifteen, I turned to point down-slope where I had seen the bubbles just a moment before. But the bubbles were gone, and there was no sign of Peter or Dan. Uh oh.

In an instant, Rob and I considered the situation, and we both reluctantly came to the same inevitable conclusion: *something was wrong.* Instinctively, we both swam towards the edge of the drop-off where we had last seen Peter and Dan, filled with dread that we would find two unconscious divers on the bottom. There is very little margin for error when conducting dives four hundred feet below the surface. Although we dive as a team to support each other in any way we can, there are a thousand things that can go wrong, and most of them can go wrong *badly.* The options for rescuing an unconscious diver from these depths are exceedingly narrow; effectively none. A far more likely outcome is that the rescuer and the victim both suffer the same fate. Swimming as quickly as we could to look over the edge of the drop-off, the feeling of dread increased dramatically. I began wondering exactly what I would do, and how—and if—I could avoid the same fate.

By the time I reached the edge of the drop-off and looked down, my heart was racing. However, instead of seeing two unconscious divers, I saw two divers who were very-much-alive and apparently well. Even though we were now more than fifteen minutes into a planned thirteen-minute dive, they showed no signs at all that they were coming up. Instead, they had their lights and cameras trained on something large that was right in front of them. As my mind reeled to understand what was happening, I suddenly saw it! At that moment of realization, all concerns about our extended bottom time (and the associated decompression penalty we would need to pay) vanished, along with any concerns about the fate of our diving companions. My heart continued to race, not from fear, but rather from sheer excitement! In my decades of exploring coral reefs around the world, this was unambiguously the most thrilling, glorious, and indescribably joyous moment of my life. We had finally found what we had spent thirteen deep dives looking for: a *living Coelacanth*!

What is a Coelacanth? Why would four highly-trained divers risk their lives thirteen times in a row just to see one? Why would National Geographic fund an entire expedition to South Africa just to capture it on video? And while we're at it, what is a rebreather, anyway? How does it work, and why does it allow divers to go much deeper than normal scuba divers can go? Why were we breathing helium? Why do divers need to spend two and a half hours ascending from a dive lasting only thirteen minutes, and how is that time calculated? Why were we so willing to extend the time on the bottom beyond the pre-determined thirteen minutes? The answers to all of these questions — and many, many, many more — rely on a foundation of skills in Science, Technology, Engineering, the Arts, and Mathematics (STEAM).

As a marine biologist, I've always been fascinated by the incredible diversity of things that live in the ocean. My fascination for fishes goes back to my earliest childhood memories. The Coelacanth is essentially the "Holy Grail" of all fishes. What makes it special is that it was thought to have gone extinct even before the dinosaurs, about seventy million years ago, until a live one was captured off South Africa in the 1930s. At the time, it had only been known from fossil specimens, which revealed special limb-like fins that scientists believe were the beginnings of what eventually became limbs for the first land-based vertebrates. Indeed, Coelacanths are actually classified along with tetrapods and other terrestrial vertebrates, rather than fishes. Encountering this elusive "living fossil" in its natural habitat is about as amazing as encountering a living dinosaur in some remote jungle. Indeed, fewer than twenty people have had the privilege. The confirmation that it was not actually extinct is still regarded as one of the most amazing scientific discoveries of the twentieth century.

Although my passion for biology and knowledge of the evolutionary significance of Coelacanths played an important role leading up to my amazing encounter four hundred feet deep off South Africa, that passion was only part of what led me there. The rest required a robust understanding of the laws of physics and human physiology, skills in developing and designing new technologies through clever engineering, and a level of complex problem-solving that can only be accomplished through artful originality and creativity.

My journey through all of these disciplines began when I was a nineteen-year-old college drop-out living in Palau. One beautiful sunny summer day, I allowed my enthusiasm for finding fishes to exceed my experience as a diver, and I ended up paralyzed from a bad case of the bends. During the year-long recovery from that incident, I committed myself to understanding the science — including physics and physiology — behind decompression sickness, and how to avoid it. I learned about Boyle's Law, Dalton's Law, Henry's Law, and the myriad physiological processes associated with decompression. I learned how pressure increases with depth, how gas molecules dissolve into my blood and tissues when diving deep, and why it takes time for those gas molecules to dissolve back out of my body during decompression. I learned the math behind how those decompression schedules are calculated, and how using helium in the breathing mixture can extend the depth to which I could safely descend. In short, through a better understanding of scientific disciplines well outside my own particular interests, I was able to understand what caused my diving malady, and more importantly, how to avoid it in the future.

Armed with this new knowledge, I spent the next several decades focused on developing the technology to allow me to dive down into the *Twilight Zone* of coral reefs, the mysterious and uncharted realm below where divers using conventional scuba can safely descend. At first, this involved taking existing scuba technology and modifying it to allow deeper diving. But soon I turned my attention to a different kind of technology: closed-circuit rebreathers. Unlike normal scuba, rebreathers recirculate the diver's breath, allowing the diver to "re-breathe" the same gas over and over. Our bodies extract oxygen from our inhaled breaths, and we exhale carbon dioxide (the by-product of metabolism). The rebreather's job is to remove the exhaled carbon dioxide and restore the missing oxygen so that the gas can be breathed again. Without wasting gas in the form of exhaled bubbles as scuba divers do, rebreathers are much more efficient, especially for deep dives. Although they are simple in concept, rebreathers are actually very difficult to design, because both the chemical process of removing carbon dioxide and the electronic sensors used to monitor oxygen do not function well in the presence of water. Even if we diligently ensure no outside water gets into the rebreather, we still must contend with the water that condenses out of our exhaled breaths. When I first started learning about rebreathers, most of the available models were extremely expensive and inherently unreliable. And so began my immersion into the world of engineering.

For the past twenty-five years, I have been helping to design and develop newer and more sophisticated versions of the rebreather technology I need to continue my passion for exploring deep coral reefs. I've learned how to use CAD (computer-aided design) software. I've learned how to calculate tolerances for different materials, and why some materials are better than others for certain tasks. I've also learned how much of engineering is actually more art than science. The real breakthroughs in design that we've come up with in developing some of the world's most sophisticated life-support technology certainly required an understanding of science, technology, engineering, and math, but none of these breakthroughs would have been possible without the raw creativity needed to see old problems in a new and fresh way. In fact, by far the most challenging obstacles we need to overcome — from ensuring oxygen sensors are accurate in real time, to developing optimal emergency techniques in case our equipment fails during a deep dive, to capturing images of specimens both on the reef and after we've collected them — all involve an aesthetic sense that cannot emerge from pure objective thinking alone.

My thirty years working at Bishop Museum have shown me that science, technology, engineering, the arts, and mathematics are all interconnected in ways that yield a whole that is far, far greater than the mere sum of its parts. Indeed, the "art" of what we do, including preserving specimens in a way that will allow them to exist for centuries, capturing their likeness through imagery that goes beyond simple photographs, and perhaps most importantly, telling stories about the natural world through documentary films, presentations, and one-on-one conversations, is in many ways more important than the science. This is what inspires people to encourage or change their ways of thinking, and allows the fruits of STEAM to escape the confines of academia and have a meaningful impact on the world.

When I first began my journey expanding the breadth of my science and technical skills, I never would have imagined where it would lead me. Perhaps what has surprised me the most is not how powerful these skills can be, nor what you can accomplish by exercising them effectively, but really how *fun* and *exciting* it is to learn new things through the educational process.

Trying to understand the subtleties of an entirely new discipline — whether that is physics, physiology, technology, and engineering for a "fish nerd," or *any* aspect of STEM for someone who does not consider him- or herself to be a scientist — can seem intimidating at first. But the truth is that it's remarkably easy. You don't need to be especially smart, or even "get" the underlying principles or complex details of any particular topic. You really need to have *curiosity* and a *sense of wonder*. Everything else flows naturally from there!

It's helpful to understand that nothing — and I mean *NOTHING* — is as satisfying and life-fulfilling as figuring out a solution to a problem that seemed at first to be insurmountable. And nothing has been as thrilling to me as a parent as watching my two children discover this for themselves. No matter how frustrated they get trying to understand how to solve a homework problem, their momentary frustration is always more than offset by the deep satisfaction they experience in figuring it out. And the best part of all for *me* is how often I learn from *their* experience. More than half the time my son comes to me with a question on his high-school physics homework, I have no idea what the answer is. Rather than making me feel uneasy, these are actually my *favorite* moments, because that's when the adventure begins. My son and I challenge each other to dissect the problem, reduce it to the basic components, and use what knowledge we do have to figure out how to fill in the blanks that we're missing. It becomes a game. Sketches are drawn, and ideas are proposed, evaluated, and either accepted or rejected. The outcome of this game is always the same: we both win.

Having strong skills in science and other subjects is about so much more than scoring high on tests or getting accepted to college. STEAM underpins every aspect of innovation, discovery, and important advancement of humanity. Without this suite of knowledge and skills, there would be no civilization. Given the immense challenges facing the future of our species, our best and only hope for long-term survival will come through ensuring our children for generations to come continue to embrace the cultivation of a STEAM mindset. Besides saving the world, an appreciation for these subjects allows us to experience wonderful adventures — regardless of whether it's discovering the rich biodiversity of your own backyard, making slime on a rainy day, or swimming with Coelacanths!

Through this book, Jayme Cellitioci has masterfully outlined how anyone, regardless of their own experience or comfort level with science (and its counterparts), can have a profoundly important impact in helping children understand and embrace its exciting possibilities. Science and exploration are a lot more accessible than most people realize, and the thrill of discovery can be every bit as exhilarating when it involves figuring out what things magnets will stick to in your own home as it is when searching for a new species of fish hundreds of feet below the surface of the ocean. The important thing to understand, which Jayme explains through hundreds of real-world, everyday examples, is that we are surrounded by countless opportunities to show our children how science, technology, engineering, and mathematics surround everything we do and can be explored with fun and excitement outside the confines of a classroom. And the Arts can play a key role in this exploration.

I will never forget those few minutes I spent swimming alongside my distant cousin (four hundred million years removed) on a reef four hundred feet deep off South Africa. Even though our dive team had gone well beyond our planned thirteen-minute limit bottom time on that dive, I was confident that the technology I helped to develop would allow me to complete my decompression. Using my math skills, I was able to determine roughly how much extra decompression time I would incur from the extended dive time, and thereby calculate that the currents would cause us to drift close to, but not far into, the treacherous waters. I marveled at the beauty of this ancient fish, as I reached out to gently stroke the rough scales along its tail. I will always cherish that moment, perhaps the most amazing of my life, which would not have happened without having applied the twenty-first-century skills of creativity, innovation, and STEAM!

Richard L. Pyle, PhD
Bishop Museum, Ichthyology

Preface

"I'M BAD AT SCIENCE."

As a science program designer, I have listened to thousands of parents state these words, offering convincing evidence to make their case. As we start to unpack the statement and replace memories of failed lab tests with new and supportive science experiences, change happens.

Whether you're a scientist by profession or you have not considered the "subject" since high school, any parent can become a successful facilitator of science learning for their child. No disclaimers. I have watched it happen time and again, and I've helped to make it a reality for many parents.

After spending my entire career in the informal science arena — closely following learning and education research, designing exhibits and programs, engaging in strategic planning and execution, and meeting hundreds of scientists, engineers, astronomers, inventors, and innovators — I realized I had a rich well of behind-the-scenes insights that could give parents shortcuts to facilitating their child's science learning.

As I began writing, I also became acutely aware that parents deserve to hear more than just my vantage point on this topic. I asked friends and colleagues from diverse backgrounds to share their perspectives on accessing and learning science. You will meet them throughout this book. Listen to their wisdom.

The internet, bookstores, and library shelves are loaded with resources for science activities and experiments. What I found to be missing, however, was the *why*, and the stories about *how* parents could organically engage with science. *Wonder is My Compass* was written to fill this gap. While you will find some examples of specific science-based activities in here, the words in this book are primarily intended to support you in cultivating a science-learning mindset.

I look forward to embarking on this expedition with you and helping you chart your family's course for science learning.

Now, let's get wondering—

—JC

Acknowledgements

In Gratitude To

~

MY HUSBAND
who is deeply committed to helping
us chase our wonder
(and often gets the equipment
to our next coordinates)

MY PARENTS, CHERYL, SOPHIA, AND FAMILY
who support our adventures and
provide a safe harbor upon return

MY FRIENDS
who inspire me to wonder deeper and further,
often for the sake of our children's future

MY COLLEAGUES
who have taught me how to make a
profession out of wondering
and contributed their expertise to
Wonder is My Compass

Introduction

I have dug up ten-thousand-year-old mastodon bones, felt the breath of ninety-thousand-pound humpback whales swimming alongside me, explored Mediterranean Sea caves in search of monk seals, and am listed as a co-inventor on a patent. However, no science-based venture has brought me deeper joy than that of being a mother.

In addition to a parent's many roles — nurse, dishwasher, taxi driver, and human napkin — the most treasured, self-appointed title on my parental résumé is *Chief of Science Learning*.

Since you're reading this book, I will assume you have a child or children in your life that you know would profoundly benefit — throughout the entire course of their lifetime — from having a positive and dynamic relationship with science. I know it can be challenging to figure out how to go about building this relationship. Fortunately for you, I have spent more than twenty years gleaning insights on doing just that, and I cannot wait to share them with you. (Along the way, we'll have more fun than a gecko on a merry-go-round wheel with bug-flavored cotton candy...or insert your own metaphor here.)

AWE-COLORED GLASSES

LET'S START WITH the facts. As parents, we want to help our children build the skills they need to be successful. We provide opportunities and give them access to experiences we think will build these skills. We sign them up for sports, dance, and music and drive them around to all of their practices, games, rehearsals, and lessons — all in the name of developing their current and future selves. Yet to be successful in the twenty-first century, our children will also need to be science literate, and we as parents should be equipping them with *science* practice, exposure, and experiences. In order to be thriving and independent adults, engaged community members, and productive global citizens, our children will need science skills and science process knowledge.

This is easier than you might think. By organically weaving science learning into everyday family life, we can give our children the tools to explore, design, and build their dreams, and shape their own (and potentially others') realities.

Every child deserves the advantage of looking at life through awe-colored glasses and finding answers that explode into a thousand more questions. They deserve to develop an innate sense of wonder that carries into adulthood, and maybe even inspires them to be a significant agent of change in the future. With this book, you can help make that happen.

There is no perfect path for enriched science learning; each person's journey is unique. There is, however, a perfect time to begin and that time is now.

Showing Up

RESEARCH SHOWS THAT children learn from the simple acts of observing and participating in the everyday things that people are doing around them. This is the incredible power of subtlety. Ready for the real irony? This means our unconscious actions and behaviors are much more likely to shape and affect the way children think than any prescribed activity that we might consciously implement. This research is based on the work of Dr. Alison Gopnik, developmental cognitive psychologist and professor at the University of California at Berkeley, who highlights the fact that parenting is not a job—it's a relationship.[1]

A good question, then, is why—knowing this—would I write an entire book about ways to consciously weave science into your family's everyday life? The answer is simple: I want to help you actively practice playing with science until it becomes second nature. In many ways, I want to raise your *un*consciousness.

Now let's get started. The first step in accomplishing this mission is to reflect on and consider your own thoughts, attitudes, and behaviors around science. Once you have made these considerations, you can then begin to work on breaking down any science-related barriers (such as feeling like you're not *good* at it), so that you may have more organic access to it.

Bringing science into your everyday family life should not be another item on your already-too-long "To Do" list, or a benchmark to make you stress about what you are or are not doing, or have or have not done. There are plenty of other sources that already exist for those kinds of stresses. Take sage advice from Dr. Gopnik: children learn much more from everyday interactions than from items on progress checklists. So give your pencil a short break. If it has never crossed your mind to consider what role science plays in your family life, here's your paid-in-full pass to start wondering (in a relaxed, non-checklist manner, that is). This includes a complimentary behind-the-scenes admission ticket to imagine what that role might be. No tricks, no gimmicks, no prior research required– I'm simply asking you to show up with an open mind and be you.

YOUR RELATIONSHIP WITH SCIENCE

SCIENCE, FOR MANY people, is a subject they took in school: a class filled with models, detailed diagrams, strange combinations of numbers and letters, and sometimes slimy things. The term "science" may trigger fond remembrances of an amusing lab partner, the eruption of a baking soda and vinegar volcano, or designing a sturdy toothpick bridge. Or it may bring up memories of failed tests, boring lectures, and out-of-reach concepts. Science is an area of beloved passion for some and of intimidation or disinterest for others.

Regardless of your existing emotions around science (and whether they arise from formal education experiences in the classroom, or informal ventures investigating bugs under rocks or tinkering with tools in a garage), science is inevitably a part of every moment, step, breath, and glance in this world.

While your prior science experiences have likely informed your current relationship with it, they do not have to define your future relationship. Many people who excelled in science class in high school no longer have an explicit relationship with science. On the flip side, there are people who failed all of their lab quizzes who now orient their lives around science.

Your relationship with science, from this point forward, is completely up to you. The degree to which you make science a more central part of your career path, personal pursuits, and parenting style is your decision entirely.

Regardless of your chosen life path (career or otherwise), you have taken on the ultimate job of a lifetime — parenting. As a parent, you are your child's first and most influential teacher. Perhaps more accurately, you are their most important *facilitator of learning*—for science and beyond. And you deserve to know one key point of data: *you are fully capable of doing this job.* (I don't even have to know you to promise you this is true.) If this excites you, read on. If it scares the living daylights out of you, *please* read on.

My promise to you is by the end of this book, you will identify and discover a million ways of embracing this mission—or at least fifty more than you had last month.

BUILT-IN SMILES

I LOVE SCIENCE. I fill my days with science. I earn most of my paycheck from science. There are certain science-based topic areas in which I feel very proficient, while other areas make me want to reach for a second-grade textbook. And this is OK. I have grown to be extremely comfortable with the art of not knowing. (I have also found de-shaming the art of not knowing, particularly as it relates to science, to be one of my favorite hobbies.)

Engaging with science feels a lot like scuba diving to me. When I'm underwater in full gear, listening to the soothing sound of my regulator, I often have three distinct thoughts: (1) I wish that I had read my dive instruction manual more thoroughly, (2) I can't believe I get to see this "secret" part of the world, and (3) I feel oddly more comfortable here than on land.

Marine life has been my draw into the world of science. The built-in smiles of dolphins were admittedly my initial hook (ah, the low-hanging fruit of marine magnetism), but they led me down a beautiful path to explore other glorious aspects of the natural, physical, and social sciences.

Your entry points, or your child's, may be different, but the doorways are there waiting for you just down the hall.

My Science Background

LIKE GEORGE COSTANZA in a memorable episode of *Seinfeld*, the dream of becoming a marine biologist has crossed many people's minds. It certainly crossed mine; I could not have imagined considering any other career throughout my K–12 schooling. Any time grade-school lessons focused on fish, dolphins, or whales, it was common for my peers to glance my way. In eighth grade, I entered an oratorical contest and focused my speech on saving the whales.

I attended an urban vocational high school and had the pleasure of studying the atypical trade of aquatic ecology. We wore hip waders and went into creeks, seining for sticklebacks and other small fish, then returned to the lab and set up aquariums. I found ways to earn extra credit by focusing on a range of conservation efforts, including volunteering at a deer check station and at the local aquarium.

As high school came to an end, a "Semester at Sea" brochure I picked up in the guidance counselor's office led me to apply to only one university: Long Island University at Southampton. Luckily, with no plan B, I was accepted. This school would serve as a vessel for pursuing my passion for marine life.

Fast forward to the end of my freshman year of college. I distinctly remember sitting in my genetics professor's office, pleading with him to allow me to do extra credit to compensate for my undesirable exam score. I was concerned I would lose my honors scholarship if I didn't maintain a certain GPA. He looked at me and asked, "Are you sure you're not more of a *social* scientist?" *Er, um, well...No,* I remember thinking, *I'm not sure.*

He was onto something. I was pulling As in all of my social science classes, and my passion for the natural sciences wasn't reflecting in my grades. But marine science was my destiny, I was certain. All of those Cousteau Society letters I had saved (in my grade-school Trapper Keeper with a bear riding on a dolphin) proved it. Much to my dismay, however, two full semesters of a marine science major had rolled by, and we had not once spoken about (much less *to*) dolphins and whales. In addition, I was drowning in my calculus lessons and my chemistry labs, and it became clear that I was destined for another major.

I switched over to psychobiology, a field that integrates psychology and biology. Despite the temporary notion that I was surrendering my destiny, it ultimately ended up being the perfect major for me. At the time, however, I felt that by making this transition, I was casting myself onto the Island of Misfit Marine Toys. I pictured myself lying at the bottom of a marina dumpster alongside other whale huggers, covered in blubber and barnacles, crying that we just couldn't hack biochemistry.

In reality, the field of psychobiology allowed me to dive into wonder-inspiring areas of study, such as sensory perception, behavior and learning, and marine mammal cognition. And because I believe that no one should ever slam their dolphin-covered Trapper

Keeper shut, I focused every independent study, research project of choice, volunteer and internship opportunity, and cooperative learning experience on marine mammals.

I delved into the fascinating space where biology and psychology overlap, and I eventually found a specific area of eternal interest: the field of creativity. The place where science and creativity overlap is my professional playground. I am happy to report that this playground is a far cry from the dumpster and barnacles image I had initially conjured up.

FALLING IN LOVE WITH SCIENCE

SCIENCE HAS BEEN an integral part of my career path, my personal life, my parenting, and my identity. I am grateful that I have found ways of accessing and integrating this subject, one that had seemed out of reach to me at times, into my work and daily life.

When I think back to my earliest memories of falling in love with science, it was not a graphic of the water cycle or the order of the planets that hooked me. It was tasting salty ocean water on my lips, being mesmerized by the Foucault pendulum at my childhood science museum, and putting together my first circuit.

Science is meant to be touched, listened to, tasted (*careful on this one*), and explored. It is meant to take us to the farthest reaches of the universe and to the deepest trenches of the sea. If we are not in awe of its presence, we likely have not opened the door and invited it in from the porch.

It is important to note that there are probably thousands of pathways into science. You may have some of your own trails that you can retrace, or you may feel that you are just beginning to forge your way by picking up this book. As I've mentioned, your path, and your family's path, will look different than mine and ours. I'm being explicit about ours so you can identify future possibilities for your family and be familiar with some of the mile markers along the way.

Whether you make science learning a major focus of your family time, engage in a few more science-themed activities and outings, or observe an elevator pulley two seconds longer than you would have prior to reading this book, my goals will have been met. (More specifically, if *your* goals have been met, mine have been, too.)

In a nutshell, be sure that you don't set yourself up to feel the way I do when I find a great recipe on Pinterest and then end up making *mookies* (accidental muffin-like cookies). If you saw my back-to-school rainforest platter made out of bananas, apples, and clementines (which was screaming to be slashed and burned), you would see that I am out here in parent-land flailing alongside you. I recognize that it's sometimes easier to focus on our shortcomings, gaps, and failures than it is to acknowledge and build upon our successes, but take a minute to focus on what you are doing well. And as you know, there is no "doing it right" in parenting.

And since there is no one "right way," social psychologist and author Brené Brown states that parents' focus should simply be on whether or not they're engaged and paying attention.[2] So steer clear of the shame game and look at your parenting glass of H_2O *(see, you know chemistry!)* as being at least half full here.

Remember, the journey we are taking together is about you and your family deepening your relationship with the world around you, and at the same time, deepening your relationships with each other. It is about celebrating the billions of opportunities to recognize and weave science into your daily lives. It is simply about *being engaged* and *paying attention.*

"SCIENCE" AND STEAM

TO HELP FOCUS on the human aspect of this journey, I default to the word "science" throughout the book, instead of calling out specific aspects of STEM (Science, Technology, Engineering, and Mathematics), STEAM (A for the Arts), or STEM+C (Computer Science). I acknowledge that each of these letters and acronyms (of which there are many more) has its own unique story, but have chosen to generalize since most of the learning and engagement tips offered in this resource apply across the board.

Many STEM educators and professionals will readily tell you that they naturally include the Arts in their assumptions and discussions around STEM. It is widely recognized that the Arts are not just a nicety to put sprinkles on top of a substantive grasp of hard science; they're critical to scientific innovation. Whether it's having visual models of data that are both user-friendly and aesthetically appealing, highly functional technological innovations, or sleeker biomedical devices, the world benefits from our recognition of the integration of STEM and the Arts (STEAM).

The good news is that this "integration" does not necessarily require extra effort on our part. We have spent centuries dividing and organizing the world into categories and silos that make learning more manageable. As we try to weave these categories back together in order to educate children in a holistic manner, we often discover that it is as simple as looking at topics in the context of real life. And in real life, all subjects are integrated.

"Your Child"

I HAVE MADE a similar leap as with "science" in referring to "your child" even though you may have two or more children, or simply have children in your life. Each child is his or her own unique learner, which is reflected in the singular approach to addressing these stories, points, and tips.

The Mouths of Babes

QUICK—THINK of a scientist who is renowned for their sense of wonder! The chances are high that Albert Einstein crossed your mind. Over the years, we have studied and analyzed his life in great detail. (In addition, I am happy to report, we are making progress in telling the science stories of individuals who have historically been underrepresented.)

At the age of two, Einstein asked his parents where his newborn baby sister's wheels were.[3] When I learned this tidbit, it deeply resonated with me. I have been jotting down many of the curious statements and questions that have come from my son (between the ages of two and seven-and-a-half) as he has been putting the puzzle pieces of life together. I am overjoyed to share many of them with you throughout this book.

When Einstein was five years old and sick in bed, his father brought him a compass.[4] He was highly intrigued by the workings of this device, particularly with the way the needle pointed in one direction no matter how he turned it (even in the dark). Einstein later spoke about the deep and abiding impression the compass made on him.

One of the reasons I love working with children in the area of science is that I know that one program, one object, or one moment can be the seed of a lifelong career interest—an interest that might have profound implications for people and the planet. I have seen living evidence that this is more than just a cliché sentiment.

While that seed needs sustained watering and sunlight to grow, it must first simply be planted to even stand a chance at eventually flowering.

I promise you that the greatest gifts you will offer are your own personal approach and mindset, your openness to exploring science with them, and your willingness to meet your child where they are. (The second-best gifts will probably come from your recycle bin, but more on that later.)

CHARTING YOUR COURSE

"TALKING STORY" IS the Hawaiian Pidgin (Hawaiian Creole English) term for chatting or conversation. I look forward to talking story with you throughout this book, as I share some of the people, places, and experiences that have shaped my relationship with science.

Consider these stories to be breadcrumbs for following a lifelong love for science learning. Use them as provocations for thinking about the types of experiences that you want to cultivate for yourself and your child.

My stories only matter as much as they support you in charting your family's course for science learning. Use the "Chart Your Course" prompts in each section to reflect, consider, and devise action steps that will help you weave science into your everyday family life.

Chapter One

Preparing for Your Science Learning Journey

"You gotta believe in yourself to do it.
You gotta be like, 'I wanna do this, so I guess
I gotta do it, to follow my dreams.'"

—Age 7½

The word "science" is derived from the Latin word *scientia*, meaning knowledge. One of the primary ways we gain *scientia* on a daily basis is by following our sense of wonder.

There are branches of science for just about every question that has been asked, and by considering some of the more common branches, your family will be able to mindfully experience and enjoy the benefits of integrating science into your lives.

If you have ever had a conversation with your child about the sun or the moon, looked at a teeth model in a dentist's office together, or kept a fish alive for more than twenty-four hours (or at least twelve), you have already scratched the surface of some major branches of science. While the possibilities for engagement are endless and potentially overwhelming, you should find comfort in the fact that you have already been facilitating your child's science learning.

THE SCIENCES

"What are you making with your LEGO?"

"A gallbladder."

(well, of course)

– Age 3

THE SCIENCES ARE typically gathered under the following umbrellas: Physical Sciences (e.g., physics, chemistry), Life Sciences (e.g., botany, biology, medicine), Earth & Space Sciences (e.g., geoscience, astronomy), Formal Sciences (e.g., logic, mathematics, theoretical computer science), and the Social Sciences (e.g., anthropology, history, psychology). As you know, however, life is not explicitly broken up into all of these different silos.

When an earthquake takes place, we find aspects of physics, geoscience, psychology, and computer science woven together in one conversation. Frameworks are simply a way of helping us get our arms around complex fields. While there is no parenting mandate that all branches of science must be given an equal share of attention, you can still use them as a reference point for overall checks and balances.

Perhaps your family already engages with earth or space sciences through fossil digs or planetarium visits. That's wonderful! In that case, you may want to consider whether or not your child has had much exposure to the life sciences, such as medicine or ecology.

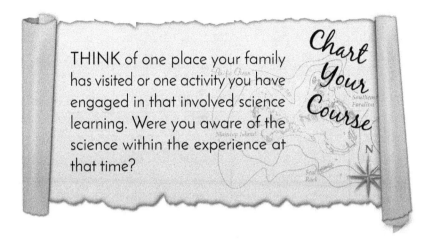

THINK of one place your family has visited or one activity you have engaged in that involved science learning. Were you aware of the science within the experience at that time?

THE SACRED ART OF FACILITATION

● ●

(facilitating my son to only compare his work to his own potential)

"Is this the coolest thing I can personally mostly make?"

—Age 5½

● ●

AS YOU START to explore the idea of being a science guide, teacher, or facilitator for your child, it is important to consider what these roles entail.

While waiting in line to make a wooden whistle at an art festival, a man overheard me interacting with my son. He leaned over and asked me if I was a teacher. While I have worked in education departments of science-based institutions and organizations for the past twenty years, I still fumble with the answer.

I typically say something along the lines of, "Not a certified one, but (fill in the blank with one of the following: I do love teaching / I love working with kids / I am passionate about education)."

Early in my career, answering this question often left me feeling subpar, like I was a pseudo-educator. I had myself back on the bottom of that marina dumpster.

As I began taking part in professional education conferences, I realized there is a whole tribe of non-certified educators like me who love sharing their science-based interests and passions with the public in ways that allow them to grow and to learn. I discovered that I was a member of the field of informal learning or free-choice learning.

I applaud the strength, endurance, conviction, resourcefulness, and tenacity of formal educators, but I never saw myself working in a traditional school setting. After teaching snorkelers about coral reefs while dangling from a surfboard, holding classes in front of a 750,000-gallon aquarium, and helping people view the sun from a museum rooftop (safely through a Hydrogen-Alpha filter, of course), my need to be in informal education settings has continually been reaffirmed.

Over the last two decades, I've worked in the education departments of an ocean-based eco-tourism company, an aquarium, a science museum, and an invention-based organization. Through these experiences, I have been able to hone my practice of designing science-based experiences for children and families. I have taught and facilitated hundreds of science-based programs. So in this respect, yes, I am a *teacher*. I identify most, however, with the role of *facilitator*.

A facilitator is someone who guides you through a process. They are not focused on delivering content, but rather on helping you take *ownership* over your learning. You are one of your child's greatest science learning facilitators, and fortunately, this doesn't mean you have to be especially adept at science or have all (or even any) of the answers.

In the following chapters, I will share some techniques, approaches, and tips that will help you feel like a better-equipped facilitator of science learning for your child.

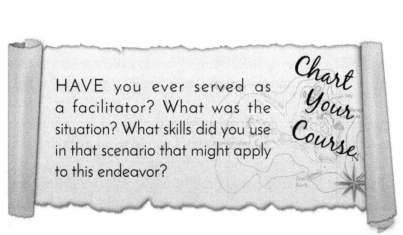

HAVE you ever served as a facilitator? What was the situation? What skills did you use in that scenario that might apply to this endeavor?

Chart Your Course

FREE-CHOICE LEARNING

"If you learn about something that you do want to learn about, it's not boring."

—Age 7½

AS YOU CONTEMPLATE embracing the role of facilitator, consider first how you facilitate learning for yourself. Think of a time when your interest was piqued about a topic or question, and you felt the urge to immediately search for answers, test out some possibilities, watch a "how to" video, or take a random field trip. What was that topic for you? How was the learning experience? How might it have been different if that subject was assigned to you?

When we learn by following our own interests, questions, and curiosities — rather than an agenda that has been prescribed for us — we are engaging in *free-choice* learning.

Since the term free-choice learning comes up so often throughout this book and forms the platform from which I operate, it is important to share its birth story.

When I began attending museum conferences, I noticed two individuals who seemed like the Mr. & Mrs. Claus of the museum

17

learning world. People flocked around them, and they were equally interested in engaging with front-of-house gallery guides as they were with museum executives. Their names are Dr. John Falk and Dr. Lynn Dierking. Years later, I would have the privilege of experiencing their consulting services during a science museum master planning process; after that, I would wind up taking part in an academic program they co-chaired.

Falk and Dierking coined the term *free-choice learning* two decades ago to capture a core idea: that people not only learn every day throughout their lives, but that learning is first and foremost a learner-centered — not a place-based or institution-centered — phenomenon.[5] They felt that *free-choice learning* best described the non-linear, self-directed learning that occurs when individuals have primary responsibility for determining the what, when, where, why, how, and with whom of learning. The term more fully encompasses the nature of this type of education where previous terms, such as *informal* and *non-formal,* could not. Over the past twenty years, the term *free-choice learning* has expanded, particularly in the out-of-school time and museum worlds.

Interestingly, since the term does not focus on where the learning occurs (as *formal, informal,* and *non-formal* do), *free-choice learning* can apply equally well to both classroom and workplace learning (and beyond), so long as the learner has some opportunity to shape his or her own learning. Thus, it is an important distinction that free-choice and informal learning styles are not synonymous.

In the mid-1990s, informal learning was considered a trifle, not a necessity with substantive value. Falk and Dierking felt that part of this misconception was packed in the name. The term *informal* has a popular connotation of being laid back. While this undertone is not inherently negative or problematic, it doesn't necessarily convey the intention and/or value that comes along with the type of learning that Falk and Dierking were trying to describe. It is therefore unsurprising that when compared to *formal learning*, *informal learning* is easily trivialized and marginalized.

Falk and Dierking wanted an educational term that people would notice, and one that strongly implied the *nature* of the learning, not the *location* where it occurred. This term, *free-choice learning*, and the rich field of research that goes along with it, has grounded me as both a professional and a parent. I am thrilled to provide you with a shortcut to access some of the research-based highlights of this field.

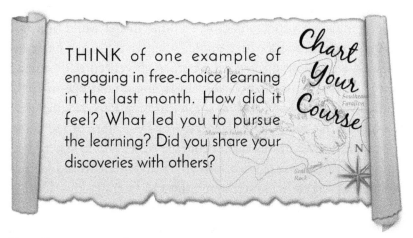

THINK of one example of *Chart Your Course* engaging in free-choice learning in the last month. How did it feel? What led you to pursue the learning? Did you share your discoveries with others?

THE POWER OF CONVERSATION

"Real Mommy, regular Mommy."

(how my son beckons me if I use a distracted tone, such as when texting)

— Age 3 ½

MANY SCIENTISTS CAN vividly recall some of the specific conversations they had on their pathways to significant discoveries and great scientific endeavors. In fact, it is often through conversations that grand discoveries are made. Talking with your child about their science interests and curiosities, as well as science in general, is at the very heart and foundation of facilitating science learning.

So how should we handle questions about the way our world works? When we give children all of the answers to their questions, we miss the opportunity to model how they can acquire knowledge and information. Showing them how to pursue their curiosities empowers them to be active knowledge seekers and learners. (Aren't you relieved to be off the hook for becoming a super genius who understands everything in space and time?)

Asking children how they think a scientist felt when he or she pursued a mission, discovered a cure, or invented a life-saving device gives them a chance to identify and empathize with the human side of science. It gives them the chance to imagine what it might be like to have the perspective and emotions of a scientist.

Having conversations that encourage your child to experiment with generating ideas (also known as divergent thinking) is a wonderful way to help build empathy and fluency skills. During a long car ride, consider asking them for their ideas to solve local, regional, or global challenges (e.g., clean, drinking water for all). Often, children see situations in a pure and uncluttered way that can be highly insightful. Reinforce for them that new ideas are needed in science and the world, and that they may be the one who will find or design solutions to some of these challenges.

The key to having a meaningful science conversation is to do so from an authentic place that involves deep listening and values your child's thoughts, ideas, perceptions, and questions. In a busy world, we have to fight our way to be present. (In the same way we have to rush to yoga class to relax.)

You will fail miserably at this some days. I sometimes hide my phone next to the napkin holder while we are playing at the table and I am waiting on a time-sensitive work email. I hope that my son is unaware of it and that he doesn't have the same

Pavlovian bell reaction that I do when the bamboo chimes on my phone summon me back to work. All of this is real life, and sometimes real life forces us to be distracted. What we can do, however, is continuously press reset and ground ourselves in the present moment as much as possible.

WHAT is the best time for you to have conversations with your child? Is it on the ride to school? At dinner? At bedtime? Cultivate a routine of using this time to explore ideas around science, the natural world, and life in general. (P.S. Make sure your phone is away.)

Chart Your Course

PASSING ON OUR SCIENCE ATTITUDES

"When you're there, and Dad's not there, I say 'Mom, you're the best!'

When Dad's there, and you're not there, I say, 'Dad, you're the best!'"

(not-so-neutral son playing the parental field)

– Age 7

HAVING RECEIVED SPECIFIC training to be a facilitator, I have learned that one of the most important qualities to embody is neutrality. A facilitator is meant to guide and balance a process, creating space for all sides of a conversation — keeping an objective stance.

As parents, we do not show up as a neutral party. We have lots of specific ideas, preferences, and opinions that are openly shared. Almost every parent has experienced the boomerang effects of their role modeling. Once, as I watched my then two-year-old son slip my sunglasses onto his face (upside down) and proceed to walk in a circle muttering, "Where are my keys?" I became keenly aware of the power and influence of my actions and behaviors. Children have a way of consistently reminding us that they are watching. And when they are watching, they are learning.

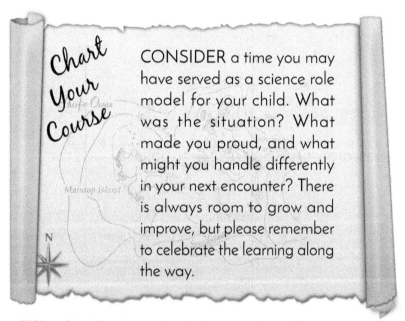

Chart Your Course

CONSIDER a time you may have served as a science role model for your child. What was the situation? What made you proud, and what might you handle differently in your next encounter? There is always room to grow and improve, but please remember to celebrate the learning along the way.

What does this mean in relation to science? It means we can easily pass our science attitudes, affinities, and aversions on to those who learn from us. Children often look to our reactions to formulate theirs. They take cues from and find answers in our behaviors. Is the worm under the log gross? Are spiders scary? Is mixing new materials safe? Our reactions help shape their interactions with and perceptions of the world. Like it or not, children often end up adopting our thoughts, feelings, and opinions—until they gain enough experience to independently form their own.

Reminding ourselves of the power of our modeling is a call to action. While my husband has an affinity and skill set for technical instructions and building, I am careful not to pass every toy box that requires assembly over to him. I let my son watch me grab a screwdriver and navigate my way through the directions, enlisting his help along the way. I know that my actions speak more loudly than my words. There are a hundred chances a week to model my willingness to learn and to share with him my sense of wonder.

Chapter Two

Identifying with Science

"You feel like love.
And he feels like fun."
(summing up his parental unit)

— Age 5

Identity, in general, is a complex construct to define. In fact, researchers from a variety of disciplines — sociology, psychology, education, and others — describe and define identity in different ways. Simply put, identity can be thought of as how we see ourselves and how others see us. Identity is both internal and external and can be both stable and fluid.

Better understanding your identity can help you more carefully pinpoint what you want and need to get out of an experience (e.g., a visit to a science museum). It can also help you better understand your relationship with science (and life) in general.

Before we begin exploring rich ways of bringing more fun, hands-on science into your life, let's reflect a bit on the role science does or does not play in your identity.

PACIFIC PONDERINGS

(describing a friend in his class)
"She's really Pacific.
You know, like serious...
she's controlled."
(aka mature)

—Age 7

I HAD SIGNED up (which sometimes means my husband, as well) to give a short presentation on Hawai'i and the coral reef at my son's preschool. "Should I dress up like coral?" "What kind of prizes do you want to hand out?" "If you expect me to make a volcano, I'm going to need more than twenty minutes." These are glimpses of my husband's stream of consciousness at three o'clock in the morning when we hadn't had the chance to catch up during the day. Some days just seem to get away from you, and the middle of the night is the only reasonable time to discuss the sitter schedule, car appointments, and fulfilling your parent volunteer responsibilities for your preschooler.

To this day, I have not figured out how to treat any form of a public presentation as a light endeavor. I felt the same way the night before my preschooler sea talk as I do when I have a major professional development workshop to facilitate for two hundred teachers. It's a combination of wishing I could spend many more hours preparing, hoping I've selected the right approach, and a desire to meet the recipients' expectations—even when they are four-year-olds.

I found myself awake in the wee hours the night before the talk, realizing I didn't have a storyline or a *Big Idea*—a technique impressed upon me through my museum exhibit design training. I thought back to a South African friend of mine, Gill McBarnet, who is a popular children's book author in Hawai'i. She had asked me to help her identify how various ocean animals reproduce so that she could be as scientifically accurate as possible in *Tikki Turtle's Quest*, a book she was writing and illustrating. I was working at Maui Ocean Center at the time, and we went tank to tank discussing the fascinating ways sea animals handled reproduction.

I decided on an adapted version of *Tikki Turtle's Quest* for my presentation. My son's rubber sea turtle from the bath and a few table tennis ball "eggs" were surely the way to go.

On the morning of the presentation, it was two degrees outside, so I walked into the classroom dressed like "Miss Frizzle Goes to the Hawai'i, But Stops by the Arctic Along the Way." My husband and son had on (clashing) Hawaiian print shirts in solidarity. For multiple reasons, I had to muster up the courage to say the word, "Aloha."

We began a beautiful journey with Tikki, as she asked Mother Whale and Mother Octopus where they have their babies. The children were all smiling and curious and enjoyed hearing about Mother Whale in the open ocean and the cave where Mother Octopus hung her eggs like a beaded necklace.

And then I told them that some jellyfish hold their eggs in their mouths. I saw a look of terror in a few of the children's eyes. I thought about how I was going to reimburse the parents for the rounds of therapy to follow. Why didn't I just sign up to volunteer for the school spaghetti dinner?

As cnidarian (the phylum containing jellyfish, coral polyps, and sea nettles) reproduction is a topic that quickly becomes incredibly diverse and complicated, I opted to stop there. In the meantime, my son, who was supposed to slowly "swim" the fish and sea creatures around me, was doing his best impression of a race car completing laps around the volcano. I pressed onward.

In the end, everyone looked more or less delighted to see Tikki make it to shore to lay her eggs in the moonlight. The moon had marker and foam stickers all over the back of it. (It was the last yellow sheet of construction paper in our house, and I assumed the craft store was closed in the middle of the night.) Nonetheless, she made it home safely—unlike the paper parrotfish and the yellow tang lying completely nauseous at the bottom of the plastic tote, courtesy of my son's Lightning-McQueen-goes-around-a-volcano performance during my presentation.

Even though I design children's science-based programs for a living and strongly identify with my role as a science-confident mother, I still get nervous and worry about how a ten-minute presentation will come together, and I still scramble with time and materials and resources. I try to give myself a colossal mistake quotient every time I tackle an endeavor of this nature. I learned this from one of my creativity professors and have since considered it a valuable tool in my toolbox.

Unless we take risks and give ourselves a chance to be comfortable with ambiguity, we will not grow as science-minded individuals or families. Be playful, experiment, take risks, and give yourself a new mistake quotient every day as you experiment with identifying your inner scientist (and simply up it when you need to).

IDENTITY

"I'm not a mammal.

I'm a boy."

—Age 2½

WHETHER OR NOT you see yourself (or others see you) as a "science person," science is inevitably part of your family's life.

Your child's comfort with science will likely play a role in their future. If you're unsure how you personally identify with science, try deliberately searching different aspects of your life for puzzle pieces and clues.

Take the time to think about what interests you in relation to the world around you, and think about the questions that you have concerning these areas of interest. Ask your child what interests them and what questions they have. You may find that some of your interests and curiosities overlap with theirs. Use these bits of data as road signs directing you toward what to explore.

As you consider the role that science plays in your identity, it's useful to consider the question, "What is a scientist?" Jacques Cousteau's answer to this question is prominently displayed in the entry of the California Academy of Sciences' Naturalist Center. It states, "It is a curious person looking through a keyhole, the keyhole of nature, trying to know what's going on."

Teaching your child how to research and explore their curiosity is ultimately a greater gift than sharing your previously-acquired knowledge of, for example, the relationship between the Earth, Moon, and Sun. You can only model this behavior, however, if you first give *yourself* permission to research and explore. Go ahead and look something up that you've always wondered about, or something you don't understand but want to. (*Really, do it now.*)

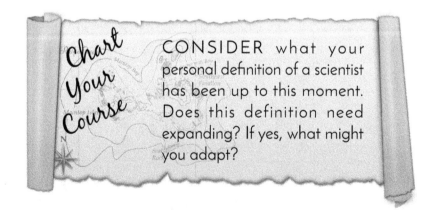

Chart Your Course

CONSIDER what your personal definition of a scientist has been up to this moment. Does this definition need expanding? If yes, what might you adapt?

MEET MICHELLE

WHILE ENGAGED IN a professional certificate for Free-Choice Learning from Oregon State University's Continuing Education program, I connected with an adjunct professor who helped me more clearly understand the critical role that identity plays in learning. I asked her to give you her vantage point on the topic. Here is what she offers:

Would you define yourself as crafty? As a traveler? As a daughter? As a parent? As a husband? As a facilitator of learning? As a learner yourself? If you are both a daughter and a parent, when are you more of one of those identities than the other? Is that even possible?

Current ways of thinking about identity would suggest that yes, it is in fact possible. Each of the above questions is intended for you to think about who you are at a given moment, otherwise referred to as your "situational identity."[6] The phrase means what it sounds like—it is an identity you employ in a given situation. My favorite example, especially as an adult, is that of being a learner versus being a facilitator of learning.

My profession requires me to spend most of my day either coordinating educational programs in a museum or being an educator in a museum. My team and I host thousands of children on field trips and oversee pre-K classes, camps, and signage at the museum. As I go through my day, my situational identity changes from "manager" to "colleague" to "facilitator of learning." Then, on a given weekend, I attend two other local museums. I walk through learning about their content—natural history, contemporary art, etc.—but I also look at the design of their signs,

I stand awkwardly to hear how a docent talks about the collection. All because I, too, am a learner.

Not only am I learning new content but also how to present different content. This example shows that depending on the situation I am in at a given point in time, how I see myself is changing as is how others see me. At my museum, I am viewed as "the boss" while at other museums I am just another visitor.

In the introduction, you were told that as a parent you "give children the opportunities that will shape their current and future selves." The self is an important part of identity. Compared to one's situational identity that changes moment-to-moment and context-to-context, the "self" refers to one's core identity, which is sticky and what we hold onto much more deeply and personally than those situational identities. Beliefs and values, which are critical components of identity, are developed at a young age and might be reflected upon later in life, further shaping a person's identity.

WHEN THEY WERE YOUNG

"Shark treuse."

(a greenish-yellow color)

— Age 6

WHEN I THINK about people I associate with having a strong science identity, Bill Nye, Jane Goodall, and Neil DeGrasse Tyson come to mind. These are individuals in the public spotlight who have made a living out of cultivating and sharing their science knowledge. They see themselves as scientists, and so do we. Perhaps lesser well-known amongst the masses is Eugenie Clark, the "Shark Lady."

Eugenie Clark was a pioneer in shark behavior research and a living billboard for the conservation of this misunderstood animal. As a young girl, she spent Saturdays roaming the New York Aquarium at Battery Park in lower Manhattan.[7] She had visions of what it would be like to swim around with the sharks in their tank. I identify with this feeling, as I spent many hours of my youth walking back and forth, following sea life in tanks, hoping they felt half as connected to me as I did to them.

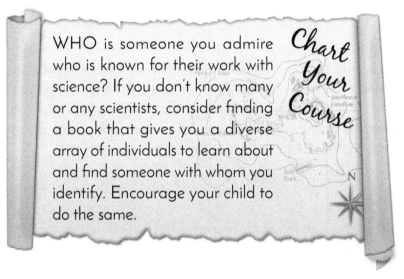

WHO is someone you admire who is known for their work with science? If you don't know many or any scientists, consider finding a book that gives you a diverse array of individuals to learn about and find someone with whom you identify. Encourage your child to do the same.

Chart Your Course

How would we parent differently if we were mindful that one day our child might trace their life's work back to one specific activity, experience, or place, as in the case of Eugenie Clark? This might be too much of a stretch on days we are simply trying to get our kid to brush their teeth after four asks, but maybe we can allow thoughts like this to enter our minds now and again. (Once their teeth are brushed, of course.)

The mere art of practicing this mindset allows us to remember that activities, places, and experiences have the power to plant the seeds of inspiration that can ignite lifelong passions — passions that may shape who children become and what they contribute to this world.

IDENTIFYING WITH SCIENCE

"It doesn't look like 'yer kind of style when it's on you."

(my son's feedback to me as I was trying on a hat in the store)

— Age 6

AT ONE POINT along my career path, as I was wrapping up a major project and beginning to seek new employment opportunities, I saw a job posting for an out-of-school time, science-based program. It immediately piqued my interest. Below is an excerpt from the cover letter I included with my application:

Perhaps this is a bit personal, but I think sharing the items in my handbag at this moment will help you glean some valuable information about me. These items include the following: two motors from the hobby shop, Make magazine Volume 3, a handful of marbles from making tag board roller coasters from Zoom, some zebra mussel shells from a trip to the lake, a couple of K'NEX pieces, and a compact shopping bag. There must have also been a wallet and some keys in there, as well.

I typed these words with a sense of pride. I wanted the hiring team to know that not only was I applying for a job, but that hands-on science and nature are at the very core of who I am and how I go about my daily life. You may or may not resonate with the items in my handbag, or with science as a regular part of your life, but the beauty of science is that we can all find ways of identifying with it.

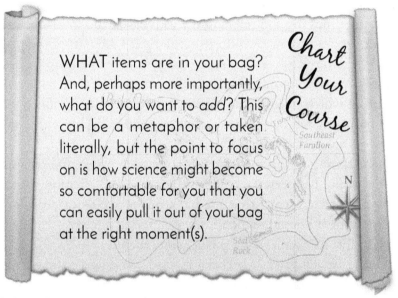

WHAT items are in your bag? And, perhaps more importantly, what do you want to add? This can be a metaphor or taken literally, but the point to focus on is how science might become so comfortable for you that you can easily pull it out of your bag at the right moment(s).

Chart Your Course

MITH JAYME

(with morning bedhead bun)
"Mommy, you look beautiful...
why is your hair shaped like a couch?"
(#passiveagressive)

— Age 3 ½

I HAVE A handful of friends that call me Mith Jayme, pronouncing "miss" as only a six-year-old missing two front teeth could get exactly right. It's a name that speaks to a piece of my identity. It comes from a longer, more fabulous phrase from a young boy who once shared the sentiment, "Mith Jayme, I made you a *tharcophagus*" as he handed me a paper Egyptian sarcophagus construction. I associate the sound of "Mith (or Miss) Jayme" with children asking me for more duct tape, baking soda, and pulleys.

Sometimes my son refers to me as Miss Jayme to his friends when we are playing outside, particularly if I am part of the play and we're having fun with science. I remember receiving a text from my neighbor one evening, following one of these play sessions in which science was prevalent. My neighbor thanked me for indulging her five-year-old daughter and said, "I love that she describes you as a scientist."

The timing of this message was somewhat ironic. Earlier that same week I had seen the hashtag #IAmAScientistBecause trending on Twitter, which put me back in that place where I was wondering if I could authentically call myself a scientist. (This is not unlike my "are you a teacher?" conundrum.)

I wondered if having a bachelor of science and a master of science qualified me to be a scientist if I didn't spend my days recording fish count data or mixing reagents. I ended up participating by tweeting with a link to a YouTube video of a song called, "I am a Scientist." It was my non-committal way of joining the conversation.

On another occasion, a different neighbor friend (whose children also play with my son) texted me a picture of an odd-looking flower. Her daughter asked her to send the picture to me because "She is a scientist. She knows things. Volcanoes. Plants. Grass. She will know what it is and why it is all prickly." I enthusiastically sent back a link to a site about pincushion flowers.

It's strange — I spend my days devoted to studying science, designing science-based experiences, and communicating science, yet I feel this trepidation about publicly identifying with science.

The more deeply I've thought about answering the question of whether or not I view myself as a scientist, the less important the answer has become. *Merriam-Webster* defines a scientist as a person learned in science and especially natural science: a scientific investigator.[8] (I personally think that sounds like an invitation, don't you?)

The power of science is not defined by how closely your degree or career path gets you to the perfect target, but rather by exploring the aspects of your identity that resonate with being a scientist. If my friend's daughters see that resonance in me, perhaps they will see it in themselves. (Meanwhile, I will continue to work tirelessly on dispelling the myth for them and others that scientists know everything.)

Chart Your Course

IF you are not a classically-trained scientist, do you feel any barriers in the way of identifying with science? (And what about if you are?) Ask your child what they think a scientist is or does and if they could see themselves as a scientist. See where the conversation goes and help them keep an open mind to exploring their ideas – and potentially expanding them.

For my friends and colleagues, and those of you who have pursued higher degrees in the sciences, I must be clear on my reverence for your efforts, intellect, resources, and training. You have worked very hard to build your knowledge and skill sets, often spending thousands of hours to help the rest of us and our planet reap the benefits of your pursuit. There are things that you *can* and *should* do that an untrained person *cannot* or *should not*. And we need you now more than ever.

Wouldn't it be wonderful, however, if everyone around you could access the field of study that you are so passionate about—if you could make the broadest impact with your work, have more advocates, have your field and work better understood, and inspire the next generation of scientists (or at least better dinner conversations)? Not to put too much pressure on you, but we are counting on you to invite everyone to the party. And, oh what a celebration it will be!

BUILDING YOUR SCIENCE CONFIDENCE

"Mom. I love you. But why are we doing this?"

(in response to me sticking LEDs
into playdough at 7:30 a.m.)

—Age 3

I ENJOY PLAYING with circuit-making materials and incorporating electronics into projects. While I'm no master, I am a willing learner who has built some skills through tinkering over time. I remember, however, initially feeling intimidated by basic circuitry items in a workshop at one of my first Association for Science and Technology Center (ASTC) Conferences.

It was an inquiry-based workshop, and even though I felt inexperienced with some of the materials, I was also excited to experiment among peers from around the country who were museum workers like me. It was fun to discuss what we were trying, and I drew inspiration from their risk-taking. (On a side note, I remember the workshop leader saying that a paper bag is a type of technology. *What? A paper bag has no cord!* I was blown away.)

Years later, I found myself at a Mini-Maker Faire, playing with Squishy Circuits. I had two lumps of salty, conductive dough peppered with colored LEDs. Each lump of dough had an alligator clip running back to the terminals of a nine-volt battery, which powered the lights.

The physical Maker Faire environment serves as a vehicle for participants to seek out the materials, topics, and people that interest them most. The environment is dynamic and playful and sets the tone for creativity, design, experimentation, and tinkering.

HAVE you ever felt very proud of fixing a broken item or putting together a complicated kit? How might you give your child the opportunity to have these types of breakthrough experiences, as well?

Chart Your Course

At the table containing the Squishy Circuits, I felt much more confident in approaching the alligator clips and LEDs than I would have a decade ago. The years of experimenting, taking the average risks of a novice, and layering my learning (one circuit board at a time) had paid off.

One night later that summer, the power went out in our neighborhood. People were coming out of their houses to see if others were experiencing the same problems. I brought out a bucket of LEDs (Light-Emitting Diodes), coin batteries, and DIY lanterns to empower the children to light their world back up. As they fumbled to figure out how to place each lead of the LED on the proper side of the coin battery (shorter, negative lead to the "-"

side; longer, positive lead to the "+" side), I remembered back to how I first felt sitting at that ASTC workshop table.

It gave me great joy to be the one providing the materials and encouraging others to explore circuit-making in a judgment-free and supportive environment. I loved seeing the looks of self-confidence and pride on their faces as their tinkering lit up the night. It wasn't until the next day that it occurred to me that the electricity had gone out after the kids' bedtime. (Perhaps I didn't need to make a mini rave in the yard with glow sticks, LED lanterns, the homemade bicycle car wash turned on high, and Bruno Mars blaring. Oh well—afterthoughts.)

I AM A PALEONTOLOGIST

(informing me of yet another
change in career choice)

He's going to be a "popcornotologist."

(checking internship listings now)

—Age 3 ½

THEY MIGHT BE Giants have a fabulous science CD, *Here Comes Science.* Our family's favorite track is "I am a Paleontologist." We now associate this song with my son in his paleontologist Halloween costume at age four. As we were selecting items for his costume, I thought about the gear and tools that I had once used while volunteering at an Ice Age dig site.

The grounds of this site bore fossils and artifacts, ranging from mastodon ribs and ice age beaver teeth (the beavers were the size of black bears) to Paleoindian arrowheads and a bead. I remember the first time that I saw a mastodon tusk emerging from the clay earth. It had a pearlized sheen, as it had not been exposed to air for thousands of years. I faintly recall hearing David Attenborough's voice in the distance.

Sporting black rubber boots and a bandana around my head, I sifted through the clay at a giant sieve, searching for other clues from the Pleistocene. The feeling that at any moment something rare, unusual, or life-altering might emerge (or be uncovered) floats thick in the air at a dig site. In fact, this "feeling"—the bottled-up potential of discovery—is the driving force for many individuals who have chosen a STEM career path.

DO you have a basket or chest in your home that is full of scarves, dress-up clothing, accessories, and large pieces of fabric or sheets? Having open-ended materials of this nature is the basis of creative play — and making a good fort is an ageless activity!

Chart Your Course

We sat in our camp chairs around a fire at night, looking up and catching glimpses of the International Space Station, talking about the history of the site and the journey of revealing its evidence. The adventure gear—from the boots to the tent—was part of the fun (for me at the dig site and for my son that Halloween) and allowed us both to experiment with aspects of our identity in different ways.

When children play dress up and engage in other aspects of sociodramatic play, they try on various roles and explore aspects of their own identity. When they put on a lab coat and mix colored water samples in test tubes, they are not just playing scientists;

they are exploring the art of "doing science." Research (and basic human intuition) shows that pretend play and role-playing are paramount to a child's development.[9]

IDENTITY MESSAGES

"Ma, ya know I have basil eyes?"

(aka hazel)

— Age 6

MY SON AND I took out his tub of astronaut toys. We flipped over our activity rug decorated with roads and community buildings, so that the gray-colored backside was face up. It was the perfect bumpy texture for our new planet's surface. As we turned his monster trucks into rovers and repurposed his toy car station to serve as the rover fix-it shop, I used a woman astronaut's voice to give the rovers direction. He told me that the astronaut I was using was not a girl. As I looked through the astronaut models, it was clear that their suits and gear changed, but their faces did not. There were approximately thirty-eight astronauts that all had the same face as Neil Armstrong. (However, they were able to change all of the other details of the mold, such as the gear and equipment.)

There are millions of messages silently and overtly communicating what scientists and engineers look like. Having an awareness that these messages exist is an important first step. Keep an eye open, as you are in the toy store and in your toy box, and look for opportunities to have dialogue and be the change. I immediately searched for an image of Sally Ride—physicist, astronaut, and educator—to share her story with my son.

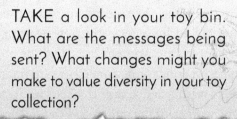

TAKE a look in your toy bin. *Chart* What are the messages being *Your* sent? What changes might you make to value diversity in your toy *Course* collection?

GIRLS AND SCIENCE

(I merely pointed to an all-boys high school,
and he was very concerned about girls)

"They can't even go on a tour or peek inside???!!!

That makes zero sense."

—Age 5

AS A SCIENCE program developer, I often see more boys registered than girls. This disparity creates a conundrum when I initially begin to design a program. We want to magnetize more girls into the programs, but not at the expense of reinforcing stereotypes. I have to consider the hooks that I'm using. Do I go after the low-hanging fruit topics (think pink!) to encourage girls to register or take more noble pathways to appeal to the masses based on what the toy aisles have already indoctrinated our youth to believe?

The Franklin Institute's 2013 publication "Cascading Influences: Long-term Impacts of Informal STEM Experiences for Girls" offers fantastic insights on the topic of young women and STEM.[10] The study, funded by the US National Science Foundation (NSF), focused on whether informal, girls-only STEM experiences have long-term influences on young women's lives, particularly women who have not historically been represented in science. While there was short-term evidence that these programs engaged girls and excited them about science, the researchers wanted to know whether these programs had long-term impacts — from five to twenty-five years out — on young women's lives. Did the programs influence future choices in education, careers, leisure pursuits, or ways of thinking about what science is and who does it?

On the upside, many women in the sample indicated that STEM continues to play a significant role in their daily lives — they either are working in traditional science careers or engage in science-related careers, interests, and hobbies.

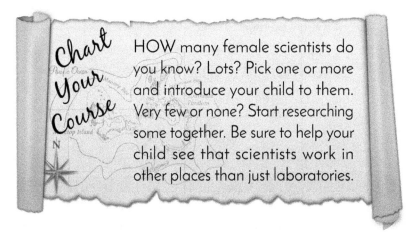

Chart Your Course

HOW many female scientists do you know? Lots? Pick one or more and introduce your child to them. Very few or none? Start researching some together. Be sure to help your child see that scientists work in other places than just laboratories.

On the downside, the study showed there were still tensions around the ways that girls and women think about what counts as science. Unfortunately, a sterile laboratory setting is still the predominant image that comes to mind for many young women when they reflect on a science career. Even the young women in this study who were fully engaged in these programs still had many misconceptions about what science is and who does it. If a young girl cannot picture herself in the sterile lab setting, she may draw conclusions that inhibit her from pursuing a science career, interest, or hobby.

One of the most concerning findings from this study is that many STEM outreach initiatives and resources being designed for girls, though well-intentioned, sometimes result in outcomes that are *opposite* to what the program is intending to achieve. According to the authors, "Our society's focus on traditional science careers, inherent in the "pipeline" metaphor, may be discouraging participation in STEM or trivializing other ways of engaging in STEM. These perceptions may prevent or limit girls from valuing the science in their life." As we focus on the science in everyday life, we help to address this challenge.

MEET MONIKA

DURING MY TIME with the Buffalo Museum of Science, I had the privilege of working with Monika, a woman who is deeply passionate about equity and access. One of the programs that Monika launched was the *Teen Skills Initiative*. This program mentored young women who spent their out-of-school time facilitating demonstrations in the museum galleries, assisting with visiting groups, and overall engaging with the public. In addition, these teens visited college campuses and built valuable life and leadership skills. The program was profoundly transformative. In my admiration of Monika as a professional; community leader; Delta Sigma Theta Sorority, Inc. member; wife; mother; and friend, I asked her to share her thoughts on families engaging with science.

Let me start by saying, I never thought of myself as a scientist. Math and science were my least favorite subjects in school, and I was glad when my schooling was over so that I did not have to sit through another math or science class again. And then I started working at a science museum. That experience changed my life.

Today, not only do I see myself as a scientist, but I make sure my three daughters see themselves as scientists as well. My experience opened my eyes to a world of new possibilities. I learned that science is about so much more than a lab coat and Bunsen burner. Science is all around us. In the water, air, and trees, in the sounds of crickets and cicadas outside, in the dog's new puppies, in baking a cake, it is everywhere.

What makes us scientists is not our level of education, but our level of inquiry, our standard of wonder. Children are naturally inquisitive. They are always asking why and how things happen and work. It is precisely that sense of wonder that helps children gain a better understanding of the world. It is our job to foster that sense of wonder and offer as many opportunities as possible for our kids to question the world around them.

An excellent way to start is by being more inquisitive ourselves. We can help children learn and grow by starting with what we already know and building from there, and you may find that you end up with more questions than answers, but that is OK. The joy is in the search for solutions together and helping your child see that it is that quest for knowledge that leads to their growth and development. The most important thing is to teach a child that learning starts by asking questions.

While museums are a great place to foster these kinds of interactions, they can happen anywhere, including the grocery store, the park, and the library. We want to give our children the opportunity to see themselves in new ways. I never thought I would see myself as a scientist, but here I am, confident in my ability to find answers but more importantly, to ask questions.

MUSEUMS AND IDENTITY

(after telling him I like to scuba dive)

"So, you are an astronaut?"

— Age 2 ½

IF YOU ARE an avid museum-goer, have you ever considered why you go to them? Dr. John Falk's research on museums and identity helps us understand that people's motivations for visiting places like museums, zoos, and aquariums have a direct effect on what they will learn and experience while they are there. And these motivations are strongly linked to their identities.[11]

How does understanding our *identity-related motivations* help us gain more from a museum experience? Falk says that the various ways that museum visitors describe their expectations and motivations for visiting fall into one of seven basic categories of leisure benefits. These classes include the following:

- *Explorers* are curiosity-driven, with a general interest in the content of the museum. They expect to find something that will grab their attention and fuel their learning.
- *Facilitators* are socially motivated. Their visit is primarily focused on enabling the experience and knowledge of others in their accompanying social group.
- *Professional/Hobbyists* feel a close tie between the museum content and their professional or hobbyist passions. Their visits are typically motivated by a desire to satisfy a specific content-related objective.
- *Experience Seekers* are motivated to visit because they perceive the museum as an important destination, so their satisfaction primarily derives from the mere fact of having "been there and done that."

- *Rechargers* are mostly seeking to have a contemplative, spiritual, and restorative experience. They use the museum as a refuge from the work-a-day world.
- *Respectful Pilgrims* visit out of a sense of duty or obligation to honor the memory of those represented by an institution or memorial.
- *Affinity Seekers* are motivated to attend because a particular museum, or more likely an exhibition, speaks to the visitor's sense of heritage and personhood.

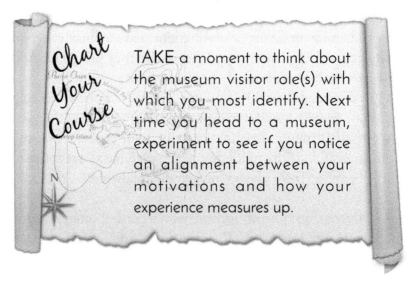

Chart Your Course

TAKE a moment to think about the museum visitor role(s) with which you most identify. Next time you head to a museum, experiment to see if you notice an alignment between your motivations and how your experience measures up.

Falk's perspective focuses on each person's immediate reasons for visiting a museum, rather than on a more constant factor such as ethnicity. In other words, the same person can visit the same museum on two different days and have two very different self-related motivations for their visit — for example, visiting on one day to support the needs and interests of their child, and on another to feed their own curiosity. What they will do at the museum, including which exhibits they visit and what thoughts run through their head, will be very different on those two days due to the difference in their visit motivation.

YOUR SCIENCE STORY

"What's the scientifical name?"

—Age 6 ½

WHEN I AM helping a group of people connect with science, nature, and culture, I feel like I am fulfilling my life's purpose—particularly if it wakes something up inside of them. I love helping people see the whole picture: the small details magnifying the interconnectedness of life's parts and pieces.

When science is (or becomes) a part of your identity, you have the opportunity to serve as a bridge for others to better appreciate and understand the world around them.

One experience I had while living on Maui, Hawai'i, impacted my science identity more profoundly than any other. There was a prominent biologist named Pauline who volunteered for the aquarium at which I worked, and whom I deeply admired. She was an avid diver and knew more about marine invertebrates than almost anyone I had ever met. She asked if I wanted to go night diving to watch the rice coral (*Montipora capitata*) spawn.

I, of course, said yes. (I mean, wouldn't you?)

Part of the beauty of this event is its incredibly precise timing. The rice coral spawns in Hawai'i approximately one to four nights after the new moon in June and July, around 8:30–9:00 p.m. While the spawning time of this species of coral was known before Pauline, she was the one to determine the specific timing of a different species: cauliflower coral (*Pocillopora meandrina*). This species spawns during daylight hours in the few days following the full moon in April and May (and a tiny bit in June). Feel free to take a minute to go mark these dates on your calendar.

I found myself in the pitch-black Pacific Ocean with my dive light illuminating a pathway ahead of me. I felt comfortable because there were several dive masters with me. Their hours of experience underwater and knowledge of how to use the fancy equipment strung off our bodies was like mental bubble wrap for me. I was genuinely not afraid. (If you are wondering whether there were sharks, they say that if you taste the water and it is salty, there are sharks. The water was, in fact, salty.)

As we swam along with the incredible introspection that comes with the sound of inhaling and exhaling through a regulator, I saw what seemed to be the entire ocean filling with millions of tiny orange dots. These dots were the egg and sperm bundles released by the coral polyps. The bundles slowly rose to the surface of the ocean where they eventually broke apart. It was there that the eggs and sperm from different colonies came into contact with each other and fertilization took place.

It was the equivalent of the coral reef giving birth. After fertilization, I knew tiny coral larvae would develop and, after drifting as part of the plankton for a while, would settle on solid substrate and form into beautiful, flower-like polyps. These polyps would excrete the stony substance, calcium carbonate, that makes many of us think that coral is a rock rather than the dynamic, living animal that it is.

The tiny buoyant spheres in the beam of my dive light reminded me of driving through a snowstorm one night in Niagara Falls, with snowflakes illuminated by my car headlights. There is a beautiful and mysterious eeriness, as well as a cold warmth, to both.

When I returned to the aquarium the next day, I stood in front of the living reef tank and spoke about the marine environment in a manner that made people feel like I knew a secret—because I did. It was a direct result of me deepening my relationship with the natural world. It impacted my identity: I saw myself as an adventurous person with the type of knowledge that could only be gained through authentic experiences.

When we take the time and the risks to experience science and nature in ways that enrich our lives, we can be better storytellers and meaning makers. You don't have to stand in front of a museum or aquarium audience to accomplish this. You can be a meaning maker for the little person in your home who is hungry for you to share your thoughts, questions, experiences, and most importantly—your time.

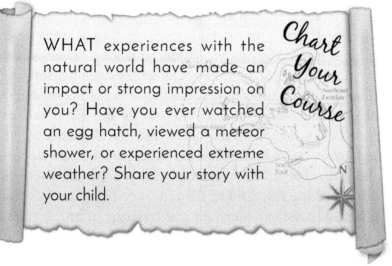

WHAT experiences with the *Chart* natural world have made an *Your* impact or strong impression on *Course* you? Have you ever watched an egg hatch, viewed a meteor shower, or experienced extreme weather? Share your story with your child.

IDENTITY SHIFTS

"What was that sound?

Was that a shoehorn?"

—Age 2½

THINKING ABOUT THE role of identity in museum visitation takes me to a memory at the Portland Children's Museum in Oregon. I told my husband that I feel most myself when I am wearing clogs and playing with our child in a museum. I was half-kidding, but...not really. As far as the clogs, there is something very grounding to me about a large sole. And as far as a museum environment, I find it comforting to be in a space that has put energy toward creating a place for my family to learn and have fun together.

Having worked in free-choice learning sites since the very beginning of my career, I was extremely excited when it was finally my turn to be on the other side of the stream table—the mom pulling apple slices from a container in the stroller instead of the person sweeping up the sand that ended up outside of the table. I was hyper-aware of my identity in this situation—specifically the shift in my identity. I relished this awareness, and the shift itself.

During this particular visit, I was much more interested in the ambience of the museum than I was in the exhibits or content. While I enjoy the stories and sub-stories that all museums tell, I also look for a nice nook where we can enjoy those sliced apples.

I find that I often begin a museum visit by going to the museum café and taking my child to the restroom. I like to work from the base of Maslow's hierarchy and take care of primary needs so that we can be fully present on our learning adventure. I most commonly identify with the role of *Facilitator*, and I like to feel grounded before beginning my journey, particularly if there is a large crowd or a high level of stimulation.

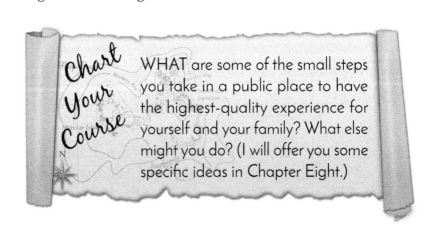

Chart Your Course WHAT are some of the small steps you take in a public place to have the highest-quality experience for yourself and your family? What else might you do? (I will offer you some specific ideas in Chapter Eight.)

YOUR SCIENCE KNOWLEDGE

"Doxin Carbon,
that's what we breathe."

— Age 4

YOUR SCIENCE KNOWLEDGE base is not the secret ingredient to your child's relationship with science. I cannot stress this enough. If you feel like an entirely inadequate source for science, rest assured that you can still be an excellent facilitator of science learning for your child. (Yes, those are two different things.) If you can identify opportunities, environments, and resources, you've got this. (Or, you'll get this. You really will.)

If science *is* your gig and you have loads of knowledge in a particular science field, and you share fun facts and experiences from your field with your child, you probably already know that this does not guarantee they will show an interest in the same topic. It does, however, give them an inside scoop that many children do not have growing up. Enjoy sharing your passion with your family and those around you, and be responsive to the clues they drop along the trail—even ones that show they might be more interested in other areas of science.

Perhaps you are motivated to weave more science into everyday family life because you understand that your child needs to be STEM literate in order to be a successful member of the future global workforce. Or perhaps you simply want your child's life to be enriched with a better understanding of the world around them. Whatever your motivation, allow it to pull you down a magnificent path of deeper science learning. And don't forget to experience the joy of inviting science to play a role in your family's identity.

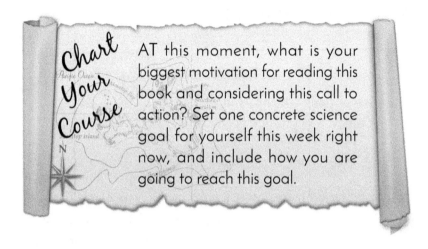

AT this moment, what is your biggest motivation for reading this book and considering this call to action? Set one concrete science goal for yourself this week right now, and include how you are going to reach this goal.

YOUR SCIENCE IDENTITY

"Even though I'm coughing,
I'm still smart."

—Age 5

BEFORE WE WRAP up this conversation, I would like to officially give you permission (in case you want or need it) to experiment with science as part of your identity. Perhaps you can pinpoint an astronomy event (like a lunar eclipse), read up on it, and share what you've learned in a social media post. Maybe you can gather some friends to discuss a favorite science topic, such as climate change, or listen to a science-oriented podcast on a subject that a family member is interested in, and again, share what you learn. Enjoy the process of finding more spaces and places for you and your family to explore science as part of your identity.

Remember, just as you're challenging yourself to identify ways to allow your child to pursue their interests, you must also give yourself the space to do the same. Don't start to integrate science only because you think it is the right thing to do, or because I'm twisting your ulna (the thinner and longer of the two bones in your forearm). Give yourself the opportunity to taste test a variety of content areas, forms of media, and places of learning, and follow your sense of wonder.

It may feel slightly unnatural or uncomfortable at first, but have patience with the process. I equate it to eating salmon. I don't enjoy salmon as much as some people, but I do know it's excellent brain food, so I sometimes elect to eat it. Over time it has grown on me, and I can recognize some of the subtle differences in the various types. Sometimes a little experimentation and discomfort are OK as you are stretching your capacity, exploring your options, and indulging in new brain food.

Chart Your Course

HOP online and type *science* in the search bar, then click on the "news" tab under the search bar. Scroll through the articles until you find one that interests you. Share your insights from the article with your child or someone else today. See how it feels to share *scientia*.

Chapter Three

Nurturing a Science Dreamer and Design Thinker

("How many legs does an insect have?")
"All of them."

— Age 2 ½

I am always fascinated by aspects of people's lives that lie beneath the surface of what they present. I am particularly curious about backgrounds and interests of rideshare drivers. I have spoken to drivers who were teachers, artists, musicians, and carpenters. During one of my rides, I got into a conversation with the driver about children and science. He mentioned that "kids these days" need more grit. After this conversation, I started thinking a lot about the meaning behind *grit*, as well as our desire for children to develop it. I also started seeing the word pop up everywhere, including in research articles and TED Talks.

Whether we call it grit, persistence, or stick-to-it-iveness, what I think we're really getting at is the ability to dig deep and see through things that aren't easy, don't necessarily have fast rewards, and may involve a long-term investment (sometimes without understanding what the end result will be). Grit is a highly coveted skill set in science. Let's take a closer look at this and some of the other skills that we can nurture, as well as concepts we can help our children explore, long before they start crafting their CVs or résumés.

Persistence and Grit

(asking my husband about finishing a
race; wanted to know if it gave him...)

"a sense-of-a-compliment?"

— Age 4 ½

THERE ARE MANY scientists who can recount working on a single problem for more than a decade. When I think about the rewards that have pulled me forward along my career path (like the opening of an exhibit or the launch of an event or program), I can't imagine waiting a decade (or more) for a return on my investment of time, energy, and other resources. Yet the story of dedicating one's life to a single question or challenge is not rare amongst scientists. This type of work takes a sense of tenacity that is not developed overnight.

While making volcanoes explode (old-school baking soda and vinegar style) can be very rewarding, children have plenty experience these days with fast payouts. What many of them are lacking, however, are hands-on projects and experiences that take the investment of time. One of the easiest ways to give your child the opportunity to cultivate their sense of persistence — and maybe even some good old-fashioned grit — is to engage them in a project that takes time and will offer some challenges to overcome along the way. This is why projects like building a robotic machine, a soapbox derby car, or an RC boat are great experiences for engaging children. They must log the time and effort in order to get the reward of a functioning device, and they learn STEAM lessons alongside lessons in failure, problem-solving, and perseverance.

Both children and adults are often too quick to give up on navigating activities, games, tasks, and projects that look challenging at face value. I have had my share of opening a toy or game, glancing at the five-point-font directions, and putting it right back in the box. However, at other times, when I have been more willing to read, learn, and problem-solve (maybe with a little help from a YouTube tutorial), I have come out the other side with some of my most rewarding experiences. Consider breaking a project or activity into steps and giving your child and yourself the opportunity to exercise your persistence muscles.

Chart Your Course

REFLECT on one way that you might support capacity-building for your child — helping them challenge themselves to push past some of their natural boundaries. Consistency and rhythm can help with this, as daily or regular practice is persistence's best friend.

Building Up

"I love my parents when they build with me."

— Age 3

THE COVETED STEAM skills of design and building begin to develop at a young age. As a baby stacks blocks, they begin to inherently learn about concepts such as the center of gravity and balance. The results of these investigations become part of their general understanding of how the world works.

Researchers from the Center for Childhood Creativity note that a child's early experiences build their brain architecture and lay the foundation for their lifelong thinking skills and approaches to learning, which are critical roots of STEM success.[12]

Children naturally build with the items around them. If you have containers in the cupboard, cardboard boxes, paper cups, or flat rocks, then no other special materials are needed. These are the everyday "scientific tools" of children.

There are also, of course, many fun and engaging building toys on the market today. Each line and set has a range of capabilities, as well as their specific pluses and minuses such as maneuverability, ease of connection and attachment, and design variability.

Many engineers and other STEM professionals refer to playing with specific building toys when they were young. Since this is also the case for many non-engineers (like myself), it is interesting to think about what motivates some people to play with these types of items well into adulthood — with plastic pieces eventually being replaced by ten-foot steel beams. Some of these early builders and tinkerers make careers out of problem-solving by applying science and mathematics, while others of us decide that we are not engineers somewhere along the way.

57

Whether or not your child decides to pursue a career in engineering is not as important as them having access to the thinking and problem-solving skills and tools that are at the heart of the field. Engineering has the power to change people's lives on a dramatic scale, and our children should understand that they have the opportunity to access that power.

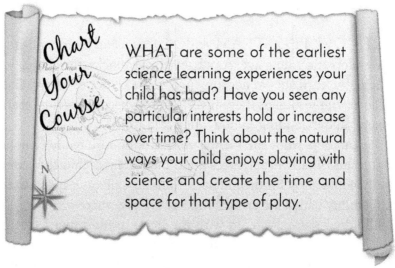

Chart Your Course

WHAT are some of the earliest science learning experiences your child has had? Have you seen any particular interests hold or increase over time? Think about the natural ways your child enjoys playing with science and create the time and space for that type of play.

Sorting It Out

"What's a tree's favorite drink?"

"Root beer."

— Age 6

I WALKED INTO my neighbor's yard and saw her and her three children with a collection of leaves, gathered from the trees around their house, and a pile of tree books from the library. They were engaged in the beautiful art of exploring the details of the world around them.

From a young age, we are taught to sort and organize items. The blocks go in the block bin, the cars in the car bin, and so on. Sorting and classifying helps us to make sense of the world, keep our environment in order, and develop our reasoning and spatial skills.

Scientists love to sort and classify. These classification systems help us learn about the world around us. Giving children the tools to help investigate their world and understand how different elements fit into a larger puzzle is a great way to approach exploring nature. For example, using a tree identification guide as you walk through a park or forest has the power to allow children to feel like outdoor detectives, as they look at clues and identify possibilities.

And this doesn't just have to happen in nature. Giving children certain objects and themes to seek out in a given environment, such as looking for all of the instances of levers that they can find around the house (e.g., tongs, pliers, scissors), can help them to zone in on the details of the world. Science is often concerned with looking at and noticing the details. Helping our kids engage in science is not about fact-collecting. It is about following curiosity, building skills, and cultivating a curious mindset.

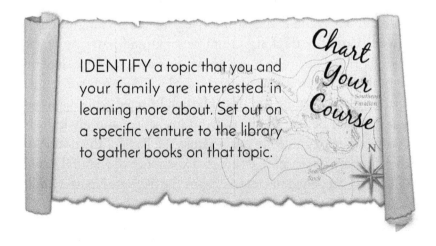

IDENTIFY a topic that you and your family are interested in learning more about. Set out on a specific venture to the library to gather books on that topic.

Chart Your Course

59

POWER OF OBSERVATION

"There were differences, and there were not differences."

(aka similarities)

— Age 6

NAINOA THOMPSON, A Native Hawaiian navigator and the president of the Polynesian Voyaging Society, reverently speaks of having observed hundreds of sunrises and sunsets.[13] He engaged in this practice in order to learn to read the signs of the weather, in preparation for being the first modern-day Hawaiian to practice the ancient Polynesian art of navigation since the fourteenth century. Thompson used traditional navigation techniques to sail the *Hōkūleʻa*, a double-hulled canoe, from Hawaiʻi to Tahiti and beyond.

Many scientists identify the art of observation — noticing and perceiving — to be one of the fundamental skills of a scientist. I think about Nainoa Thompson lying on the warm ground in Hawaiʻi, carefully tracking the movement and patterns of the constellations, becoming one with nature's cycles. I once slept on the Hōkūleʻa when it was docked on Maui. As I felt the gentle rock of the water in the Māʻalaea Harbor, I peered out, imagining what it would be like to rely only on my senses and my knowledge of nature to guide me safely across the Pacific. The notion of expanding my observational skills to experience the natural world at this level deepened my reverence for the degree of mastery that Nainoa Thompson was able to reach.

Ethnographers systematically study people and cultures from an insider's perspective. One of the critical skills they use is observation. Learning to observe, just as learning to listen deeply, can take a lifetime of practice, coaching, and training.

Providing our children with the opportunity to practice, develop, and hone their observational skills is a gift to last a lifetime. No matter how we go about strengthening and honing these skills, we will undoubtedly benefit our children and ourselves in ways that go beyond science.

Chart Your Course

TRY the following: (1) Spend time sitting still in one place for a given period of time and see what you notice; (2) pay attention to the information taken in by your various senses (observations should go beyond what is taken in visually); and (3) use tools or resources (like a sketch pad, notebook, or a checklist) to record observations — drawing or writing out information from the scene in order to capture it.

N

PATTERN-FINDING

(Asking at bath time if he would like
to play an instrument one day, like the
violin, or the guitar, or drums...)

"I want to make bubbles with my butt."

(#classyguy)

— Age 3

AS I WAS designing and coordinating a museum bubble festival, I had the arduous job of finding large-scale ways for the public to play with bubbles. (I can almost feel your empathy.) I had to think about activities that were grander than backyard bubble blowing and took advantage of the size and scope of the museum venue.

In one particular experiment, I blew bubbles between two pieces of plexiglass in a tray of soap solution using an aquarium tube. The *tessellation* of bubbles that formed amazed me. A tessellation is a plane where nothing is overlapping, and there are no gaps (think M.C. Escher's lizards in his "Reptiles" lithograph). The order of nature that presented itself in soap bubbles gave me the same sense of scientific excitement as when I peeled apart two plastic CD cases glued together by fingerpaint squished between them. It made a fractal pattern that became more detailed each time I pressed the case sides together and then separated them. Try this with your child and display the results. (Finally, something that you can do with those CD cases you've been keeping around!)

Mathematicians are trained to see patterns, and there are many ways that we can enjoy fostering this skill in our children. Similar to making connections, recognizing patterns is at the heart of many scientific and mathematical discoveries to date.

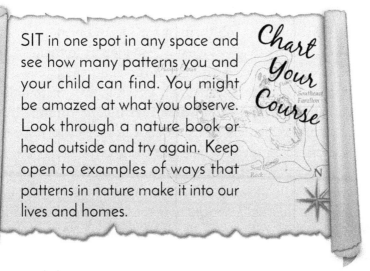

SIT in one spot in any space and *Chart Your Course* see how many patterns you and your child can find. You might be amazed at what you observe. Look through a nature book or head outside and try again. Keep open to examples of ways that patterns in nature make it into our lives and homes.

INTRINSIC MOTIVATION

"Are you glad of me?"

— Age 2 ½

HAVING YOUR CHILD engage in meaningful, grit-building activities is an excellent way for them to tap into their intrinsic motivation (the self-driven motivation that comes from within). As they are working, comment on their efforts versus showering them with a sugar-coated praise parade.

Early childhood guru Dr. Lilian Katz[14] and renowned psychologist Dr. Carol Dweck[15] emphasize the importance of avoiding praise language, such as "Good Job!" and "You're so smart!" Ironically enough, terms of this nature do the opposite of what so many of us intend when we say them.

Praise can be a subtle form of manipulation and can also create "praise junkies." It makes children rely on us for evaluation and validation rather than relying on their own judgments. In a nutshell, the term "Good Job!" leads to kids feeling less secure. We also sometimes rob them of the joy and pleasure of having the opportunity to assess what a "good job" is to them.

Katz warns of the effects of praise on children's interest, stating that when the praise and attention are withdrawn, many kids won't touch an activity again in which they initially showed interest. Praise can also interfere with how good of a job children do — putting pressure on them to "keep up the good work."

Observation statements that are more productive and enriching, while still allowing us to give supportive feedback, include sentiments such as, "I noticed how you tried a number of different ways to connect that circuit" or "I saw how hard you worked at getting that rubber band to stay in place." Dweck notes that, unlike being smart, effort is a variable over which children have control.

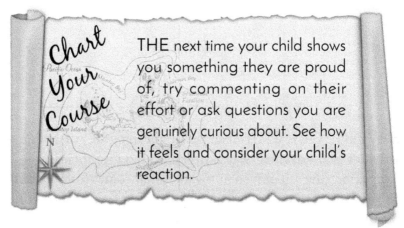

Chart Your Course

THE next time your child shows you something they are proud of, try commenting on their effort or ask questions you are genuinely curious about. See how it feels and consider your child's reaction.

Questions, such as, "Can you tell me about some of the symbols you included in your drawing?" or, "How did you decide what materials you were going to use when you created that sculpture?" give us the opportunity to demonstrate interest in our children and their endeavors without setting them up for unhealthy external reward needs later in life.

When I began to understand the implications of praise language more deeply, I felt a small pit in my stomach. I am sure if I listened to a recording of myself with my son at age two, I would find that I was giving a lot of sugar to my adorable little rat. When I first started to shift my language, it was awkward and uncomfortable, and I didn't feel like I was supportive enough of my son's mini-accomplishments. I missed my, "Oh, you tied your shoe? Woohooo! Let me run and bake you cupcakes!" at first. The more I practiced, however, the more I realized what a powerful shift this would be for both of us.

My hope is that my son feels like he has the space to take risks, fail, and not be great at everything he engages in and that he is learning to be the judge of when he does a good job. I still occasionally give him a little "cheese" (but I try to at least serve it on whole-grain crackers).

STEAM AND DESIGN THINKING

(comments on my evening music
selection of Diana Krall)

"Neh, this is too fancy

I want like rocket style

I don't like la la la la la

I like deh deh deh deh deh"

(said in an unusually dark tone)

—Age 6

WHEN MY NEIGHBOR-FRIEND (the one who had thanked me for indulging her science-loving daughter) came back from a trip to Florida, she told me about a marine mammal rehabilitation center they had visited. Their daughter was quite concerned about one particular turtle who had been bitten by a seabird. My friend and her husband had listened at length to her concerns about this turtle, as well as her idea for a life-saving device that she wanted to design to protect turtles in the future. I set up some sea turtle activity stations in my yard (table tennis balls in sand to mimic egg laying, sketching notebooks, colored pencils, marine life books, plastic and stuffed turtles, recyclables, tape, scissors, netting, and a wading pool filled with water and plastic boats) and invited her over to further explore her ideas along with my son and some of their friends.

We read through marine life books that I pulled off the shelf, discussed turtles in Hawaiian and Native American culture, and looked at shells and coral pieces under a magnifying glass as we spoke about the coral reef ecosystem. We also sketched potential designs, modeled prototypes out of clay and recyclables, and tested her model in a pool of water. As it turns out, the natural process of inquiry and the investigation of a question or idea often integrates a variety of subjects — including those which make up STEAM (Science, Technology, Engineering, the Arts, and Mathematics).

From my perspective, the bridge to help someone cross over from STEM to STEAM is the concept of *Design Thinking*. According to Tim Brown, CEO and President of IDEO (a San Francisco-based design firm), Design Thinking is a discipline that uses a designer's awareness and methods to match people's needs with what is technologically feasible, as well as viable as a business strategy and market opportunity.[16] Design Thinking can be applied to nearly every domain imaginable, particularly those that develop products, processes, systems, and strategies.

I initially learned of this concept in a Creative Studies course, where we watched an ABC *Nightline* clip featuring IDEO employees re-designing the shopping cart. The IDEO team members put on their ethnography (the systematic study of people and cultures) hats and headed to a grocery store to observe people using existing shopping carts. They observed the behaviors of individuals, noting how many shoppers will park their cart, collect items from a shelf, and return to their cart with the items. The end design of their new cart empathized with this challenge and featured a detachable basket. Empathy is a core tenet of Design Thinking and is a skill set that is invaluable to cultivate in young people.

When you look at the essence of STEAM in the broadest and brightest light, you can begin to understand how your child's future career will require at least some form of these skills. The importance of STEAM goes beyond job tasks: it represents what the world will be asking of them.

THERE are opportunities every day in every setting to develop empathy skills through basic observation. Spend time people-watching with your child and practice reading facial expressions. Discuss clues that can be read to help better understand people's emotions.

Chart Your Course

EMPATHY

(Uses various tools and devices to give his stuffed animals...)

"patience"

(patience, patients, it's all very confusing)

— Age 3

THE HIGHLY-REVERED STANFORD d.school, a school dedicated to design education, describes empathy as being at the core of the human-centered design process. Many of the challenges that d.school designers work on are not necessarily their own personal challenges. They must, therefore, make an effort to put themselves in others' shoes and attempt to feel what another person (or group of people) is feeling, and experience what life is like from their perspective.

A scientist sometimes wears their designer hat. They may design a multifaceted research project, a model for working cross-departmentally, a series of experiments, or a device that improves or saves lives. In the role of designer, they must learn to empathize. The fantastic news is that like creativity, empathy can be learned and developed. And this, as with most (if not all) of the skills we are discussing, can start from a very young age.

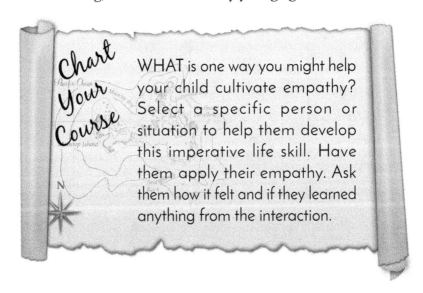

Chart Your Course

WHAT is one way you might help your child cultivate empathy? Select a specific person or situation to help them develop this imperative life skill. Have them apply their empathy. Ask them how it felt and if they learned anything from the interaction.

Chapter Four

Cultivating a
21st-Century Learner

"My listening ears are on.
They just need two minutes to load."

— Age 5 ½

The "Four C's" are a major focus of twenty-first-century education. Can you guess what they might be if you don't already know? Take a second and a risk, and see if you can identify at least one. (For those of you who already know, play restful interlude music in your mind for a moment.)

The Four C's are *Critical Thinking, Creativity, Communication,* and *Collaboration.* The folks involved with the Partnership for 21st Century Learning (P21) are thought leaders in this arena.

Information changes at a rapid rate, and we are lucky enough to have it at our fingertips—making it more beneficial for children to spend time developing inquiry and critical thinking skills than memorizing facts and figures. In addition, technological advances are rapidly changing the landscape of the workforce, placing a higher value on the human skill of creativity than rote tasks that can be performed more efficiently by machines.

MOm and Me (and the seals)

ONE OF THE most profound experiences I had during college that helped me understand the power of the integration of science, creativity, and other "soft skills" took place in Greece. While I was engaged in a learning co-op focused on seal rescue and rehabilitation in the Netherlands at Zeehondencreche (now known as Zeehondencentrum), the founder of the organization asked me if I was interested in going to Greece to write a report on the Hellenic Society for the Study and Protection of the Monk Seal (better known as MOm). Needless to say, I was very interested.

I flew into Athens and made my way to Allonisos, a Greek Island that is in the central northwest Aegean Sea. I was met by researchers who focused their efforts on trying to protect the Mediterranean monk seal (*Monachus monachus*), one of the world's most endangered marine mammals. These conservationists embodied a fascinating blend of the space where science meets culture meets economy.

I learned that one of the greatest challenges of protecting the monk seal was helping the local fishermen understand that this seal was not their enemy; overfishing the waters was the culprit that led to fewer fish for the seals and fishermen alike. In their approach, the researchers did not take a defensive stance against the fishermen, nor did they attack their views. They ate dinner with them, met them at pubs, and listened to and empathized with their needs and issues on and offshore. I deeply admired this approach, and it has served as a lifelong reminder of socially and emotionally intelligent change leadership.

During my eight-day stay, we spent a lot of our time conducting research on boats, my favorite being the inflatable dinghy used for up-close ocean research. As we zipped through the water, I remember looking up at the rugged limestone cliffs and feeling as though the pages on Greece in the *Encyclopedia Britannica* had come to life. It seemed like the land had given birth to a coral reef that was trying to touch the sky. As for me, I felt like a pirate looking for hidden treasure (the monk seal) in the sea caves.

In these caves, which were primarily inhabited by gulls and wild pigeons, we checked on the electronic cameras that had been installed by MOm researchers. The camera network was a great way for them to better understand the seals' day-to-day happenings without interfering with their natural behavior. We collected otoliths (the small ear bones of fish that seals tend to spit out) to record data on and better understand the monk seal diet. Understanding the behavior and ecology of an animal is often critical to being able to help protect it.

Later, as I sat in one of the researchers' houses, we lined our eyes up with the windowsill so that we could look out at the water and pretend we were still on a boat. It was in front of that house that I snorkeled in the sea for the first time. I remember the trepidation I had as I stood on the shore, geared up in a wetsuit and fins, fearful of heading into the unknown. It was everything I had dreamed of doing, yet when the opportunity presented itself, I was as frozen as a shy freshman at their first high school dance. I eventually made my way into the water. While it was fairly murky that day, my career calling toward free-choice science learning was becoming crystal clear to me.

When I reflect on this coming-of-age experience, I think of sleek black seals, goats and wild dogs, authentic feta cheese, learning to drive a stick shift on windy cliffs (yikes, sorry Mom), and listening to my Tracy Chapman and Cranberries cassette tapes over and over on my portable cassette player. I also think about the way that life is highly integrated, not sectionalized. We are often taught about subjects in formal education settings, yet this one small internship experience demonstrated for me how science, culture, nature, and economy are interwoven and interdependent.

As I learned from the trepidation of my first snorkeling experience, when we have roadblocks and inhibitions around science, knocking down these roadblocks and dissolving these inhibitions is often as simple as gaining a little experience.

In retrospect, I have come to realize that the offer to go to Greece was more so a gift from the Zeehondencreche founder than an actual need for a report. (I believe she knew I would pay it forward in some fashion—namely to the environment—in the future.) For me, it was one of the most impactful instances of mentoring that I have ever experienced. I still keep tabs on the work that MOm is doing and am grateful for people who dedicate their lives to serving as the advocates and voices for animals in peril on this fast-changing planet we so strongly impact.

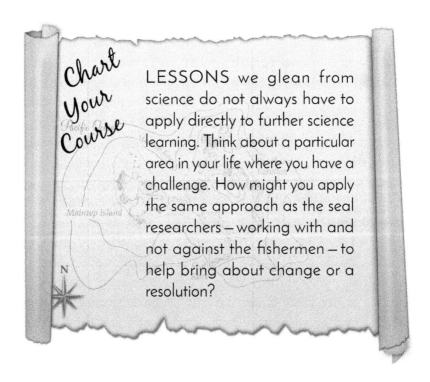

Chart Your Course

LESSONS we glean from science do not always have to apply directly to further science learning. Think about a particular area in your life where you have a challenge. How might you apply the same approach as the seal researchers — working with and not against the fishermen — to help bring about change or a resolution?

THE EVOLVED SCIENCE THINKER

● ●

(after eating rice, somewhat against his will)

"It just tastes like eating a cloud.

Clouds don't taste like anything."

—Age 5

● ●

THE MONK SEAL researchers were called upon to use skills outside of their educational training to keep accurate biological data reports. They were called on to be emotionally intelligent, creative problem solvers.

As we engage our children in science learning, we have to ask ourselves what it means to be a practitioner of science in the twenty-first century. To be a practitioner of science is to be a practitioner of problem-solving. By problem-solving, I mean finding a solution to a challenge, meeting a need, or filling a gap.

A key ingredient to problem-solving is creativity. Harvard professor and creativity scholar Teresa Amabile describes creativity as the production of novel and appropriate solutions to open-ended problems in any realm or domain of human activity—ranging from the arts to the sciences, to business, and education.[17] Amabile highlights the fact that while ideas must be novel (different from what has been done before) in order to be creative, that doesn't mean any bizarre or outlandish idea will fit the bill.

Creative ideas must, in some form, be related to addressing the problem or challenge at hand. Most creativity facilitators, practitioners, and scholars that I know employ this working definition of creativity. And if you are interested in applying for a United States patent, or encouraging your child to do so, you ought to subscribe to this definition as well. To receive a patent, your invention must be new, non-obvious, and useful.

I have found that the space where critical thinking, creativity, and science come together serves a Petri dish for the ultimate experiment of human potential. It is in this space that I have produced each one of the science-based programs, exhibits, and experiences that I have ever designed.

By pursuing a master of science in Creativity and Change Leadership through the International Center for Studies in Creativity at SUNY Buffalo State, I was introduced to research and first-hand evidence that creativity can be both taught and learned; it can be enhanced and amplified; and we can examine not only our levels of creativity but our blocks to creativity and our creative styles. There is ample opportunity for every person to develop their creativity and apply it to their life in both small and grand ways. It is precisely these opportunities that make creativity a foothold for families looking to weave science into their daily lives.

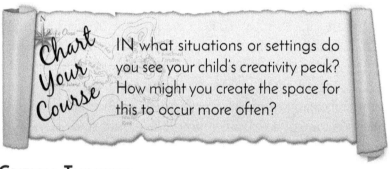

Chart Your Course

IN what situations or settings do you see your child's creativity peak? How might you create the space for this to occur more often?

Critical Thinking

(discussing inventor, physicist, and engineer Nikola Tesla)

"What made him dead?
Did he run out of blood?"

—Age 3 1/2

MOST PEOPLE ASSOCIATE critical thinking more closely with science than creativity. Let's look at the whole picture. Critical thinking involves using reason, drawing on data to make insightful arguments and informed decisions. It often involves intentional thinking, careful consideration, analysis, and evaluation. Many of us naturally associate this type of thinking with scientists.

While the word *critical* may trigger some negative connotations, it does not equate to criticizing. It simply means to look closely and logically in a thoughtful manner. Critical thinking involves thinking with direction, intention, and purpose.

Children are asked to think critically when they crack a code, organize information, or provide reasoning for the way they solved a problem on a test. Oftentimes, critical thinking requires us to take a position based on what we see as truth and acceptability. As adults, we are asked to do this every single day.

Being a critical thinker, however, does not exclude us from thinking creatively. Analyzing information often allows us to generate more novel and applicable solutions for real-world challenges. Successful scientists and innovators have learned to harness the power of critical and creative thinking: the dynamic duo that underpins many great advances in society.

We can support children in developing critical thinking skills by helping them: (1) formulate good questions (that get to the heart of a matter), (2) gather and harvest information (with an open mind), (3) apply the data (experiment and test it out), (4) analyze the results (what implications are there?), and (5) use the insights to consider other vantage points (demonstrate empathy).

When we ask our children to make data-informed decisions and describe their line of reasoning for these decisions, we not only give them practice in a critical life skill, we also glean important insights about their thinking process. This is the most invaluable data a parent can possibly have, in order to help shape, encourage, and inspire a smart decision maker.

ASK your child to share what
they think are some of the biggest
challenges that people face
around the world. Ask them what
they think might be some of the
solutions and encourage them to
make a prototype (model) of their
idea(s) using recyclables or crafting
materials. Have them place the
model somewhere special to
remind themselves that they have
the power to shape the world
through their critical and creative
thinking.

Chart Your Course

N

FURTHER DEFINING CREATIVITY

(arms and legs slathered in yogurt)

"I'm using my smoothie as lotion."

—Age 3½

SCOTT BARRY KAUFMAN is a well-known researcher and
author in the fields of positive psychology and creativity. He has
helped clarify that creativity is a whole-brain process and not
simply a right-brain function.[18] He explains how much of a fallacy

and myth this "right-brained" misconception is and why it is critical to embrace the messiness of the creative process and the dynamic, interconnected workings of the brain that make it all possible. Follow his lead to learn more about the neuroscience of creativity—an awe-inspiring arena that is exploding with new insights.

Fascinating biology aside, let's look at creativity from a very basic Psych 101 perspective for a moment. In one of my first graduate school courses in creativity, we were asked to write our own definitions of creativity. While I can't remember exactly what I wrote, I remember that every definition my classmates and I identified was different. The term meant something unique to each of us in that classroom, and I suspected in the world.

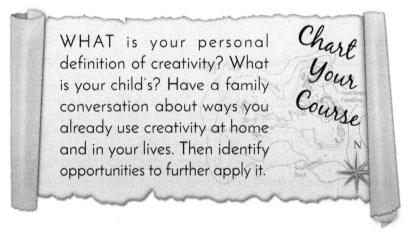

WHAT is your personal definition of creativity? What is your child's? Have a family conversation about ways you already use creativity at home and in your lives. Then identify opportunities to further apply it.

Chart Your Course

Throughout the program, my definition of creativity evolved from being highly esoteric to much more grounded and tangible. The best part of this evolution is that the latter was much more inspired. Vague musings were replaced, or at least substantiated, by tools, techniques, and processes that were proven to build and enhance imaginative thinking and its application. (I did discover, however, that applying these elements still offers a golden invitation to the random inspiration of the muses.)

Of late, I subscribe to "potential originality and effectiveness"[19] as the definition of creativity that most resonates with me. While

I wasn't sold ten or fifteen years ago on the aspect of usefulness or effectiveness being critical to defining creativity, I stand by it now. It is the "so what?" aspect—which is where and how the power of originality is unleashed.

CREATIVITY RESEARCH

IN A 2010 IBM research study of fifteen hundred CEOs, creativity was determined to be the most important leadership skill for dealing with the complexity of the future.[20] More and more people are recognizing the critical value of creativity in the twenty-first century. While it may seem to some to be at the opposite end of the spectrum from science, it is imperative that the two function together to solve some of the greatest challenges of our time. As a trained facilitator in creativity, the first question that I ask a potential client is, "Is creativity really needed here?" This question seems simple, but sometimes it leads to the answer, "Actually, no." If this is the case, we do not move forward with the creative process. Some challenges require solutions that are more straightforward and obvious. Other problems, however, require novelty and originality—in other words, creativity.

Also in 2010, a *Newsweek* article highlighted "The Creativity Crisis," reflecting a trend in the decline of creativity testing scores since the 1990s (note: there was previously a rise between the fifties and the nineties).[21] The scores were measured as part of a longitudinal study (a study that takes place over a long period of time) using E. Paul Torrance's Torrance Tests of Creative Thinking (TTCT).

The TTCT have tracked hundreds of children into adulthood, recording their number of businesses started, patents and grants received, research published, buildings designed, music composed, leadership positions held, and more. The article noted that childhood creativity was three times stronger than childhood IQ when it came to predicting lifetime creative achievement. (Insert "mind blown" emoji.)

Since many people still associate creativity with the Arts (though this view seems to be expanding and evolving), data of this nature helps reframe creativity as an essential part of our everyday lives that extends beyond the paintbrush. From deciding how to navigate a social challenge to figuring out the best way to implement positive changes at home or at work, creativity plays a crucial role in shaping the quality of our lives.

Making changes, solving challenges, and identifying opportunities for growth requires novel thinking. It requires finding and creating solutions that do not yet exist. Regardless of you and your child's style or level of creativity, the great news is that research has proven time and again that creativity can be taught, learned, and developed. The first step is to acknowledge and recognize yourself as a creative being.

One barrier that prevents some people from thinking they're creative is that they associate being highly innovative (i.e., a paradigm shifter) with being creative. A man by the name of Michael Kirton developed a measurement scale called the Kirton Adaption-Innovation Inventory (KAI). The KAI helps people understand where they fall on a continuum, from extremely adaptive all the way to incredibly innovative. This measurement has allowed many adaptors (people who make changes by tweaking instead of throwing the whole thing out and starting fresh) to realize that they aren't any less creative than their innovator counterparts. We have a tendency to celebrate innovative creativity, in American culture in particular, but adaptive creativity makes your smartphone that much more functional than it was three years ago.

Helping your child see the merit and value in their style—whether it be in how they creatively express themselves, what they need to maximize learning, or how to work well with others—is a remarkable journey to help them navigate. One of the best ways you can do this is to help frame the context in various situations. By helping your child understand the bigger picture, such as the dynamics that may occur when they play or work with others with varying styles on a project, you are helping them learn to use higher-order thinking skills.

Developing creativity skills is a rewarding and lifelong journey. Take the time to consider ways that your family might explore enhancing their creativity. Investing twenty dollars in a sheet of melamine at the hardware store, screwing it to the wall, and getting some dry-erase markers is just one way you can get started.

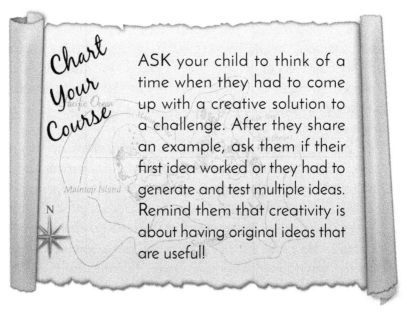

Chart Your Course

ASK your child to think of a time when they had to come up with a creative solution to a challenge. After they share an example, ask them if their first idea worked or they had to generate and test multiple ideas. Remind them that creativity is about having original ideas that are useful!

CREATIVE THINKING

"Can I have another cookie-you-guess-so?"

(way to lead me to the water...or the cookie jar)

—Age 3 ½

WITH CREATIVITY COMES creative thinking, and with creative thinking comes creative thinking skills. Identified by creativity master educator E. Paul Torrance and creativity researcher Dr. Tammy Safter,[22] these skills include:

- Recognize and Define the Problem
- Produce or Consider Many Alternatives
- Be Flexible
- Be Original
- Highlight the Essence
- Elaborate—but not Excessively
- Keep Open
- Know Emotions
- Put Your Ideas in Context
- Combine and Synthesize
- Visualize it—Rich and Colorfully
- Enjoy Fantasy
- Make it Swing! Make it Ring!
- Look at it Another Way
- Visualize the Inside
- Breakthrough—Expand the Boundaries
- Let Humor Flow and Use It
- Get Glimpses of the Future

Whenever I am trying to infuse a situation, program, or project with creativity, my mind goes straight to this collection of skills. They allow me to consider the many ways in which we can bring novelty to the table. Over time, I have seen how many of these skills, such as keeping open and making connections, have a critical role in science and scientific thinking.

Scientists are often required to remain open to possibilities. One way that we can foster this skill in our youngest scientists at home is to help them to continue to generate options beyond their initial "good idea." Take notice in your day-to-day life at how often you (or those around you) act on the first idea that comes to mind. When we keep open, we allow for new information to come into play and for ideas to "simmer," allowing the power of incubation to take place.

Whether it be putting information together in new ways, connecting two or more ideas to come to a new solution, or using a metaphor to aid in arriving at a new idea (e.g., biomimetics—mimicking nature), making connections is another critical skill in science. Many types of technology we use today result from scientists, technologists, and designers making new connections, both literally and figuratively. See what connections you and your child can make together.

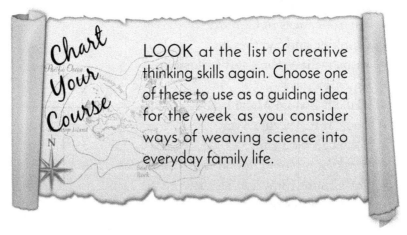

Chart Your Course

LOOK at the list of creative thinking skills again. Choose one of these to use as a guiding idea for the week as you consider ways of weaving science into everyday family life.

CREATIVE PROBLEM SOLVING

"Just press here, and fa la la la la!

It turns on."

(aka, Voila!)

— Age 3 ½

IN 2010, I watched the news in sadness and disbelief as millions of gallons of oil were spilling into the Gulf of Mexico. One aspect of the entire story stood out above the rest in my mind: the desperate need for solution-finding. Scientists were heavily debating how to stop the constant gushing of oil into the Gulf, while most of us watched and waited. What was needed in this situation, besides STEM skills? Creative Problem Solving.

The real art of Creative Problem Solving (CPS) stems from a model seeded in the 1940s by advertising executive Alex Osborn as a method for solving problems creatively. He teamed up with academics Sid Parnes and Ruth Noller in the 1950s and put form to this notion in a process that depicted three distinct stages: fact-finding, idea-finding, and solution-finding. Scholars have continued to evolve the CPS model to this day, and the evolution will continue.

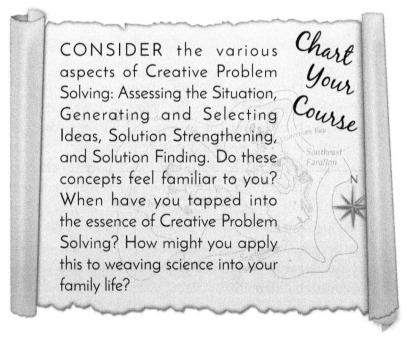

CONSIDER the various *Chart Your Course* aspects of Creative Problem Solving: Assessing the Situation, Generating and Selecting Ideas, Solution Strengthening, and Solution Finding. Do these concepts feel familiar to you? When have you tapped into the essence of Creative Problem Solving? How might you apply this to weaving science into your family life?

When I facilitate groups, *Creative Problem Solving: The Thinking Skills Model* is my framework for knowing where to begin and where to go with the process. This model projects a dynamic balance of generating ideas, selecting the appropriate ones, and strengthening them. Brainstorming, a divergent (idea generating) tool that is commonly associated with creativity, relies on the yin of generating ideas being met with the yang of selecting, strengthening, and implementing them. Creative Problem Solving keeps this balance in check and reminds us that creativity must match up original thinking with effective solutions.

MEET JOHN

My friend and Creative Studies colleague from Singapore, John, has given me many insights on education from an international perspective. John is the Chief Edimpactor of EdImpact and has deeply contemplated the space where creativity and science meet. He shares the following:

> I am a very blessed father of two very wonderful teens—Joshua and Joanna. But before I was a father, I was a science teacher and a pretty crazy one. I love making science come alive for my students in the classroom. Perhaps a large part of that came from my dad's love for crafting and spending hours as a kid observing him at work, and occasionally breaking apart some of his art pieces. But through my own growing up years, seeing Dad's devotion to drawing and making his drawings become three-dimensional artwork shaped a large part of how I view science education differently.

> *HOW MIGHT THAT HAVE SHAPED MY CHILDREN'S CREATIVITY?*

> There is no shortcut to becoming a better parent. We need to involve and engage them from a young age. Through understanding our own children, we naturally

recognise how they learn best. I firmly believe that before we can ignite our children's passion, the home is the best place to provide that personal space for them to feel safe, have fun, and to question, explore and create. Children who grow up in an encouraging and supportive family environment at a young age are more likely to discover an area of interest that they will continue to deepen. Among a variety of factors, many studies have reinforced the impact of parental involvement in learning in the home with better cognitive development, particularly in the early years.

As a father, I love my children asking questions, but I am not one who offers answers and solutions easily. While each of my kids discovers their own interests differently, I take it upon myself to extend their curiosity by getting them to think and do their own research. For example, my son became highly motivated in science by reading biographies. I would follow up by asking him what have they invented and offering a more concrete experience with either bringing him those objects or to those places to further arouse his curiosity. Engage them in activities that will exercise the whole brain. Stimulate their creative consciousness by allowing them to see that there is always more than one way of getting things done!

Progressive educational philosophies such as those of Reggio Emelia and Maria Montessori fascinate me. While these liberal philosophies advocate the need to allow children to play with their imagination, I feel we need to first believe in the child within ourselves. All children love to play, and until we recognise that play in and of itself is the purest way to stimulate creativity, we will struggle with bringing that childlike imagination to fruition. However, there is also a big part of me that tends to over-rationalise (even at the expense of compounding a mistake) which may at times kill "fun ideas."

Thomas Edison is attributed with saying, "Opportunity is missed by most people because it is dressed in overalls and looks like work." The deliberate work to affirm our children's new ideas lends such an opportunity. I remember that I once bought a chunky-shapes puzzle for my girl when she was just a toddler. While little Joanna was toying with the pieces, my wife with all good intentions commented, "Sweetie, you cannot fit a round block into a square hole." However, my little baby amazingly took some scrap cloths to pad the base of the block and managed to make that supposedly impossible fit! I can't help but diverge into the immense possibilities of such a sacred moment of exploration. What if my girl one day finds that fundamental insight of technical importance into the larger physical world or that of atomic and subatomic discoveries of quantum mechanics? As the former UCLA basketball coach John Wooden said, "Do not let what you cannot do interfere with what you can do." The question lingers, "What if?"

As our kids grew older, the pressure to do well academically in school became a very real concern, especially for us Asian parents. While hard work may not always lead to success, at the same time, getting children to take some risks does encourage them to be more inventive. It isn't at all easy to see your own child make mistakes, and of course, it often pains me to see them tear with every failure or setback. However, I firmly believe that the best gift I can leave for my children is simply to support their curiosity and create different opportunities for them to think on their own. I feel that we need to think hard and recognise what is worth learning. As a biology teacher, I used to make my students memorise the sophisticated processes of mitosis and meiosis in order to score well for their essays. Yet underpinning that, have I done my part to get them to inquire about nature and what these natural processes hold? More importantly, I wonder if I have done my part to share that practical knowledge of helping children draw insights and make connections to better appreciate how the world works. Have I helped them to amplify that wow-factor to learning? I see my role as that of a catalyst to getting them to think more deeply in a scientific way. Give them a handle on scientific concepts and see where they are going before I present the problem scientifically. As that human catalyst, I manipulate the scientific formulas or algebra in order to involve them: to extrapolate or find solutions or make predictions. The divergent mind might even stretch it further and seduce them to confront taboos—inviting them to potentially dangerous or even forbidden kinds of knowledge. Get them to question the social and moral implications to genetic mutations and ask, "What might possibly happen if...?" and we can enjoy that little brainstorming together to explore implications for personal health management. (Clearly, I would fly on an all-time high if my kids start questioning about issues of genetic variation, selection, and inheritance!)

WHAT'S THE GAME HERE?

With the advent of technology today, there are also more distractions on the internet. Looking around, we can see many children contented with being consumed in the little world within that device between their fingers. What makes things worse is to see many parents themselves not only indulging their children with their mobile games but to see these phones or tablets as a tool to buy some peace and quiet for themselves. I dare say, while these short-term gains may seem useful for busy and tired parents, they do little to help a child develop their own passion and interests. Quite honestly, I am guilty of that too. Given a chance to turn back the clock, what would I do differently? I think I would give my children a musical instrument rather than a smartphone to coax or stimulate their creative minds. Psychologists have studied that learning to play a musical instrument is far superior to computer instruction in enhancing the kind of abstract skills which are needed to excel in mathematics and science.

I asked the question earlier, what is worth learning? Speaking as both a parent as well as a science educator, I think there is so much more we can do to help children connect ideas to the real world around us. But we need to give them time and space to mull over problems and for themselves to distill that relevance. While the quest for scientific knowledge is not a matter of taste or even choice, children themselves need to be brought to a deeper level of connection in all learning. Our challenge today is to help them find relevance to what they are doing, else no meaningful learning can really take place.

SCIENCE AS A VEHICLE FOR CREATIVITY

(asking him not to swing on the door)
"I'm a rudder.
Do you like rudders?"

—Age 4

MY FAVORITE PROFESSIONAL way of applying my creativity is to design programs and exhibits for children and families. I deeply enjoy the challenge of thinking about intergenerational interactions. I imagine a grandmother and her three-year-old granddaughter standing next to each other, exploring a material, referencing a label or graphic, or using a piece of technology. I try to think about what they might want and need in order to have a meaningful and positive experience. I also like the idea of helping families extend their experience, whether or not all family members were present, beyond their museum visit.

For my Creativity and Change Leadership Masters Project, I focused on utilizing a science museum camp as a vehicle for encouraging meaningful conversation and creativity skill development.[23] Admittedly, this title looks way too long embossed in gold on a binding, but it spoke to the heart of what I was exploring.

For this project, I selected four of the Creative Thinking Skills as identified by Torrance and Safter—Visualize the Inside, Keep Open, Combine and Synthesize, and Enjoy Fantasy—to individually pair with hands-on science activities.

Ultimately, twenty-three of the fifty-eight families registered for science camps at the time of this research project fully participated in the study, completing a workbook that they filled out in the evenings following camp. Children were introduced to one of the four creativity skills during the day in camp. The parents then initiated conversation with their children using three given conversation starter prompts (e.g., "What do you think Earth will be like in five hundred years?") and collectively completed a CreActivity, an exercise that explored the skill they focused on in camp. Finally, the parents were asked to jot down their reflections in a workbook that I gave them.

For the skill *Visualize the Inside*, families completed the experiment of letting an egg soak in vinegar (which breaks down the shell and reveals the inner world of the egg). For the skill of *Keeping Open*, they made predictions about how the raisin bugs the kids designed during camp might change overnight (they swell from absorbing water). To engage with the skill *Combine and Synthesize*, participants called three friends, asked them what

HOW comfortable are you with facilitating a simple science experiment? If your true answer is *not very*, it is so important to start simple and small. Grow one bean sprout. Gain confidence. One of my greatest life hacks is to hire a trusty eleven- to thirteen-year-old to serve as a mother's helper for a couple of hours. I can be home working and acting as head of safety, and they can be pretending they are dinosaurs with my son. Plus, their rates are great. (You can even pay some of them in unlimited pizza and yogurt tubes!) Procure their help with this experiment thing.

Chart Your Course

their favorite sandwiches were, and designed a new sandwich by combining and synthesizing their favorite ingredients. To *Enjoy Fantasy*, participants engaged in a CreActivity with their family to design their dream science museum.

Through this process, I found science to be a highly-effective vehicle for families to have meaningful conversations around creativity and other twenty-first-century skills. The phrase "awareness is half the battle" rings more true to me now than ever. (Ironic side note: I just burned the chicken nuggets in the oven because I lost track of time while I was typing about awareness.)

I must remind you that there is no perfect recipe for science and creativity skill building. Simply being mindful that these opportunities exist in everyday life and can happen through play, experimentation, and conversations is a fantastic first step. Reaching for them is the second. (I am now going to find a vegetable to go along with the second batch of nuggets I am committed to not burning.)

COMMUNICATION

"Telecommunications is when you...uh

...wiggle your tail around."

(insights I receive when working
from home around my son)

— Age 2 ½

MORE THAN EVER, scientists are being called upon to be effective communicators and storytellers. Gathering and having the data is one side of the coin, but getting others to understand the data, care about what it means, and ultimately use it to shape their behavior (e.g., committing to reducing, reusing, and recycling) is another. There are many fun ways to help our children practice their storytelling and communication skills. Museums and other public learning places can be the perfect places to do so.

Consider testing out the following activity the next time you are in a natural history museum: Head to a case displaying multiple objects that interest you. Take a moment to see what you notice. Consider if any of the objects seem familiar to you. Objects tell stories through their shape, adornment, textures, materials, sounds, and other variables. See what stories the objects you are observing have to tell you.

Here's another test: Think of the smell of a familiar object — the tree near your house, your jacket after a campfire, or your grandmother's sweater. Objects often make us think about

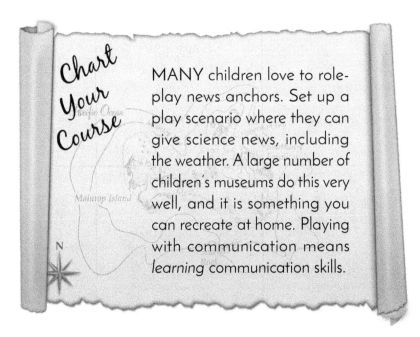

Chart Your Course

MANY children love to role-play news anchors. Set up a play scenario where they can give science news, including the weather. A large number of children's museums do this very well, and it is something you can recreate at home. Playing with communication means *learning* communication skills.

memories, and smell is one of the most important senses in memory recall. While sight and sound signals must first be interpreted as they make their way to the brain, smell signals have a direct shortcut to the brain from the nose.

Objects can do more than trigger memories. They can also inspire the creation of new stories. Creativity practitioners often use a technique called "Force Fit" or "Forced Connections" to pair seemingly unrelated objects to generate new ideas. Try it for yourself: identify a goal, wish, or challenge that is on your mind. It could be something as simple as deciding what to eat for lunch or as complex as solving all of the world's energy issues. (I suggest starting with lunch so that you can gain practice in this technique and then eat the solution.) Next, select an *unrelated* object to help you generate ideas for achieving this goal or wish or solving this challenge. For example, maybe you choose a window sill as the object to connect with lunch. An image of a steaming pie cooling on a summer day floats into your head… why not try shepherd's pie for lunch or a pizza pie?

Forced Connections is a great tool to master. If it is difficult for you, keep practicing; if not, keep applying. There is no challenge that is out of bounds for this technique. It's a fun and empowering way to approach challenges as a family.

Storytelling

(why scientists should practice being good storytellers)

"They can tell their kids, if they have some, about what they did that day."

— Age 7 ½

I ONCE FACILITATED a panel on the topic of Communicating Reef Science at the Ninth International Coral Reef Symposium in Bali, Indonesia. While there, I went scuba diving and was blown away by the rich array of colors and shapes that existed below the water's surface. The blue-spotted rays (*Taeniura lymma*) stand out most in my mind, as each individual blue spot looked as though it had an LED lighting it up. My emotions were equally struck by the visibly high degree of coral bleaching that was present on the reefs.

Reef-building coral polyps have a symbiotic relationship with a marine algae (technically single-celled, photosynthetic dinoflagellates, if you're one for details) called *zooxanthellae* (zoh-zan-thell-ee). Greatly oversimplified, this is a mutually beneficial relationship whereby the zooxanthellae live in the polyps' tissues and provide most of the coral's food through photosynthesis, and the coral provides nutrients and a protected, sun-exposed place for the zooxanthellae to live.

Zooxanthellae have highly specific light and temperature needs.

When the water temperature and light intensity are above a certain threshold, the zooxanthellae photosynthesize at a higher-than-normal rate. Free radicals, a byproduct of photosynthesis, build up to a level that is damaging to the coral's tissue.

To prevent tissue damage (a means of survival), the corals sometimes expel the zooxanthellae (like spitting out bad orange juice). Since the zooxanthellae are what bring color to the polyp's tissue, the coral usually loses its color when its habitators are expelled — thus the term "coral bleaching." The bright white coral skeleton becomes visible beneath the living coral tissue and gives the reef a bleached appearance.

Interestingly enough, if the temperature and light intensity fall back below a certain threshold, zooxanthellae from the surrounding water can repopulate the coral's tissue. If this does not happen at a rapid enough rate, however, the coral polyps will have starved to death during the time they were without their zooxanthellae (a primary source of food), and all or part of the coral colony will die. With our oceans warming at an unprecedented rate, this has become a major issue.

The panel I facilitated at the conference was focused on the responsibilities and approaches of communicating science related to coral reefs (like bleaching) to the public. We spoke about a variety of topics: the awareness of technical jargon and its barriers for government decision-makers; the impacts of sensationalized-type headlines; the value of timely research result reporting (sometimes information is only useful if it is reported in a timely fashion); and the critical role of quality interpretation of the earth's environment and ecology for the general public.

Scientists are being held more and more accountable to be able to explain their science to the public at large and to help people understand what it means and why it matters. Issues pertaining to the environment have made this exceedingly more imperative.

Practicing the art of storytelling with your children, particularly after they have had an experience or taken in new information, is a wonderful way to support them in developing their communication skills. Asking them questions about what they identified as the big idea, the main challenge, or the point of an exhibit or documentary after viewing it is another way of encouraging them to assimilate information and articulate meaning. And there are many ways to record these stories—from keeping a journal to making video diary entries to creating books. There are a wide variety of book-making kits for children on the market that encourage them to write and illustrate a story and then mail it in to be turned into a bound book. There are also books with blank comic strips that provide a template for your young person to create their first graphic novel.

Another excellent tool for storytelling is a *zoetrope* (a mechanical, rotating device with vertical slits for viewing the images placed inside), which allows children to experiment with the basic elements of animation. (There are relatively inexpensive toy ones that you can purchase.)

Scientists are often called upon to present their research and findings in a variety of ways, such as poster presentations and workshops at conferences. If your child has a science class project or is participating in a science fair, use this opportunity to help them think about some of the ways they can capture people's eyes, minds, and hearts. Assist them in thinking through the most important points they want to make and the visuals they want to use to convey those points. This activity can be a fun, creative, and enriching process. Would a model be helpful? A role-play scenario that involves others? Is there an opportunity to dress the part? Help your child consider the possibilities of their presentation delivery methods as much as the content that is going to be shared.

Perhaps your child might benefit from interviewing a scientist and then posting the interview on YouTube. When I was at the Bay Area Maker Faire, I watched a tween boy with a tablet, a microphone, and his grandfather in tow, walking around interviewing various techies at their booths. The wide variety of skills he was practicing and building—from experience with the technology to articulating his questions to the self-confidence he was building as he approached various adults—was highly evident.

A science project or fair is also a great chance to help your child work on their public speaking skills. Record a practice run of their presentation and then sit down with them over some popcorn and play it back. Ask them what they thought they did well, what they would like to work on, and what new ideas they have that might enhance their presentation.

This approach does admittedly take some extra time and planning. Taking projects to this level is not always possible in the busyness of day-to-day life. As I was writing these ideas, I pictured an evening from my childhood where my mom and I were up late into the night making a paper maché puppet, trying to blow dry it to completion so that I could paint it before morning. The point to ongoing skill building is to maximize opportunities and to do what you can when you can, in whatever incremental steps are possible.

Chart Your Course

FOLLOWING an experience with science, encourage your child to tell someone about it. Support them in remembering and adding the details. Storytelling is a craft that benefits from practice.

Nonverbal Storytelling

GIVING YOUR CHILD opportunities to play, build, and do science alongside children that speak other languages is also a wonderful way to develop their communication and storytelling skills. One of my favorite sites to test out-of-school time programs has a large English Language Learners (ELL) population. I am always amazed at how giving children materials and holding space for them to be makers, designers, and creators is a universal language. The power of non-verbal communication is especially sweet between children in these situations.

Communicating through mediums other than words is a highly important practice. Any inventor with a patent will tell you the value of sketching. If your child does not have a propensity toward drawing, they may need extra support to put their ideas in sketch form. Remind them that there is no critique of their work, that it is simply for them to explore their thoughts, get their ideas from their minds out into the world, and remember their process. Giving children or adults who do not see themselves as "artistic" permission and encouragement to express themselves and their ideas with crayons, pastels, or paints is a powerful gift.

Chart Your Course

IF your child wants to sketch, draw, or color, do they have easy access to materials? The simple act of making materials easily accessible and available is an important first step.

COLLABORATION

*Told me he gets a lot of "comments"
from his friends at school.*

*Like that he's
"the best tire swing pusher,"
for example.*

(aka compliments)

— Age 6 ½

TEAMWORK AND COLLABORATION skills are a significant need in research laboratories and other places where scientists carry out their work. We cannot begin early enough to cultivate these skills within our children. Working with others can be both rewarding and challenging. Our interactions — and our reactions to those interactions — can sometimes determine our success in a given situation. They can provide launch pads, or barriers, to entry.

There are profiles that allow us to better understand how we interact with others, and with the world around us — from our thinking, problem-solving, and innovation styles (FourSight) to our preferences in how we perceive the world and make decisions (MBTI). While the plethora of profiles available to us have varying degrees of reliability and validity (I highly disagree with the result of which *Princess Bride* character I would be), one of their primary benefits is to reflect on our strengths, as well as consider where our gaps and weaknesses might be. Going through this process often helps us understand the light and dark sides of our styles and gives us insights as to how we "chemically combine" with others.

HELP your child navigate the muddy waters of compromise. Identify a situation where they were successful in reaching a compromise and point out how their willingness to push through to the other side (particularly if they sacrificed a little) helped move a situation along. Helping your child understand the actions and results of positive compromise will aid in reinforcing a framework in their mind that can be tapped into over the course of their lifetime.

Chart Your Course

N

We all have our own set of values, opinions, and beliefs. Throughout one's lifetime, it is highly advisable to look at the world through others' lenses and vantage points. The earlier we begin to help our children see the extreme value that lies within diversity—in all its forms—the earlier they can start to understand how partnership and collaboration can lead to success that is sweeter than what any one of us is capable of achieving on our own.

Flexibility and adaptability, particularly as they relate to agreeing on a similar goal and direction, are key factors in collaborating.

THE ART OF REFLECTION

"Mom, when you say no,
it takes the happiness right out of me."
(#sorrynotsorry)

—Age 5½

THERE WAS A week in late summer when it seemed like every night I needed to talk to my son (who was four years old at the time) about different situations that had gone awry during the day. I imagine we were all craving the rhythm of fall at that point and were tired from a summer of heavy travel. The issues at hand were all the classics, ranging from trouble with sharing toys to not losing one's marbles when it's time to come in for dinner. I was grateful to have my old trusty friend, the *Learning Cycle*, on hand.

The Learning Cycle is the harvest of a seed planted by John Dewey in the 1930s that has been cultivated by many individuals since. I have extracted the essence of this plant and adapted it to fit the needs of my family. There is no hard science here regarding my family's experimentation with using the cycle, but perhaps our trial results will benefit your family's experiment design.

The Learning Cycle empowers an individual to look at what took place, what went well, what didn't go so well, and what can be learned for next time. Each evening of that trying end-of-the-summer week, I facilitated the Learning Cycle at bedtime. My son was able to self-identify the challenges from earlier in the day. I did not even have to point out one of them. I was not the expert on life, and he was not the recipient of my critique and judgment. I only asked him questions, and he answered them. He sometimes asked to change the subject, and I kindly let him know that I wanted to have this conversation with him first and then we could read a book of his choosing. I like the quietness of night for reflection, yet I want his last interactions with me to be warm, light, and positive. (I reserve my cold, dark voice for the tenth time I have asked him to put his shoes on.)

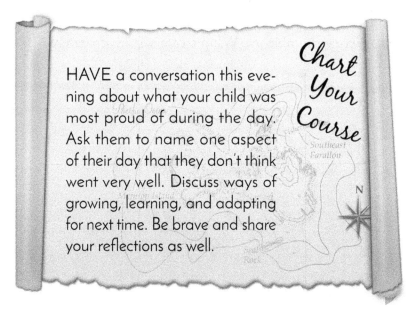

HAVE a conversation this evening about what your child was most proud of during the day. Ask them to name one aspect of their day that they don't think went very well. Discuss ways of growing, learning, and adapting for next time. Be brave and share your reflections as well.

Chart Your Course

The Learning Cycle is not unlike the affirmative judgment tools that I often use to facilitate a group after a program or event to think about what went well, what might be improved, and what opportunities might exist for next time. There are different terms and versions of this tool (e.g., PMI: Pluses, Minuses and "Interestings"; and LCOB: Likes, Concerns, Opportunities, and Brainstorming to overcome the top concerns), but they all have the same goal of methodical reflection.

You can use these techniques to debrief science and life experiences at home. They are ideal for hearing out your child and other family members and organizing thoughts to apply learning to future situations.

Having experimented with this for a while, my first piece of advice is to lightly test it out for yourself. You know your child best. See what they are responsive to and adjust to incorporate the language that makes them feel safe to share and supported in growth and learning.

My second piece of advice, as you experiment with the Learning Cycle, is to be prepared to have it turned back on you. I have been facilitated by a four-year-old, and it is equivalent to eating a nice piece of humble pie. Whip cream served separately.

Chapter Five

Navigating Science Learning Experiences

"The North Star is not like a regular star.
It's more special.
But regular stars are pretty special.
But North Star is even specialer."

—Age 6

The main steps in navigation are determining your current position, identifying your destination, and then plotting your course. The word *navigation* itself exudes adventure. Beyond wayfinding, it seems to suggest overcoming obstacles, problem-solving, and adapting one's approach to the surroundings and other variables at hand.

As we navigate our family's science learning expedition, we find ourselves sometimes at the helm (the wheel) and other times at the stern (back of the boat)—with intermittent moments of prepping food in the galley and taking naps in the berth. Every now and again, as we approach the shoreline, we are rewarded for our efforts. We step off the boat, look back at our tattered ship tied to the dock, and breathe deeply as we bask in the accomplishment of completing another leg of the trip. When this moment comes, we must seize it, revel in it—because soon, we will have to reload supplies, muster up new energy, and re-hone our focus so that we can jump back on board and head out for the next leg of the adventure.

I once purchased a compass for my son in the Yosemite National Park gift shop. Earlier that day, we were discussing tools one might use for navigation. His ideas included the North Star, other stars, a mirror (to see if a bear is behind you), maps, a thermometer, GPS, the wind, a compass, and a whistle (to tell people where you are). While some of these tools seem to fit more clearly into the navigation box than others, his list broadened my perception of navigation. It included ways of taking in more data about one's immediate surroundings before plotting a course.

I invite you now to consider your family's starting place with science. In order to chart the best course for navigation, we must orient ourselves around this point.

ALL AROUND

"How do molecules form?
And what are demigods?"
(light conversation at bedtime)

—Age 6

WHEN IT COMES to learning science in an organic manner, life is your classroom. Every bridge you drive over, every piece of heavy machinery you pass, and every time you discuss the probability of rain, there is an opportunity to enrich your family's relationship with science.

As with most skills with which you become proficient, one of the keys to successfully integrating science into your daily life is practice. Learning science is most often about practicing the art of not knowing the answers and modeling ways of pursuing them. This is the magic of curiosity: the desire to learn or know about something.

Creativity scholar Mihaly Csikszentmihalyi (affectionately referred to as Mike by his colleagues) defines *curiosity* as the individual differences in the likelihood of investing psychic energy into novel stimuli, and interest in investing that energy into one set of stimuli over another.[24] In other words, it is the odds that you'll move toward investigating the dangling carrot that seems most unique, interesting, and shiny to you.

As you invest energy into activities that feel novel (new or original) to you, be explicit with your child about *your* process for learning new information, making discoveries, and gaining insights. Do you call someone and ask for their knowledge and experience with the topic? Do you search the internet for information or use an app? Do you test out your predictions? Do you go somewhere to learn more? Share these steps when you pursue your own curiosity. Your child may or may not remember the answers you come upon, but they will likely remember you modeling how to pursue them.

(As a side note, it may be comforting to hear that most professional scientists typically know a great deal about their respective areas of focus, but they are often in the same boat as the average novice when it comes to exploring a completely different branch of science.)

One of the first steps to upping your family science game is to recognize that you are very likely already doing many things to encourage science learning. If you have let your child help you bake a cake, you have given them the opportunity to build math skills (through counting, measuring, and estimating) and chemistry skills (by observing the changes that take place through heating the batter). It is important to realize the value in these simple, everyday activities: they form the foundation for deeper science learning experiences later on.

The more you start to look at the world through a science lens, the more opportunities you will see for fostering comfort, curiosity, and an appreciation for this wonderful arena. For instance, helping your child notice the slow process of liquid water changing into solid ice in the ice cube tray (by checking every few hours) can turn an invisible task into an activity that cultivates their sense of wonder. It can also help you to slow down, be more observant, and more in tune with your surroundings—all foundational characteristics of a present parent.

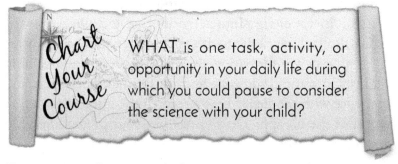

Chart Your Course

WHAT is one task, activity, or opportunity in your daily life during which you could pause to consider the science with your child?

FOLLOWING CHILDREN'S INTERESTS

"Following your interests can help you feel better because you're actually doing what you want to do."

—Age 7

I OFTEN ENJOY listening to TED Talks when I am exercising. It helps me to have someone in my ear talking about how they swam from Cuba to Miami (Diana Nyad) or traveled across India on the back of an elephant despite being visually impaired (Caroline Casey) as I move my body with a mediocre stride. It makes me put my exer-whining in check and inspires me to pick up the pace a little. TED Prize talks are particular favorites, as they are calls to action from some of the most prominent thought leaders of our time.

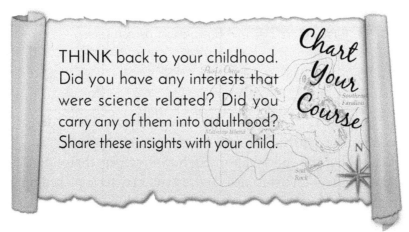

THINK back to your childhood. Did you have any interests that were science related? Did you carry any of them into adulthood? Share these insights with your child.

Chart Your Course

I was deeply moved by E.O. Wilson's TED Prize Talk. Wilson is a biologist, researcher, theorist, conservationist, naturalist, and voice for millions of tiny organisms. He is primarily known as the world's leading authority on ants. He is to biodiversity awareness what Elvis is to rock 'n' roll. In Wilson's "My Wish: Build an Encyclopedia of Life" presentation, he points out that "We live on a mostly unexplored planet. The vast majority of organisms on Earth remain unknown to science." When describing where his interests began, he shared the following: "As a little boy, through my teenage years, I became increasingly fascinated by the diversity of life. I had a butterfly period. A snake period. A bird period. A fish period. A cave period. And finally, and definitively, an ant period."[25]

In my household, we have gone through truck, tiger, train, spider, shark, dinosaur, and robot periods, to name just a few. Wilson's talk is a reminder to take the interests of our children seriously, giving them access to books, people, experiences, and resources that allow them to explore these interests. The person holding a major key to unlocking a piece of the biodiversity puzzle just might be sitting at your dinner table playing with their peas at this moment.

APPLYING WONDER

"Has there been, in Buffalo, an ostrich seen?"

– Age 5

MY SON HAD a research project assignment for his kindergarten class. The parameters were very loose and supportive, and it was all about the children learning how to pursue their interests and curiosity. I love this idea (and, as you may have picked up, I even wrote a book encouraging this sort of thing).

And yet, I was stumped at how to help him get started. I did my best to procrastinate. After all, it wasn't my fault the library was closed on Monday. The only alternative I saw was to go and get ice cream.

Then, I reminded myself of the title of the book that I was writing (this one). And so, we began by filling in the blank of, "I wonder...." It was so painful (like facilitating a five-year-old writing a large batch of thank you cards kind of painful) to not control the process. I wanted to tell him what to wonder. I wanted him to question things I already knew the answers to and already had pictures of for his poster board. It would all be so much easier. But, this approach wouldn't serve anyone. And so, I sat back and let him take the lead.

The research topic he chose was "Buffalo, United States." When this assignment came up, we were just eight weeks into a move to northern California from Buffalo, New York. I had just reached the point where I wasn't afraid to say the word Buffalo without triggering my son's tears, or my own. While the move was exciting and purposeful, it was nonetheless an emotional process. This project gave us a way to own our sense of place in these two different worlds, and I realized that taking on a new location did not diminish our feeling of connectedness to our hometown. We realized that we could still build our knowledge and connections, but from a different vantage point.

The questions my son crafted included the following (in his words): "Is there any tsunamis that have reached the Californian Ocean? Underwater? It would take a few hours." (From Buffalo, that is), "Has there been, in Buffalo, an ostrich seen?" "Have legends be told in Buffalo?" "When they came alive, how did they make the first building? Where were the materials?" And, "How many girls did it take to make one boy?"

Whew, I had my facilitation work cut out for me. I heavily promote the practice of taking children seriously and validating their questions, but I cannot say I was able to keep an entirely straight face during this question-identification round. I had to take a small break at one point with my head under the table, quietly slapping my hand on my knee. I composed myself, brought my head back above the table, and carried on. The pure joy and innocence of creating the space for my child to explicitly wonder caught me off guard.

We used the no's to some of his questions (e.g., tsunamis and ostriches) to find our way to related yes's (e.g., snowstorms and white-tailed deer). In the end, I learned new facts about my hometown right alongside my child—as a result of his wondering. I also had the chance to watch him build his research and learning skills.

I was reminded in that moment that as we help our children with their formal learning experiences, they develop skills that can be applied in informal learning situations—life outside of the classroom. In fact, a staggering 95 percent of our science learning takes place through informal learning experiences.[26]

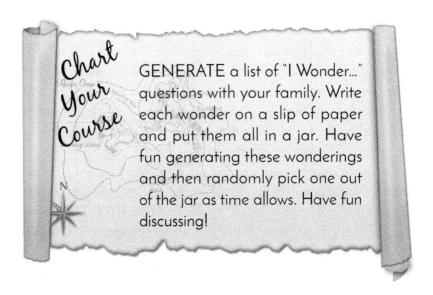

Chart Your Course

GENERATE a list of "I Wonder..." questions with your family. Write each wonder on a slip of paper and put them all in a jar. Have fun generating these wonderings and then randomly pick one out of the jar as time allows. Have fun discussing!

BEFORE, DURING, AND AFTER

"Ma, do you know what lives after us?"

("Uh, no.")

"Yeah, me either."

—Age 5

AS YOU BEGIN to seek out more science in day-to-day life and potentially engage in more science experiences, events, and outings, it can be fun to think about the before and after of these encounters.

When designing science programs, I often call to mind an organizing framework I learned in a creativity course in graduate school. The framework is called the Torrance Incubation Model of Creative Teaching and Learning (named after master creativity educator E. Paul Torrance) — better known as TIM. This model has significantly shaped my parenting, particularly in the realm of facilitating science learning. I am sharing it with you so that you will have a reference point for creating enriched outings with your family that do not simply start and stop with admission and exiting.

The model depicts three phases: Heightening Anticipation, Deepening Expectations, and Extending the Learning.[27] According to Torrance, there are the aspects that prepare us for an experience (*Heightening Anticipation*), elements that exist and occur during (*Deepening Expectations*), and opportunities that arise following the experience (*Extending the Learning*).

When I am preparing to take my son on a nature-based excursion, such as a public viewing of a lunar eclipse, I consider what I might do to get us ready and help build and capitalize on our excitement and learning. We might check out books from the library, watch YouTube videos, or simply have a conversation about what we know, wonder, or predict. Taking the time to do this heightens our anticipation for what's to come and primes us for a learning experience. It also gives us a more focused mission once we arrive.

In order to get the most out of a learning experience, I try to be prepared and equipped in a manner that allows me to be present. It is important, however, to note that this does not always work out as I plan (like the time when my son was hyper-focusing on the corn chips we left back in the cabin while juvenile orcas were breaching in front of us), but parenting often seems to be about minimizing risk and maximizing opportunity.

Sometimes it's about having the simple items on hand, like a blanket to sit on or a jug of water to drink from, that allows family members to be more comfortable, relaxed, and present at a site or event. Other times, having resources and materials (like a sketch pad, checklist, or identification guide) can enhance the engagement by encouraging your family to dig deeper. And sometimes it is simple actions, such as deciding to turn your phone off or giving up on picture-documenting an experience in order to actually have it.

Of course, while putting the camera away at times has merit, giving your child a lens through which they can capture the world can also be an empowering experience. Take the time to extend the learning by printing and appreciating the pictures afterward so that your child can see the fruits of their creative labor and science interest.

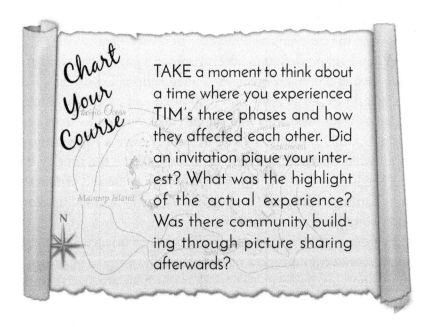

Chart Your Course

TAKE a moment to think about a time where you experienced TIM's three phases and how they affected each other. Did an invitation pique your interest? What was the highlight of the actual experience? Was there community building through picture sharing afterwards?

I sent my son on his kindergarten field trip with a disposable camera. It had been years since I had film developed. When the pictures came back with random shots of the environment, he looked at them with a great deal of pride on his accomplishment of capturing what he saw. (And there was a fun irony in him and his friends attempting to take selfies on the instant camera.)

Getting Ready and Digging In

"When I grow up I want to be a
man that makes books.

That's my big dream."

— Age 3

ONE EXAMPLE OF a resource that *Heightened our Anticipation* and inspired a way to organize a family experience in Seattle is the book *A Day at the Market*. A friend had given us the book years before we traveled to Seattle and it was one of our favorite bedtime picks. The fruit in the bins on the pages was palpable, and the rhythm of the story was based upon, and successfully captured the essence of, Seattle's famous Pike Place Market.

The characters in the book range from the fish throwers to the apothecary workers. We read it (for the hundredth time) on the airplane to Washington and spoke about what we were excited to find and what we wanted to do while at the market. When we arrived, it was like the pages of the book came alive. We entered the *Deepening Expectations* stage of TIM as we went through the labyrinth that is the market set-up, seeking out the various stores that were depicted in the book.

We learned that bumbleberry (mentioned on one of the pages) is simply a mix of whatever berries are left over at the end of the season, we purchased a stuffed snake that resembled one from the book, and we revealed to the owner of the House of Jade that his storefront starred in the story. We went back three times during our one-week Seattle stay to unravel the mysteries of the pages. This one simple book served as a GPS of sorts for a multi-layered experience.

For those of you who have ever experienced the joy of finding a "hidden track" on a CD (aging myself), there is a hidden track that comes along with engaging with your child through the lens of science. It plays as a dynamic soundscape of deepening your connection with your child and better understanding who they are, as you witness them unfold into a curious individual with unique interests and perspectives.

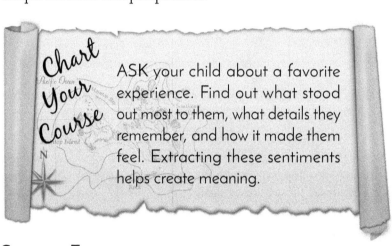

Chart Your Course

ASK your child about a favorite experience. Find out what stood out most to them, what details they remember, and how it made them feel. Extracting these sentiments helps create meaning.

SCIENCE, EXTENDED

"It goes 900,000 degrees speed."

(referring to his clay jet)

−Age 6

PREPARING FOR AN experience can help you get more out of it, and following up on the experience can be equally, if not more, powerful for learning.

On a sunny, crisp Sunday in October, my family picnicked with some friends at Aquatic Park in San Francisco and watched the Blue Angels—the US Navy's flight demonstration squadron.

As we watched planes swoop in formation, free fall, and make beautiful contrail patterns in the sky, science was also in full flight.

My son's entire torso shook when the jets flew in from behind our heads.

While he was thrilled with what he saw when he looked up, he was equally engaged in building jets out of clay on the blanket. Perhaps we diluted his interest with three hours of apple juice tailgating on the grass before the show started, but there's probably more to it. It can sometimes be challenging to get him to look out to sea or up into the sky to share an experience in the exact moment, in the exact way I want him to, with the exact same feelings as me. I mean, what is wrong with this kid? Oh, yes. He is his own person, with his own interests, and ways of experiencing situations.

Over time, I have learned that the highly tangible aspects of my child's environment (e.g., pretzels and trucks) are sometimes equally or more appealing than the far-off spectacle(s) I desire him to observe. I have also learned that the most powerful experience is sometimes the combination of these two elements.

It was my son's choice to start making planes out of the clay that my very-prepared friend had brought. I had never seen him sculpt airplanes before this moment. The details mirrored what he was gleaning in those nanoseconds when he was looking up.

That evening, we *Extended the Learning* by watching videos about the jets we saw (and felt). We also looked up instructions for paper airplanes and made an *F-16* that flew across the living room with the agility of a swordfish. My son's eyebrows were up near his hairline. While building an airport for this paper airplane, along with the clay ones we made earlier (placed in empty plastic popcorn containers and dragged home) and a small Blue Angels souvenir plane, we talked about our fantastic day. My husband asked if we noticed how we heard the planes after we saw them pass. All of this led to a great discussion about breaking the sound barrier and how the extra fuel is burned in the jet exhaust.

When my son asked which plane I thought was better—the metal one we bought or the paper one we made—I told him it was all of the planes together that were my favorite. I explained that this was because the collection of planes represented the beautiful day we had together.

It is the *Extending the Learning* phase of the TIM model that typically has the longest and most indefinite timeframe. This is where you assimilate the experience, share it with others, build onto it, have the opportunity to frame and recall various aspects of the experience, and put it together with other puzzle pieces to create new meaning. In a nutshell, it is often where the magic of the learning happens.

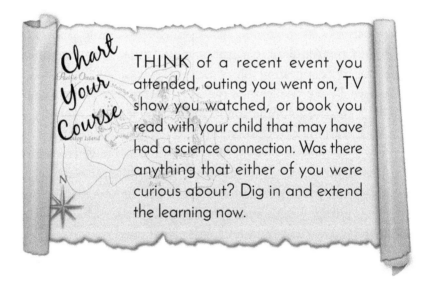

Chart Your Course

THINK of a recent event you attended, outing you went on, TV show you watched, or book you read with your child that may have had a science connection. Was there anything that either of you were curious about? Dig in and extend the learning now.

Some of the same actions can be taken in the *Extending the Learning* stage as in the *Heightening Expectations* stage (like checking out library books or watching YouTube videos), but there are new opportunities afterward to apply the insights from those resources to actual experiences (which often generate specific questions to guide the pursuit of knowledge-finding). Once again, the art of conversation can be one of your most powerful tools during this learning stage.

LAYERING EXPERIENCES

"Should all the plankton be forgot,

keep your eye on the grand ole flag."

(slight misinterpretation of the lines
in "You're a Grand Old Flag")

—Age 5

ONE OF THE primary reasons that it can be impactful to think about the before, during, and after of an experience is because learning happens in layers. Think of it as one of those delectable desserts that take all day to make, adding one layer at a time. The deliciousness is in the fullness of the bite — all of the layers combined and gelled together.

During the same trip to Seattle where we visited Pike Place Market, my family and I headed north to the San Juan Islands. We took the car ferry to Orcas Island to do a little camping and whale watching. My son was enamored with the majestic steel structure of the vessel and adjusting ramps as we loaded and unloaded.

The next morning at our campgrounds, we awoke to an active intertidal zone—the shoreline area that is covered during high tide and exposed at low tide. It was as if a veil had been pulled back from the ocean and the sea was giving us a behind-the-scenes tour. It felt as though we were snorkeling on land, without the intrusion of equipment. Barnacles, juvenile rock crabs, and chitons lay exposed to the morning sun.

The light mist and tall evergreens (along with hot coffee in my favorite blue and white speckled camping mug) put me in a state of bliss as we searched for sea life and watched a man build a perfectly balanced rock tower. It inspired us to create towers the following day using flat, barnacle-encrusted rocks and pieces of kelp. I used a multi-tool to cut the kelp into wide slices, making them ideal tower pillars. (I have since learned that building and leaving random rock towers in nature is frowned upon for a variety reasons, ranging from potentially misleading hikers looking for rock towers that serve as trail markers, the potential of increased erosion, and conflicting with the notion of leaving no trace in wilderness.)

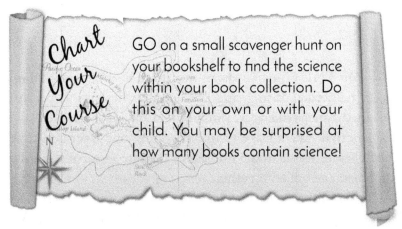

Chart Your Course

GO on a small scavenger hunt on your bookshelf to find the science within your book collection. Do this on your own or with your child. You may be surprised at how many books contain science!

My son had already seen many of the creatures in this intertidal zone at aquariums. I tried not to compare the experiences out loud or in my own mind; it's easy to say that learning about these animals in nature is a much better experience. While I do, in general, agree with this sentiment, I also think that these experiences can be complementary. When we learn about science and nature, the learning is layered. Information we gather from books, documentaries, museum-type visits, and in-context experiences (like a walk through the woods) create a tapestry that is ever expanding and in many ways superior to information gathered from a singular source.

That's why, on the way home from this trip, I read to my son one of our favorite books about tide pools. Books often seem to bridge my family's adventures with our day-to-day home life in a manner that allows us to continue creating meaning long after the laundry from the trip is finished. And when we pull those books off the shelf and open them at a later date, they release bits of the past experiences that seem to have been waiting to be reactivated.

Chapter Six

Science is
Better Together

*"It's good to do science with other
people because you might be able to
learn something from someone.*

*And that can lead you to a
bunch of other stuff."*

— Age 7½

Take a moment to go with me on a very short mental excursion. Close your eyes. (Wait, I'll save that for the audiobook version.) Keep your eyes open and imagine a scientist doing his or her work. OK, do you have a clear image? If you imagined them alone at a lab bench looking into a microscope, your imagination matches what is depicted by a quick online image search for "scientist" (or swap out the microscope for safety goggles and flasks of rainbow-colored water).

When I think about science, I think about collective exchange.

I think about teams on research boats, people networking at workshops, and telescopes set up in a constellation-like pattern on a museum rooftop. I think about togetherness. Let's explore some ways of learning science together and tapping into each other as resources and co-conspirers of wonder.

PEOPLE AS RESOURCES

"You 'tend you a people and..."

(fill in the blank with a wide variety of role-playing scenarios)

—Age 3

WHEN WE THINK of enjoyable family experiences, it is often our interactions with people that made those experiences special — a helpful staff member, new friends we met at an event, or a performer who inspired us.

I once launched and managed a neighborhood-based science studio that served as a satellite site for a science museum. It was an experiment to explore how a hub-and-spoke model might work—if the satellite would act as a feeder, if relationships could be built that enhanced the museum experience, and how programs might be complementary.

One experimental program at the satellite was called Sidewalk Astronomy. On select Friday evenings, volunteers from our local amateur astronomy association would set up their telescopes in front of the studio. People stopped by as they headed to and from restaurants and cafés in this walkable neighborhood.

More often than not, however, people would go out of their way to completely circumnavigate the telescopes, sometimes walking in the street to avoid them. They assumed this arrangement was not meant for their usage.

It was a sincere pleasure to invite them to walk closer or come back to look at the moon or a planet, and to make a personal connection with the night sky. Many people asked how much the experience cost. When they found out it was free, they were pleasantly surprised. Becoming more intimate with an object like the moon, which is part of our daily existence, can be profound. I carry around a certain physical feeling in my torso for days after solar and lunar viewing, as if I am holding bits of the sun or moon's light within me. It feels like a unique combination of atmospheric waviness, inspiration, and connectedness.

One does not need to be a full-fledged expert in a subject in order to be a good facilitator of learning for it. (In fact, being an expert can sometimes impede this.)[28] While the volunteers facilitating the Sidewalk Astronomy were considered "amateurs" or novices, they were very knowledgeable and passionate about their subject matter. Some of them had a newfound interest in astronomy, while others had been part of the association for decades. Their novice orientation seemed to be to their advantage, as they spoke to people in tangible and digestible terms. These volunteers weren't so immersed in the technical aspects of the field that they lacked the perspective of the everyday person's understanding of astronomy.

Of course, technical experts and accomplished science professionals who are also highly gifted at communicating their science do exist (and seem to be on the rise). But the power of the amateur science enthusiast is in the natural way they connect to people, through their passion as much as their content knowledge.

As you come upon individuals, both expert and novice, in your day-to-day life, take the time to connect with them. Invite them to be part of your family's science learning. Science knowledge is held by mechanics, grocery store seafood preparers, carpenters, and other members of your immediate community. As you engage these individuals in conversation and ask them questions about their jobs, you are very likely to gather science-based nuggets that you can add to your family's gold mine of *scientia*.

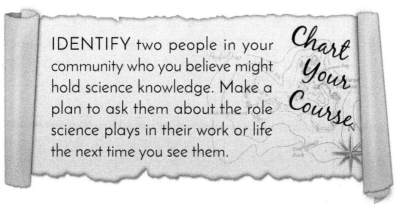

IDENTIFY two people in your community who you believe might hold science knowledge. Make a plan to ask them about the role science plays in their work or life the next time you see them.

MEET BRIJHETTE

I AM FREQUENTLY amazed, humbled, and inspired by others' stories about the cultivation of their relationships with science. One of the people involved in this amateur astronomy club was an African American woman in her twenties named Brijhette. Brijhette has a fascinating array of interests ranging from astronomy to architecture, and I have had the privilege of learning from her and calling her a friend. Like everyone who has a passion for a certain subject, Brijhette has a backstory:

> Our culture tends to, at least outwardly, worship scientists and their work. Because scientists are at the forefront of innovation, new knowledge, and technologies—this "worship" is rightfully earned. But it may lead to misconceptions about the average person's ability (not just the smartest or the richest) to enjoy, understand, and engage in science.

I grew up poor. Having enough food in our fridge and our electricity working were important events worthy of note. My great-aunt, who raised me, completed her education only through the seventh grade before entering the workforce to help her parents provide for her siblings. She always emphasized the importance of an education and believed that education was the best way to break the vicious cycle of poverty.

She pushed me always to do my best in school. This continual pursuit of knowledge extended to objects around the house. I was, as all kids are, intrinsically curious. How does a metal spinning disk make music or movies? What makes a car's lights come on when it slows down? Why did my brother's headphones stop working in one ear? Even though folks in my neighborhood had very little, the common adage was to fix it rather than throw it away. This experience gave me plenty of practice in taking apart all kinds of things—from electronics like radios and CD players to pliers and wrenches whose central bolts were loose—and experimenting with putting them back together again so that they worked.

There was nothing special to us about fixing things; it just was. It was a necessity. As I grew older and attended high school in a different neighborhood, I was astonished to learn that, in some households, if an electronic or part stopped working people threw it out and got a new one. Worse yet, fixing it or "jerry-rigging" was considered "low-class" or "ghetto." I know now, though, that it was in these moments that I had my first introductions to science, imagination, logic, and working confidently with my hands.

The root of what would eventually steer my career aspirations towards structural and earthquake engineering likely stems from these early moments. I'm not (yet) a parent, but the advice I leave for parents is this: sometimes, it's OK to let your kids play with and take apart and tinker with the real thing. I'm sure my aunt's heart sank as yet another radio or TV didn't work again after my tinkering, but the feeling of accomplishment and usefulness of successfully fixing one was unparalleled. For me, knowing that each thing I took apart had value, knowing that the ultimate goal was to get it to work again, motivated me to proceed with caution, pay attention to detail, and engage in experimentation before implementation. These are highly prized skills in just about every activity and profession.

Curiosity is the engine which powers imagination and dreams and, consequently, scientific enterprise. It is intrinsic, as old as intuition itself. The universe has no shortage of wonder; our world, no lack of beauty. It's up to us to not let its bright fire to be extinguished in ourselves and our children.

INTERPRET THIS

(advice to first-time whale watchers)
"Watch and listen for a whale,
so maybe you see it before the instructor does,
which will be a good thing for you."

— Age 7 1/2

WHEN MY SON was two, we went on a highly-enjoyable Birch Aquarium whale watch tour out of San Diego Harbor. While I had seen the distinctive heart-shaped blows of the gray whales from afar on previous watches, this was the first time I was close enough to see the barnacles on their heads. I observed them in awe, aware of the impressive journey they were making from their Arctic feeding grounds thousands of miles away.

We selected this particular whale watch because of the aquarium's reputation and their connection with Scripps Institution of Oceanography. With a balanced mix of informative narrating, quiet ocean viewing time, and respectful whale approaching, we were given a wonderful experience.

Chart Your Course

VISIT a science destination and find a staff member or volunteer with whom you can chat. Encourage your child to ask him or her questions about the content, or their experience with the content.

While on board, we chatted with two passionate and authentically engaged naturalists, as well as a volunteer from the aquarium, Mr. Art. They were very kind to my toddler, who was clearly interested in taking over one of their jobs. My son was mimicking Mr. Art as he showed the other whale watchers the model of the gray whale. We were able to look at a piece of baleen (the long brush-like filters that hang in grey whales' mouths) and jars of krill and amphipods (their main source of food). These types of demonstrations help people imagine what it would be like to see these sixty-thousand-plus-pound animals dredging up their muddy dinners.

Mr. Art and the naturalists embodied the power of first-person storytelling and the value of human-to-human interaction. Science museums and science centers often have docents (volunteers) and staff in the galleries who are there to support your learning. The breadth of their backgrounds spans from teens having their very first work experiences to retired PhD engineers who want to continue having rich social interactions around science.

SCIENCE AS A COLLECTIVE EXPERIENCE

"You know what they say,

the outer the sea the calmer it gets."

(yep, that's what they say)

— Age 5 ½

AS I HAVE shared with you some of my favorite science-themed endeavors, you may have picked up on a common thread: they are often centered on sharing a collective experience around science. As I was growing up, I had the idea that all scientists wore lab coats and worked alone at long benches. While this is one face of science, it is not the *only* face.

Children need to see the adults they most look up to demonstrating a willingness to take risks and be open and vulnerable learners. It is a gift, a privilege, and a responsibility we have as adult caregivers. And the best part? You need not know any of the answers ahead of time. You can seek them out together. Remember, the more that we can give others an open door to our process of science learning, the more likely they are to come along with us.

Chart Your Course

FIND another family with an interest in engaging more with science and set up an experiment time or field trip to learn together. What are they up to this weekend?

Chapter Seven

Science Museums, Natural History Museums, & Science Centers

"Do bone people go to the science 'zeum in heaven?"

— Age 3 ½

Think back to a time where you were in a museum. What motivated you to visit that day? How did you decide your path? What piqued your interest and how did that affect how you spent your time? Did you come across anything that inspired you? And did you follow up on that inspiration in any way?

Free-choice learning experiences allow individuals to pursue learning that is relevant to who they are and how they want to grow — or what interests them in the moment. Museums and other non-formal education environments often lend themselves to these types of experiences. Galleries filled with fascinating objects that have only been seen through media, rich storylines that immerse visitors in other times and places, and opportunities to choose how and where to spend time provide fertile soil for free-choice learning.

What do you picture when you hear the word *museum*? Perhaps pillars and people standing around objects displayed in glass cases, or children with smocks and messy hands.

The term *museum* is broadly used to describe places such as science centers, aquariums, nature centers, and even zoos. In some frames of reference, there are more than one hundred different categories of museums, with various target audiences and subject-based themes, including children, history, and art.

When I use the term *museum*, I am speaking to the broadest range of platforms that readily lend themselves to free-choice learning.

MUSEUMS AND MEANING MAKING

"Museums can actually make you learn a lot of stuff."

—Age 7

WHILE VISITING THE Field Museum of Natural History in Chicago some years ago, I came upon a label that described a West African *Jeli*—a type of storyteller, historian, poet, and musician. In addition to this impressive résumé, the label called the Jeli *meaning makers*. I remember thinking that there might be no job more important or title more distinguished in the world than *meaning maker*.

As a professional in the museum community, I have found museums to be an amazing platform for people to make connections and meaning. Science museums and science centers, in particular, help us to make meaning of how our world works.

My goal is to empower you to make the most out of tapping into science-learning resources, so that you may serve as a facilitator and *meaning maker* for your family's engagement with science.

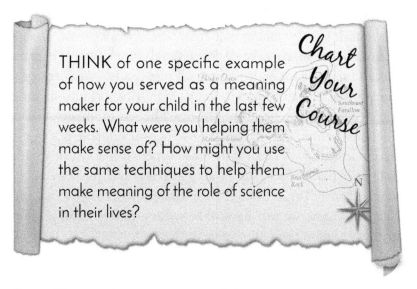

THINK of one specific example of how you served as a meaning maker for your child in the last few weeks. What were you helping them make sense of? How might you use the same techniques to help them make meaning of the role of science in their lives?

FREE-CHOICE LEARNING AND MUSEUMS

"I go to museums just to basically have fun."

— Age 7

WHILE FREE-CHOICE SCIENCE learning can take place in any setting, including a formal education classroom, some places and spaces more overtly lend themselves to science learning than others. Science museums, science centers, nature centers, zoos, and aquariums rise straight to the top as places that are natural Petri dishes for science learning.

Research from John Falk, the papa bear of free-choice learning, showed that the California Science Center has had a significant impact on the science literacy of the greater Los Angeles area.[29]

As of 2009, more than half of the area's residents had visited the Science Center since it opened in 1998. According to the data collected, visitors believe that the Science Center strongly influenced their science and technology understanding, attitudes, and behaviors. It is important to note that these Science Center visitors are broadly representative of the general population of greater L.A. and include individuals from all races and ethnicities, ages, education levels, and income levels. Minority and low-income visitors expressed some of the strongest beliefs of impact.

Science centers are, by design, useful and valuable places for science learning. We can visit these types of institutions with confidence that our science learning interests and needs are being taken seriously. It's as though these centers want to give us a big science hug, and we just have to be willing to step through that entryway and be ready to receive it.

Most science museums and science centers are staffed by people with a rich variety of backgrounds that cover a broad range of science themes and topics. As my colleague Karen (who you will meet in a moment) taught me, they serve as a buffet for allowing children (and their caregivers) to sample a variety of options and select their favorite "foods" for a sit-down dinner.

Science museums and centers primarily exist to support your family's science learning. Consider purchasing a membership and looking at your engagement as a relationship. You and your science center(s) will get more out of a deeper, long-term relationship than a quick visit to see the latest blockbuster exhibit. As with any relationship, communication is a key factor to success. Take the time to give meaningful input and feedback that can help shape your future experiences and relationship with the institution.

Be creative with your relationship. While many of us look at our science museum or science center as a great spot to go on a rainy Saturday or a humid Tuesday with the kids, it can also be beneficial for us adults to have our own connections with the museum, ultimately strengthening our role as facilitators. So, go ahead and round up a few friends for the latest Science of Beer event or Science Café conversation night and send the kids to Grandma's. After all, it's all in the name of science!

Consider other ways that you might like to tap into your local museum's many offerings (such as a team-building experience for work). Museums are often open to reverse engineering the program process. If there is an audience that has a particular wish, even if it's out of the norm (like an adult group birthday party), museums will often work with them (as in you) to arrange a program experience.

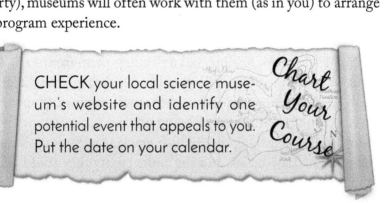

CHECK your local science museum's website and identify one potential event that appeals to you. Put the date on your calendar.

Chart Your Course

ENGAGEMENT LEVEL

"What are cow's favorite thing to put on pizza?"

"Mooshrooms."

— Age 7

I OVERHEARD A conversation one day between two parent friends of mine about a children's museum and whether or not it was age-appropriate for the first parent's one-year-old. My immediate (internal) reaction was, "absolutely." The responding parent, however, gave a more cautionary reply. I incubated on our differing opinions about the suitability of the museum for this child, and I realized our differences were primarily based on two things: how we viewed utilizing museums, and some of the practical logistics.

Many of the exhibits at this particular institution are aimed at preschool-aged children. I was thinking about the safe, open pathways, the large plastic rocks and trucks located in a sectioned-off space, and the giant aquarium that would be wonderful for a one-year-old to stand in front of and observe. I could imagine the child (who was highly verbal) and his father practicing colors and looking for hidden sea life in the aquarium. I pictured my hard-working friend, a teacher, relaxing as his son sat in a pile of the plastic rocks, loading and unloading them from a truck.

I also envisioned him following his son through the building, walking over indoor bridges and through interesting spaces. I pictured the social aspect of being around other parents with their toddlers snacking on goldfish crackers and mini pizzas at the museum café tables, and the connectivity this would bring. It's nice sometimes to have a gentle reminder that others are in this giant social experiment with you.

There is another version of this story, however. Maybe this father would attend the museum and find that his child was too rough with the items in the role-playing areas. He might fear losing his son as he tried to run ahead, and the amenities might not allow him to quickly change his diaper or take care of other matters that were important to him. As parents, we know that the amount of rest, arrival of new teeth, and lunar cycle can all have their random effects on the quality of our outings with our children.

I have found that one of the keys to having a successful day out is being able to manage my expectations as we head into scenarios with many different variables and potential outcomes (which goes back to our conversation about visitor motivation). We all have our safety nets (like bringing granola bars, spare clothes, adhesive bandages, and race cars). In addition to thinking about your visit-related motivations, try to also consider some of the specific operational aspects that contribute to a positive or negative museum visit for you. Can't think of any specifics? I've got you covered in the next chapter.

CONSIDER a negative experience you had at a museum or other venue. How was that experience affected by expectations? Are there any measures you can put in place to manage your expectations of an experience (science or otherwise) in the future? There are learning opportunities at every turn of the bend.

Chart Your Course

Chapter Eight

A Museum Visit

*(after reading the extinction
page of his dinosaur book)
"I have an idea where they all went.
To California.
Does that surprise you?"
(no, no it doesn't)*

— Age 3

A family's visit to a museum can be made or broken by a broad range of experience factors. The following factors, when pre-considered, can contribute to a more fruitful and positive visit (or at least up the odds). Many, if not all, of these factors, apply to aquariums, zoos, and other public science-learning places.

Before we can get into ways of maximizing science learning in museums and other places, we need to think about the basics.

TRANSPORTATION

MANY MUSEUMS HAVE a bus stop located very close to, if not right in front of, their site. Consider potential public transit route options in your area. Not only can this be more cost efficient than parking, but it can also add to the overall adventure.

PARKING

MUSEUMS VARY IN parking arrangements. Many museums have their own parking lots, with costs ranging from free to ten dollars or more, so take this into account. Think about the best arrival situation for your family or group. You may want to drop everyone off at the front entrance before parking. If the weather is inclement, think about what gear you may need or have in tow and how you will deal with it upon arrival.

MEMBERSHIP

I WILL SHOW my bias and encourage you to purchase a membership if you plan on visiting an institution more than one time. Some museum memberships pay for themselves in two or so visits. The economic intelligence, advantages of being brought into the family of the organization, and investment in the cultural aspects of the community combine to make a winning formula. There are organizations, like ASTC (Association of Science and Technology Centers), AZA (Association of Zoos and Aquariums), and ACM (Association of Children's Museums) that have reciprocal memberships, allowing you to get into other similar institutions for free or at a discounted rate. Our family has visited dozens of science museums, science centers, children's museums, zoos, and nature centers across the country for free or at a significant discount (often 50 percent) because of our memberships.

You can fill out membership information before your visit by applying online, picking up the application from the museum in advance, or printing it and filling it out at home. Many institutions will even allow you to turn in your receipt of entry within thirty days of a visit and subtract your admission costs from your membership purchase. This discount can be a great option if you want to try a place out before making the investment. Museum memberships often come with other perks, ranging from museum store discounts to free passes to bring a friend.

TICKETS

CONSIDER BUYING YOUR tickets ahead of time versus on site. Many museums offer the option of purchasing them on their website. Be prepared that you may still need to wait in some form of line to pick them up when you arrive, but this wait should be shorter than the regular line. Also worth noting is that many museums offer discounts on tickets (e.g., for military families).

ITEMS TO BRING

DEPENDING ON THE weather, you may show up at the museum with umbrellas, coats, hats, and more. Most museums have some form of coat room. This area may or may not be monitored or have lockers (bring quarters), so be prepared to bring only items that would not devastate you if they disappeared. Many mittens look similar, and there is the chance that they could go home with the wrong owner as an unintentional museum souvenir.

BABIES ON BOARD

WHEN IT COMES to babies and toddlers, one of the most important aspects of an outing is the locomotive equipment. Think about how you and your little one will move around the museum—from slings to wraps to strollers to walking.

When my son was a baby, I loved using a sling. As he aged, I used a soft, backpack-type carrier (which I wore on my front) to cruise around with him attached. I enjoyed the kangaroo-esque feeling of us taking in the sights together. I also experimented with various strollers. When he was a baby, I enjoyed a stroller with a large undercarriage. Gradually the ever-important snack tray was the key dominating factor. Later, the fifteen-dollar umbrella stroller was the most important object in my life, as it was light-weight and I could leave it anywhere and not worry about it disappearing. It actually became so disheveled that, at one point, I hoped someone would take it; yet alas, I just couldn't lose that thing.

There was also a short phase during which I found myself bringing a potty seat in a plastic bag and sanitizing wipes in my backpack, so I would not lose momentum on our potty training efforts. While this might not seem ideal, it allowed me to leave the house without regressing to using training pants. And yes, I used a lot of soap and hot water on it when I returned home. I will be honest and say that this little scheme made me feel like a potty-training MacGyver.

SCHEDULE

KNOWING A MUSEUM'S schedule, and the schedule of its visitors can help manage expectations.

Most museums have free days. These are a wonderful way to remove the financial barrier to accessing a museum and its resources. If you enjoy a collective experience, this might be the right type of day for you. If crowds make you uncomfortable, however, you may want to consider your visitation mindset, plan, and approach. It's also a good idea to pay attention to the local school calendars, as school breaks are busier than other times. Also, consider the flow of the museum's traffic throughout the day. School field trips generally take place up until lunch hours.

This one sounds like a no-brainer, but be sure to check your museum's open hours and closed days. Nothing is worse than standing at a locked door with a group of children who were expecting an adventurous day out. I have been that person, and it is not fun.

Times of demonstrations, performances, and movies are also important to take into consideration as you organize your museum experiences. These offerings and their times are often posted on the museum's website, and staff members frequently have helpful tips about attending these shows, so don't be shy about asking for their insights on crowd size and timing. (Bonus: Sometimes there are member perks in these situations, like member-only events.)

EATING

MOST MUSEUMS HAVE a café, a food kiosk, or at least some snacks available for sale in the gift shop. Consider what will be the best option for your crew and budget. I like to throw granola bars, apples, and water in the backpack, no matter what. Some museums also have designated areas for families who have brought their food. Having a picnic lunch at the museum can add to the fun of the outing. It also gives you time to talk about what you've seen or experienced, look at the map, and plan the rest of your day. Taking time out to eat can also help recharge and cleanse the auditory, visual, and mental palettes.

RETAIL

MOST MUSEUMS HAVE a gift shop or some other form of retail on site. You should be prepared for this before being caught in front of the polished rocks barrel with your guard down. Some museums have gift shops (or multiple kiosks) that you can choose to visit should you wish, while others have exhibits that end with an inescapable retail experience you must pass through to exit.

While making a retail purchase is often an excellent way to take a piece of your experience home, it can also lead to uncomfortable moments for parents who do not wish to purchase items as part of their visit. As with any situation of this nature, the choice is in your hands, and you should feel empowered to make an informed decision. You may also want to have a conversation with your child about any parameters before arriving at the museum.

I once found myself outside of a science museum with my kid wailing that I had broken my promise. We had needed to leave the museum and he just could not choose something in the shop for under ten dollars within this epoch. It was one of those moments I had to mentally repeat the mantra, "stick to your words" over and over again and force my muscles to keep propelling me forward so I wouldn't run back with him into the store. I'll admit, I'm not always great at avoiding the renegotiation.

In between sobs to go back for the astronaut ice cream and his critiquing of my promise-keeping skills (I promise you that I had promised nothing), I was reminded of how important it is to know for myself whether an outing could include a souvenir purchase, what price range would be appropriate, and if so, to communicate all of this before thwarting an otherwise perfect day. I see time and again how when I flail, so does my child (not that navigating ambiguity isn't another important life skill).

Members typically receive a discount in the museum store, and most institutions will allow you to shop at their store (member or not) without purchasing museum admission. Consider buying birthday gifts, holiday gifts, and other merchandise in the shops, as the profits benefit your local museum and sometimes even the causes they support, such as conservation efforts.

SAFETY

AS WITH ANY public space, it is important to consider a safety plan for your family. If you and your child get separated, what will they do and what will you do? We tell our child to freeze where he is and to identify a worker that can help him. A good safety talk about strangers also accompanies this. (I find the Berenstain Bears to be useful for help with messaging in these situations.)

Take the time with your child to help them learn as many important details about your family as possible. Make sure they know you and your spouse, partner, or other guests' full names. Knowing phone numbers and addresses are also valuable information.

Your immediate action should be to notify museum personnel to assist you. Give clear direction to others in your party, regarding splitting search duty. It is important to know how to describe your child's features and characteristics concisely before being in a situation where this is important. Also, pay attention to what your child is wearing, so you can add these details (although they are second to physical characteristics) if they are needed.

In fact, take a photo(s) of your child before going to a large event or venue so that your child's appearance is accurate to that day. The National Center for Missing and Exploited Children (NCMEC) has an app that allows a parent to upload their child's photo in a safe and secure manner. The benefit is that it can be shared with law enforcement should that step be necessary.

When it comes to educating your child about strangers, it's good to talk to them about important phrases to use, such as, "I don't know who this is" and, "they're taking me against my will." Tell your child that if they are unsure who is a worker, they should feel empowered to speak out to adults around them that are not a part of a negative or potentially dangerous situation. Encourage them and give them permission to be loud and bring attention to their situation of being separated from your group.

Most family separations in museums are momentary and can be quickly resolved by communicating a few details to those around you. And most museums have paging systems that can be useful for these situations, and the staff is often in radio communication with each other.

In thinking about other dimensions of safety, consider any medical and emergency items you may want to have on hand. I have a child with a nut allergy and once found myself waiting for my husband to run back from the parking lot with the antihistamine. That was not a fun moment—I was trying to keep my son and myself calm while simultaneously brainstorming how I would mail back my parent-of-the-year trophy. (I have extra return address labels printed if you ever need one.)

When it comes down to it, I am a parent first and a science facilitator second. As we engage in learning experiences, we have to have the basics covered so that we can move into the fun stuff and the deeper knowledge. So go out there and explore, but remember that awareness is an essential skill of science.

TOURING WITH TECH

MANY MUSEUMS, SCIENCE or otherwise, have the option of using audio guide tours. They are typically available for a rental fee and give a behind-the-scenes scoop on the exhibits through a wand-type instrument or at well-placed audio stations.

Some sites also offer smartphone apps you can download before your visit. If this is available for a museum in which you are interested, take the time to explore the functionality of the app before the tour so you can maximize its usage.

Many museums also have low-tech versions of tours, such as a backpack with items for discovery-making (like a magnifying glass) that can be checked out, or a simple scavenger hunt. If your museum doesn't offer this, you can make your own scavenger hunt. It can be as simple as deciding to look for all items that have a connection to a theme (e.g., water), or as complex as pre-making a booklet that has images of items from around the museum (most museums have something of this nature for school groups).

Taking photos and designing the scavenger hunt, perhaps for other family members or friends, could be just as fun as completing the activity. Tasks can range from finding objects to answering trivia questions, the answers to which provide clues to a puzzle. The opportunities are endless.

And if you can't make it out to a museum, more and more institutions are offering virtual experiences. The Field Museum, for instance, has online virtual gallery tours that feel like the next best thing to a museum visit.

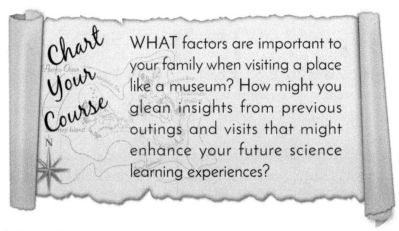

WHAT factors are important to your family when visiting a place like a museum? How might you glean insights from previous outings and visits that might enhance your future science learning experiences?

MEET CHIP

I ONCE WAS involved in a National Science Foundation-funded project called *Math Momentum*, which was centered on highlighting and bringing more mathematics into science-based institutions. I was particularly impressed with one project participant, Chip, and his openness to playing with math. Chip is now the Executive Director of Science at the Children's Museum of Pittsburgh.

I asked Chip to share his insights on what he would like families to know about engaging in math and science learning in a science center setting. He shared the following:

> It turns out that a math exhibit was difficult to do well, because of where the math exists. It doesn't exist in a physical space or experience. You can't ensure that the visitor is innately mathematical. Math happens in the space between the exhibit and the visitor. Great math exhibits, like all great exhibits, allow the guests to find themselves in the experience.

In an exhibit of dinosaurs, we had a component that encouraged visitors to measure the length of a fossil leg to estimate the creature's running speed mathematically. It is an elegant bit of extrapolation. There is a complicated relationship between leg length and top speed. In the accompanying computer interactive, the formula scrolled on for lines and lines, far too long for some people.

The exhibit compelled visitors to measure the fossil leg and put their data into the computer. It then "took over" and flashed the data in a long, complicated formula. It frustrated visitors when they couldn't see how the method worked. We were forced to redesign the interactive for a longer look at the math. They wanted to see their data move through the equation and reveal the answer. They cared about the process; they were doing math socially.

This social dynamic within museums and science centers carries a subtle and profound benefit. Children see their caregivers doing science, being mathematical, and expressing curiosity and wonder. Adult caregivers and parents see their children excited by phenomena and building new understandings of the world. These simple, pleasant interactions hold revelations that can last a lifetime.

In a simple exit survey of parents at a family science event, we included an open question, "What surprised you most about your visit to the Museum?" There were many answers given: "I didn't know you could blow a bubble that big!" "I learned I could lift myself with pulleys." And on and on. But it also held a surprise. About 5 percent of the more than 250 surveys had a response that said something like, "I didn't know my son/daughter liked science/math." These parents discovered that the children they will live with for the next decade love science and are proficient at mathematical reasoning.

These parents learned something important, and it wasn't what we were expecting when we built our exhibits. They discovered who their children are. In fact, it works two ways. Our children also learned that their adults love mathematics and science, and that they ask questions and remain curious. We are role models on our visits. Be interested, wonder aloud, and share the joy when you don't know something.

A visit to a museum can change what we know about science and math, and it can also change what we know about each other.

Chapter Nine

"Behind the Scenes" of the Museum Experience

"Ask the workers about the stuff at the museum

because then you'll know about it."

— Age 5

As a museum professional, there have been many times when I've wished for the opportunity to explain to people how much conversation goes on behind the scenes of a museum about the need and desire to be relevant. This wish is at the very top of the staff's minds. Regardless of their specific mission, museums want (1) to be interesting and appealing to you, (2) to matter to you, and (3) to be used by you. Without being relevant to you, they cease to exist.

There are entire programs and degrees that prepare people for careers in museums (and they make for the most fascinating internships!). Allow me to share some insights around the inner workings and offerings of most museums. You can apply this knowledge to your next visit or program, or you can apply it to play. My family has made mini museums out of our brick blocks, novelty toys, and clay. Making a "Museum of Curiosity" is the perfect usage of that random bucket of figures and birthday party booty.

Now, back to those life-sized museums...

AWARE OF ENTRY

I don't find it offensive at all that my son walks in front of me and pretends that he's the "little car with the flag" that warns people that I (the big hauler) am on my way.

And I'm completely fine with the beeping.

— Age 5

MUSEUMS OFTEN HAVE signage, objects in cases, or sculptures that help you make sense of what is to be expected in the space you are entering. The fancy museum term for these elements is *advance organizers*. Advance organizers help you get a taste of the topic you will explore once you enter. It's often worthwhile to stop and look at these items or displays, to gain deeper meaning of the following experience, and to think about what you might like to explore.

I have experimented with evaluating the qualities that make advance organizers successful in a museum setting. One of my earliest professional experiences with this was trying to figure out what the best stories were that we wanted to tell about the Buffalo Museum of Science's Ice Age Dig site.

When fossils and artifacts were discovered at this site, the staff covered them in plaster casts for safe transport back to the museum. Most of the items were placed in the museum collections, while select others were prepared for display. To explore which aspects of the site's story might be interesting to the public, we dedicated a gallery at the museum to experimenting with how to tell the story. We set a large case outside of the exhibit hall and placed various items in it to help catch visitors' attention and draw them into the space. We also drafted various welcome signs and observed people's reactions, listened to their conversations, and engaged them in follow-up conversations after they read the signage and experienced the hall.

Museum workers often spend a lot of time and energy selecting objects, writing label copy, and preparing visitors for an experience within a select space. When the opportunities arise, take a moment to stop at these advance organizers, heighten the anticipation of your next steps, and engage your curiosity.

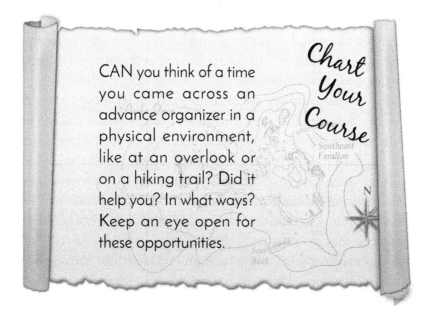

CAN you think of a time you came across an advance organizer in a physical environment, like at an overlook or on a hiking trail? Did it help you? In what ways? Keep an eye open for these opportunities.

Chart Your Course

On Exhibit

(after getting a pep talk about making good choices)
"It's just really hidden in my body.
And only my heart can find it.
My heart found it.
And now I can be good now."

—Age 4 ½

ONE DAY AT work at the science museum, most of the staff were searching for a lost child. We eventually found him sitting contentedly inside of a giant nose. It was part of a traveling exhibit called *Grossology*, themed on the children's book by Sylvia Branzei.

Thousands of people flooded the museum to experience the science of gross, and we gave them what they came for. I personally made two people faint by giving a cart demonstration about how to create fake wounds (ingredients: petroleum jelly, cocoa powder, and red food dye).

Most modern-day science museums and centers have a mixture of permanent exhibits and traveling or temporary ones. In the 1980s, traveling exhibits became all the rage at science museums. They seemed to be the golden ticket to drawing in the masses.

These come-and-go experiences, however, have proved to be a challenging model for museums. Traveling exhibits can be extremely pricey to rent, there are not always a wide array of blockbusters on the circuit (making them unstable revenue sources), and they don't always help build meaningful relationships with desired audiences (visitors). Many institutions are now putting more effort and resources into their permanent spaces, particularly those that can serve as platforms for changing programs and experiences.

While traveling exhibits can be a great motivation for a museum outing, I would encourage you to also take the time to connect with other aspects of science museums. My son and I love the Foucault pendulum and the brown bear at the Buffalo Museum of Science. When I was a little girl, these objects helped me mark what floor I was on as I ventured through the museum. I distinctly remember how the building felt five hundred times larger than it feels to me today.

Consider the range of experiences that are offered at the museums closest to you. Remember that you don't have to engage with every corner of a museum during a single visit. Sitting in front of a natural history museum diorama and having a conversation about what your child notices might be just what the doctor ordered for focusing, connecting, and building their observation skills. Another visit might focus on fully experiencing a traveling exhibit while it's in town.

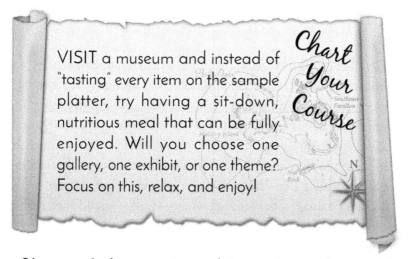

VISIT a museum and instead of *Chart* "tasting" every item on the sample *Your* platter, try having a sit-down, *Course* nutritious meal that can be fully enjoyed. Will you choose one gallery, one exhibit, or one theme? Focus on this, relax, and enjoy!

I have watched parents, time and time again, spend most of the visit saying, "Come on, let's go, we need to get to the next exhibit," as their child is engaged in an activity. As parents, we spend a lot of time hustling our children along, taking them away from activities that engage them, only to follow an arbitrary agenda. We then struggle to help our kids focus and spend extended periods of time completing tasks, such as homework or practicing an instrument.

As a mom, the words, "Come on, we have to go..." come out of my mouth on a regular basis. The struggle is real. But if I'm being honest, my push to keep my child "on course" is not always based on true need. There are times that I am prodding us along simply to get to the next place or predetermined task for no good reason but to "cover it all." It is important to be both honest and reflective about our intentions and actions in these spaces.

PROGRAMS

(takes socks off in the car, looks at his feet)

"Ma, is this what a teenager looks like?"

— Age 3

MUSEUMS TYPICALLY HAVE a broad range of school and public programs. The public programs are often divided into categories such as toddler, youth, teen, family, and adult. Designing science-based programs for a variety of audiences, particularly ones that successfully engage a family's age span, is a passion area for me. These programs serve as bridges to more deeply experiencing places that offer free-choice science learning experiences.

When I managed the satellite science studio I mentioned earlier, I loved having parents and their little ones pile into the five-hundred-square-foot space for Open Studio hours on Saturday mornings. With hot cups of tea or coffee in hand, they would gather around activity tables — the children building marshmallow toothpick bridges, looking into microscopes, and snapping circuits together, and the adults connecting through conversation about movies, news, work, creative projects, and more. Science-based materials and activities provide great substance to gather around.

Museum programs allow us to dig deeper into focused topics and give us the opportunity to look at the world through a particular lens. One of my favorite public programs that I coordinated at the museum was called Bubblefest. It was a festival of everything bubbles and indeed appealed to all ages. The audience ranged from babies to grandparents, and everyone was equally engaged. Bubbles offer an array of experimentation and investigation. From scented bubbles to candy bubbles to glow-in-the-dark bubbles, the options are endless. I must say that the glow-in-the-dark dance room stole the soapy show. (Yes, you can purchase glow-in-the-dark bubble solution for your bubble machine and set up some black lights right in your very own home. Seriously, do it.)

Bubbles are a beautiful example of how you might deeply explore a simple yet multidimensional topic. Beyond some of the conventional types of bubble play available at this festival, many other fun connections to bubbles were made, such as bubble tea, bubbles in glass blowing, and astronomy with our bubbling sun.

SEARCH science programs in your area and online, as many take place virtually. Sample a few experiences and see what types of programs best suit your family.

Chart Your Course

Most museums have programs that operate during school holidays and breaks. Use their event calendars and sign up for their e-newsletters to find fun science opportunities, such as celestial happenings, engineering and chemistry weeks, and themes that connect us globally. As I've mentioned, most science museums also have adult-oriented events that offer fun social opportunities, including events centered around fermentation (yep, beer).

Whatever your age, interests, or social group makeup, there are very likely programs that have been designed with those particular "specs" in mind.

MEET KAREN

MANY OF THE science museum programs, exhibits, and experiences I designed and coordinated were under the mentorship of a woman named Karen. Karen has a deep reverence for nature and for the process of making discoveries in the natural and physical world. Among the many ways that she inspired me was her conviction to start explorations with the use of the term, "I wonder…"

"

> At an early age, I had a "good fairy," as Rachel Carson hoped for every child, to instill a "sense of wonder so indestructible that it would last a lifetime." My dad, an automotive worker, was not book smart but he had a keen appreciation for nature that manifested itself in walks in the woods too numerous to count. No matter the weather or season, found a dad, a little girl, and her dog hiking the paths, stopping to roll over a log in search of critters, watching a crow build a nest, or listening to the angry chirps of chipmunks bothered by our intrusion. My dad's education did not advance much beyond middle school, but he was the smartest person I knew for he knew how to listen to the world around him. His love for the outdoors permeated through his veins and found its way to his little tomboy that looked forward to our adventures, asking question after question about the plants, rocks,

and animals we saw on our daily walks through parks, fields, or our backyard. He sparked my sense of wonder that allowed my curious nature to manifest itself into a rewarding career in informal science learning.

My educational approach to learning stems back to my meanders in the woods with my dad, having entered the academic world through the back door with muddy boots. I found myself teaching how I learned with my dad: to see, wonder, and discover. "To know something you need to see it," my dad would tell me whenever I asked him the name of that tree or bird. He didn't focus on names, for a name is merely a means of communicating, and did not teach you anything about the object. Observation: touching, smelling, and looking ever so closely at the shape of a leaf, or color patterns on a flower, tells you so much more than any label, for it leads to wonder. "I wonder why the leaves are waxy, or I ask myself how a bee finds nectar." Observation, actually seeing things, leads to wonder which leads to discoveries and more wonder.

Instilling a sense of wonder in a young child is not difficult since we are born with an innate connection to the natural world, something naturalist E.O Wilson called *biophilia*. Just spend a few hours outdoors with a young child, and you will see through their eyes: the mighty ant carrying a large crumb; the white, foamy "spit" on the blade of grass; or the hard, green ball on a stem of goldenrod. A sense of wonder that lasts a lifetime begins with observation. Start by asking your child when you come across a squirrel in a tree or museum case, "What do you notice?" Perhaps it's the bushy tail or sharp claws. Then model how to take their observations and turn them into I wonder questions ... "Hmm, I wonder why the squirrel has a bushy tail?" "I wonder why its claws are so long?" Wonder leads to discovery. "What do you do when you walk a balance beam?" "How does that squirrel scurry on that branch without falling?"

It never grows old to see the light bulb turn on when a child makes a discovery by themselves and takes ownership of learning. That is the magic of a sense of wonder; it stays with you for a lifespan, for each "I wonder" leads to another question that leads to another discovery. Every day is filled with awe. All you need to do is look for it and "I wonder" together.

COLLECTING & TRADING

(my son informing me of his career
aspirations; he's going to be...)

"A man. A big man. A mailman.

A mailman who delivers letters to husbands."

(#prayforthehusbands)

—Age 2

SOME MUSEUMS HAVE a collectors' depot, where children can bring in and trade items. This concept has been around for years and is a wonderful way of helping children feel connected to their museum as a personalized place of learning. Proper collecting techniques are an important part of the learning exchange, as there are some important elements to consider, such as protected habitats, live animals in shells, and so on.

Collecting, in general, can be an amazing way to engage your child or family in science. When I was younger, I was an amateur philatelist (stamp collector). I would attend stamp and coin shows and my mother would give me one dollar to spend on the penny stamps. That dollar would keep me busy for hours, as I sifted through suitcases filled with postmarked stamps from around the world, trying to find the perfect one hundred artifacts for my collection.

I can still recall the rewarding feeling (and hear the crunchy sound) of placing them in the vellum rows in my collector's book. But even more, I remember the sense of global connection and infinite possibility that filled my imagination as I did this. It made me hungry to connect with the world in a way that I would later act upon with my passport in hand.

DOES your child have a collection? Spend time understanding how they organize their collectables. Help them draw comparisons between the ways that scientists organize the natural world and how they organize their collection.

Chart Your Course

ULTIMATE BACKDROP

"So...have you been to the children's museum?"
(his opening line for a young lady in the sandbox)

— Age 3 ½

I HAVE ALWAYS looked at books as toys. I love when my child is sitting next to me, enraptured by a story. Museum-type settings can be incredible backdrops for engaging in simple activities that you might typically do at home, such as reading books, coloring, and putting together puzzles.

Imagine your family reading about snakes as you view the reticulated pattern on a python, or learning about how the mother Maiasaura guarded her eggs as you sit amongst other dinosaur skeletons. Perhaps you have a child that loves to draw or color. Bringing a sketchbook and colored pencils along to a museum, zoo, or nature setting can transform an experience. One of the greatest gifts that an activity of this kind provides is the opportunity to sharpen your child's observation skills. Just as we often notice more details about the world around us when we are on a bicycle versus in a car, we tend to see more details when we need to know an object well enough to draw or sketch it. Any scientist will validate the value of building skills in observation and precision. And these skills can be developed organically from a very young age.

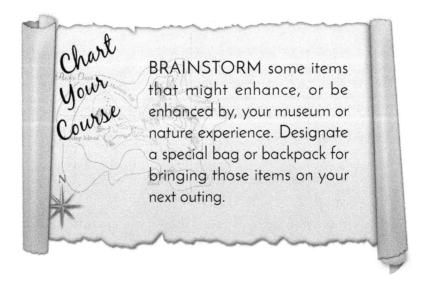

Chart Your Course

BRAINSTORM some items that might enhance, or be enhanced by, your museum or nature experience. Designate a special bag or backpack for bringing those items on your next outing.

My first memory of strategically pairing a book with an outing was reading *Stellaluna* by Janell Cannon in front of the fruit bat exhibit at the Buffalo Zoo. The pages came to life as the bats swooped around in the background and my toddler and I were immersed in imagining their world.

Just as we can bring elements of the museum home, we can also bring aspects of home life to the museum.

MAXIMIZING EXPERIENCES

(When asked what he is excited
about in the coming year...)

"Dessert."

—Age 3

THERE ARE MANY ways that museums can support your child's learning. This includes preparing for or following up on another science experience. As we considered with the Torrance Incubation Model (remember TIM?) in chapter 5, information or activities that *Heighten Anticipation* and/or *Extend Learning* can enrich and deepen our overall learning experiences.

For instance, you might explore the physics activities at a science center prior to visiting an amusement park, in order to heighten awareness about simple and complex machines. Or you may visit an exhibit that covers a science topic that your child will be exploring next in school. Imagine how much better it will be for your child to take in new science information after they have had hands-on experiences that will give them context for that information. Learning happens through this type of layering.

Museums and science centers can also be wonderful resources for extending the learning after your science-based experiences. Two days after going on a whale watch around the San Juan

Islands, my husband, son, and I headed to the Pacific Science Center. As we investigated a model of the Puget Sound under the skeleton of a killer whale, we were able to gain additional context for our whale watch experience. I stared up at the skeleton and replayed my mental video of the giant fin of Blackberry from the J pod (one of the resident orca whales in the Pacific Northwest) rising out of the water. On-site resources, ranging from objects to hands-on exhibits to knowledgeable staff members, allow us to explore topics further and build onto our learning.

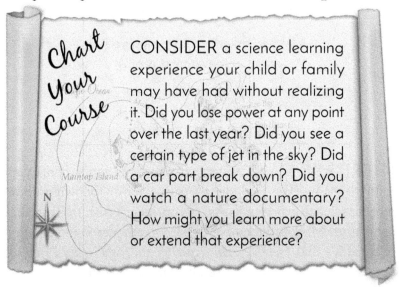

Chart Your Course

CONSIDER a science learning experience your child or family may have had without realizing it. Did you lose power at any point over the last year? Did you see a certain type of jet in the sky? Did a car part break down? Did you watch a nature documentary? How might you learn more about or extend that experience?

ENRICHED HANGOUT

(after I inquired about what he was doing in the other room)

"Do you think I was out drinking a motorjito?"

(thank you, movie with the talking planes)

—Age 4

DURING A SAN Francisco visit, I reconnected with a dear friend that I had met on Maui. We shared an idyllic time there in our twenties. Knowing that we'd have children ages one and four in tow, the California Academy of Sciences was a unanimous first choice for a meetup location. We would be able to talk and catch up in a visually-rich setting, and the kids would be engaged. While at the Museum, we sat on a bridge with sharks swimming under our feet and were reminded of the ocean environment where our friendship had originally blossomed. Museums are great places to engage with our kids, and also great places to connect with other adults.

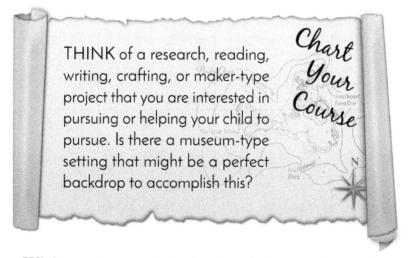

THINK of a research, reading, writing, crafting, or maker-type project that you are interested in pursuing or helping your child to pursue. Is there a museum-type setting that might be a perfect backdrop to accomplish this?

Chart Your Course

While my primary mission here is to help you embrace science learning, I would also like to encourage you to tap into science museums, science centers, libraries, and other spaces for more than just their obvious uses.

Use them as places to energize, focus, change up your environment, and get inspired, as well as for their ambience. There is no rulebook stating that you need to make discoveries about Newton's three laws every time you visit (but kudos if you do make that happen). You can go to these places to catch up on letter writing (how cool to write to your traveling aunt while you're amongst gems from around the world) or to read your mystery novel in a setting surrounded by mummy tombs. These public science institutions are there — ready and waiting — for you to find *your* favorite ways of engaging with them.

Chapter Ten

Aquariums and Zoos

(referencing octopus)
"They're even intelligenter than a raptor,
which are really intelligent."

—Age 5

While I was on Maui working for an eco-tourism organization, I was asked to serve as the first education manager of a newly built aquarium. It was a dream come true for an ocean-loving girl in her mid-twenties from Buffalo, New York.

After staring at Lake Erie for most of my life up to that point, with a stint near the Atlantic while attending college on Long Island, sharing and interpreting the incredible marine life and ecosystem of the Hawaiian Islands was both exhilarating and daunting.

What I personally love about aquariums is the way they transport people. It's not just the way they take us from being on land to underwater, but rather the endless sense of possibility that one experiences from this immersion. For a wide variety of reasons, many people have never seen below the water's surface firsthand. In this respect, aquariums can serve as an introduction to an entirely unseen world.

It was not so long ago that the ocean was a complete and total mystery to us. Through the passion, engineering, artistry, and innovation of individuals like Jacques Cousteau and Emile Gagnan (co-inventors of the Aqua-Lung), we have portals to experience this out-of-reach world. Many aspects of the ocean still remain a mystery, but we have a much greater opportunity today to see and know this aspect of our blue planet than we did fifty years ago.

AQUARIUMS

SITTING IN FRONT of a tank with my child (or, truth be told, anyone's child) and observing the dynamic interactions within an ecosystem is one of my very favorite activities. It's the perfect scenario for a game of "I spy with my little eye," as well as a great example of a concept that nature teaches us best: interconnectedness. As you view a coral reef and watch the interactions between marine life and the environment, you can see the interdependence of life. Looking into a single tank can help us show this important concept in a manageable footprint.

Like zoos, aquariums are often highly engaged in conservation efforts. At Maui Ocean Center, we raised green sea turtle hatchlings and, once they ate their limu (seaweed) and grew big and strong, we released them into the wild. Many people are surprised to learn that we also raised corals. The art of growing corals has taken on a critical role as reefs have been decimated by such threats as warming ocean waters and unnecessary human contact. One of the most compelling aspects of an aquarium setting is the opportunity to discuss these types of issues with the public.

Aquariums also provide the feeling of being transported away from one's day-to-day life. This small effect has the potential for great impact; the otherworldliness of the marine environment is an amazing stimulant for the imagination, and people seem to have a certain receptivity when they are in such an environment. Researcher Wallace J. Nichols writes in *Blue Mind* about the surprising science that shows how being "near, in, on, or under water can make us happier, healthier, more connected, and better at what we do."[30]

Aquariums are amazing resources for introspection and science learning. Yet just because you may be in a science learning setting, that doesn't mean science has to be your sole focus. As with science museums and science centers, you can use these spaces to accomplish other personal goals, such as relaxing, enjoying your time with loved ones in a present state of mind, incubating on a dream, or looking for ideas to solve a challenge.

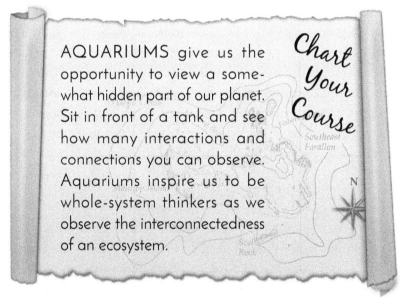

AQUARIUMS give us the opportunity to view a somewhat hidden part of our planet. Sit in front of a tank and see how many interactions and connections you can observe. Aquariums inspire us to be whole-system thinkers as we observe the interconnectedness of an ecosystem.

Chart Your Course

A fun experiment you can try is to have each family member identify a personal goal, wish, or challenge that needs a creative solution before an aquarium visit. Once inside, see if each of you can use the experience to generate twenty-five options for reaching your goal or overcoming your challenge. Tap into the specimens or objects you come across, observations you make, interactions you may have with activities or guides, and so on.

I once tried this experiment with a group of elementary students in an art museum. I was touched by the challenges they identified before visiting the museum—questions such as, "How might I become a better dancer?" to "How might I make more friends?" What was even more profound were the ideas, insights, and solutions that the paintings and sculptures held for these students. As you play with this approach, you will see that there is no challenge that falls outside of its range.

MEET CLAUDIA

ONE OF MY most powerful career learning experiences was pursuing a professional certificate in Free-Choice Learning. Through this program, I was able to connect with museum professionals around the country—from executives to playologists—and more deeply explore the various dimensions of learning. One person I met through the program was Claudia, the Senior Bilingual Education Communications Specialist at one of the country's most prominent aquariums. She shared the following about how she wants families to feel when they are at the aquarium.

> I want parents to feel comfortable visiting the aquarium together while exploring and engaging in learning more about the ocean. Young children are always reminded to behave a certain way when they're out of the home, but at the aquarium we encourage learners of all ages to use all of their senses and ask questions about what they're observing. When parents model this inquiry behavior, they're showing their children how to engage in scientific exploration and wonder.
>
> The great thing about science is that all you need is a sense of wonder. Parents shouldn't feel like they need to

know everything about the natural world because their role should be to help facilitate the discovery. When your child asks you a question, ask them what they think and why. By helping our children make sense of their ideas, we're empowering them to communicate "why." "Why do you believe that this animal is a fish?" "What body parts do fish have to help them to survive?" "Can you see those body parts on this animal?"

It's also important to remember that science can happen anywhere — from our backyards to the beach. Use these spaces to engage in learning conversations with your child. You'll be surprised by all of the things they wonder!

SCIENCE MUSEUM & AQUARIUM HYBRID

(While trying on a pair of harem pants, my son tells me...)

"I like your yoga circus pants. You can go to yoga. And then to the circus."

(#myperfectsaturday)

—Age 5

SOME SCIENCE LEARNING institutions are a hybrid between a science museum and an aquarium. The California Academy of Sciences is home to the Steinhart Aquarium. When we "submerged" ourselves to the lower level of the facility during our first visit, I was enamored with the *Twilight Zone* exhibit. The

Twilight Zone refers to a section of the ocean that is too deep for the average diver and often too shallow for the large investment of a research vessel.

When I lived in Hawai'i, I remembered hearing about Richard Pyle, who studied under the godfather of fish identification, Dr. Jack Randall. (Psst...you met Richard in the Foreword. I reached out to ask him to help set us up for this deep dive into science learning, and gratefully he accepted!) Pyle helped design a rebreather that allowed him to dive at depths of around five hundred feet. I heard how he was discovering marine species by the dozens on these deep dives. And now, here was an entire exhibit about this mysterious region of the ocean.

While my son rotated a mechanical wheel to try to catch virtual fish, I thought about how the career opportunities he will encounter in fifteen years may not even exist yet (one popular estimate places this likelihood at 65 percent, as reported by the World Economic Forum).[31] The areas of science where we know a little, but not a lot, are my favorite. I like to have a certain amount of substance or content to leap from, but I also like the sensation that I might somehow be part of making discoveries and contributions, pushing the frontier in that area. The elusiveness of the Giant Squid (*Architeuthis*)—which swim in very deep and cold waters—was one animal and topic that hooked me early on.

One benefit of a hybrid science museum and aquarium is seeing the dynamic interconnectedness of life. As we searched for geckos in the rainforest exhibit on the upper level, we read about the adhesive properties of their feet. We later saw urchins down in the aquarium and made connections between their tube feet and the gecko feet we had seen upstairs.

We had sketch pads and colored pencils in tow and sat down to draw a reef scene at one of the large windows. My son asked if I could draw the reef for him. I did not oblige. I assured him that it was much more about the fun of trying to draw what we saw, about how imperfect mine was going to be, and that it didn't matter if it looked exactly right. This advice was enough to make him willing to draw. The resulting picture—which was fairly to scale with recognizable fish, seaweed, and anemones—is probably my favorite picture of his to date.

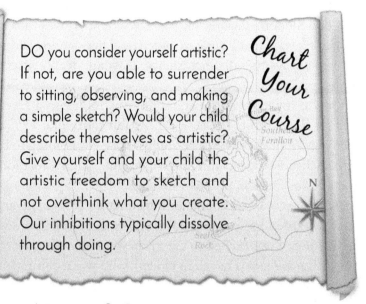

DO you consider yourself artistic? If not, are you able to surrender to sitting, observing, and making a simple sketch? Would your child describe themselves as artistic? Give yourself and your child the artistic freedom to sketch and not overthink what you create. Our inhibitions typically dissolve through doing.

Chart Your Course

SCIENCE, NATURE, & CULTURE

(After a conversation about race, ethnicity, humanity, and how our blood and bones all look similar underneath our skin)

"So every body is everybody?"

(I answered him with deep conviction, "Yes!")

—Age 5

WHEN I WORKED at Maui Ocean Center, one of my favorite topics to share with visitors was the formation of coral reefs. As I described a polyp settling on the substrate and producing its own calcium carbonate (think chalky) home, I was keenly aware that the *Kumulipo*, an ancient Hawaiian creation story chant, captured this process hundreds of years ago with untouchable accuracy and beauty. The Kumulipo reveals an indigenous knowledge that rivals that of a modern-day marine science scholar. It was through my time in Hawai'i that I came to understand how culture and science are not always two distinct arenas. They are deeply interwoven in these islands.

One of my tasks at the aquarium was to design a *Hawaiians and the Sea* exhibit. The assignment felt more like a *life calling* than a work project. My intuition was that I was going to have to actively listen to the community, invest in building relationships, and employ creative problem-solving.

At the time, I was taking an introductory Hawaiian language class. I learned basic conversational terms, as well as a few children's songs. I was excited to use my newly acquired knowledge on one of the *kupuna* (Hawaiian elders), who was a cultural advisor of the aquarium. As I walked by him, I asked, "*Pehea 'oe?*" ("How are you?") He looked at me with surprise and did not answer. He then saw that I was wearing a fish hook necklace. He asked me what I had caught with it. I told him nothing; I had picked it up in a gift shop. He told me I should not be wearing a fishing hook if I did not catch anything with it.

I took this interaction to heart, and decided I needed to be more reverent in my practice and usage of the Hawaiian language and customs — and also that I needed to catch something with my hook if I wanted to continue to wear it! A short time later, I flew to an environmental education conference on O'ahu, where one of the evening activities was a fishing excursion. I jumped at the chance to authenticate my hook. While embarking on the excursion, I took my hook off of my necklace and tied it to a line. After a few solid pulls, the line broke, and I returned to Maui with no fish-catching story or hook. A Hawaiian friend made me a hand-painted slipper-shell necklace to wear in its place—a wonderful consolation prize.

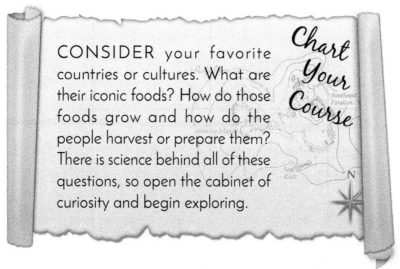

CONSIDER your favorite countries or cultures. What are their iconic foods? How do those foods grow and how do the people harvest or prepare them? There is science behind all of these questions, so open the cabinet of curiosity and begin exploring.

Chart Your Course

I continued investing the energy to learn more about the Hawaiian culture and accepted the cautiousness of Hawaiian elders. I had to jump many hurdles to prove my intentions when designing the *Hawaiians and the Sea* exhibit. I remember sitting on the couch of one of the most revered kupuna on the island, pleading with him to give me the guidance and answers I needed to create this exhibit. What I was mostly asking for, in retrospect, was his approval.

Months later, on the evening of the opening of the *Hawaiians and the Sea* exhibit, all of the elders who had challenged me (some of whom prefer not to occupy the same space at the same time) showed up for the blessing. It was a very emotional night for me, as I had persevered and earned the respect of these individuals who served as cultural gatekeepers.

In the Hawaiian culture, like many other cultures, science and nature are not seen as separate. If you are more intrigued by the social sciences, perhaps this is a key gateway to science learning for you.

Zoos

• •

(discussing how snakes lay lots of eggs)

"Humans only lay one human at a time."

("But what about twins?")

"Still, only one human at a time."

(fair point)

— Age 4

• •

AS I HAVE visited various zoos around the country with my family, the leading message of conservation at most facilities is loud and clear. After a day at the Buffalo Zoo, my son told me about the plight of the rhino, how people hunt them for their horns, and how they are endangered. The facts he knew—and the emotion that was in his voice—were the direct results of his zoo visit.

During that same visit, we had explored an Arctic exhibit and made some exciting discoveries about energy conservation. Reading the display panels motivated me to go home and conduct the "dollar bill test" on my refrigerator (place a dollar bill in the seal of the fridge door and make sure it doesn't slip down) to see if we were wasting any energy.

Like aquariums, zoos give people the opportunity to see animals up close and personal, and to observe physical details and behaviors they would likely never see otherwise. For some children and adults, viewing these animals connects them to places they may have seen only in books and movies. For others, zoos provide education about animals and their habitats, and inspiration to care about these creatures in nature. They serve as record keepers and repositories of data on captive and wild animals that inform conservation efforts, and can even serve as breeding centers for endangered animals. Take the bongo, for example. This native African forest antelope is facing extinction and was bred in captivity and introduced to the wild to help bolster the population.

MANY zoos have online resources, *Chart Your Course* including webcams set up in various exhibits. Log on and check out these resources for yourself. These direct observations can be particularly helpful if your child decides to study a particular animal for a project.

MAKING CHOICES

(swiftly pulling his coat off after I asked him to please leave it on)

"Are you happy Mom, are you happy? You happy?"

("Well, I would be happier if you left your coat on as I asked you.")

"Choose to be happy, Mom."

(please put your coat back on, Dalai Lama)

– Age 3

YOUR FAMILY'S OPINIONS, ethics, and values may affect which public places you choose to spend your dollars and your time. Some individuals are uncomfortable with animals in captivity and may avoid platforms that feature a living collection; other families may find it acceptable to view fish in an aquarium setting, but not marine mammals. The range of variables that impact one's decisions to engage in an activity is as broad as it is personal.

When my son was around three years old, we were reading a story about horses in a circus. I was telling him how I preferred to see horses running wild in a pasture. He looked at me and said, "So, do you like zoos?" Gulp. These conversations are fantastic opportunities to explore your own thoughts, feelings, and opinions openly—while supporting your child in drawing his or her own conclusions.

Ethics, values, and parameters vary from person to person and family to family. Regardless of where you land on your feelings toward science and nature-based spaces and places, the options we have touched on up to this point all lend themselves to science learning, should you choose them.

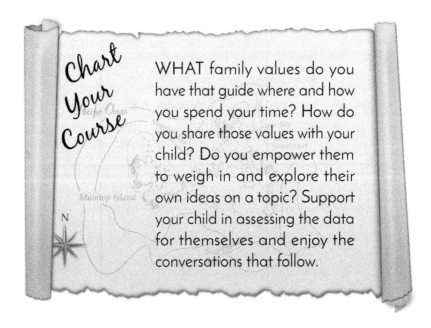

Chart Your Course

WHAT family values do you have that guide where and how you spend your time? How do you share those values with your child? Do you empower them to weigh in and explore their own ideas on a topic? Support your child in assessing the data for themselves and enjoy the conversations that follow.

Chapter Eleven

Nature-based Science Learning

*(telling my son to put his hat
on to play in the snow)*

"I'll just wear my head outside."

(umm, no, please put your hat on)

—Age 2

Humpback whale fins have inspired windmill blade design, lotus leaves have inspired fabrics, and termite structures have inspired ventilation systems. More than ever, scientists, engineers, architects, technologists, and designers are turning to biomimetics (mimicking nature) to identify solutions for design challenges around the world.

Scientists travel to both densely populated and remote areas of the globe to obtain data to help us understand our complex environment. Each and every PhD scientist was once a child who played outside, picking up stones and sticks, likely climbing trees and possibly walking through creeks or woods or along shorelines. They got their start somewhere, at some point, and many of them remember and have written about these early moments.

It is important to be mindful that we are often the main facilitators of getting our kids outside. This might mean turning off the TV and going into the yard. Or, it might mean putting in a little extra effort to pack up the backpack and head out on a trail. These outdoor experiences are often where our very best memories are created, impressions of the natural world are made, and seeds are planted (literally).

A G'DAY FOR ECO-TOURISM

- -

"What is rain's favorite place to rain?"

"The rainforest."

— Age 7

THE TERM *ECO-TOURISM* has been defined in many different ways. Some feel that a tourist destination's environmental impact must be nominal to none in order for it to be considered eco-tourism, while others use this term loosely to describe anything that allows people to connect with nature.

During my senior year of college, I spent three months engaged in an internship at Tangalooma Island Resort, an eco-tourism resort off the coast of Brisbane, Queensland, Australia. I had worked all summer in the Hamptons (Long Island, NY), serving as a house caretaker, nanny, and children's marine educator at a beach club. I worked day and night and saved up the eighteen hundred dollars I needed to buy my plane ticket. That left me with around four hundred dollars in my pocket as spending money for three months on another continent. At the resort, they gave me room and board. A pillow on which to lay my head and vats of dry cereal were all I seemed to need for a high quality of life. (Oh, the basic needs of a twenty-one-year-old.)

Tangalooma was primarily an old whaling station converted into an eco-tourism destination. Wild dolphins came into the harbor each evening, expecting us to enter the water with our buckets of fish. As dusk fell, my fellow interns and I donned our wetsuits, light blue polo shirts (worn over the wetsuit), and Madonna-style microphones.

We took tourists into the water and helped them feed fish to the dolphins. I learned how to say, "take two fish," "please wash your hands," and "please don't pet the dolphins" in Japanese. (I am sure this will get me far one day, should I ever visit Tokyo.)

WHAT aspects of science, nature, and culture capture your imagination? Express these to your child and see where the conversation goes. Perhaps you have shared interests that will lead you to your next destination – through books, movies, or on air, land, or sea!

Chart Your Course

I am forever grateful for the example of seeing how a place that was once known for its flensing decks (where whales were processed after being hunted) could be turned into a place that connected people with the power and beauty of nature. (The flensing decks, by the way, were turned into tennis courts.) The transition from whale hunting to whale watching is a powerful transformation.

As I think back on this experience, several highlights come to mind. Sitting on the grass learning to play the didgeridoo in my

Blundstones, watching the sky turn violet from the southern lights, and dancing to the Counting Crows' "Mr. Jones." I was nearly ten thousand miles away from home, but I felt secure under the watch of the humpbacks and the bottlenose dolphins. I often wonder what gave me the confidence to be so far away from everything I knew, and I've come to the conclusion that it was the combination of my mother making me feel like I was capable of doing anything I set my mind to, and the sheer fulfillment that I received from pursuing my sense of wonder at a resort that helped me connect others—and myself—with nature.

NATURE CENTERS

"You should bring a flashlight, a backpack with food and maybe, like, friends that have been there."

(advice on what to bring to a nature center)

— Age 7 ½

BEFORE I HAD the chance to be with the dolphins and whales, I connected to nature through beavers, white-tailed deer, and peregrine falcons.

I attended a vocational high school that featured majors ranging from plumbing to advertising arts to my (beloved) program, aquatic ecology. My classmates and I put on waders and seined for fish, hiked along boardwalks through cottonwood trees, and planted evergreens on rolling hills at Tifft Nature Preserve, a recovered brownfield turned nature center in downtown Buffalo. During high school, it never crossed my mind that decades later I would walk these same trails with my own little naturalist.

When we grow tired from hiking the nature trails, we can sit on the dock and fish, or warm up by the wood-burning stove inside the interpretive cabin. In the winter, we can snowshoe our way through the trails.

I held my son's fourth birthday party at Tifft, complete with a paleontology theme. The program space in the Visitor Center has the perfect science and nature research feel—complete with reptiles and amphibians in tanks all around. One of the biggest hits of the party was the tent and sleeping bag area we brought in and set up on a large piece of artificial grass. The second biggest hit was the miniature plaster "dino digs"—plaster casts with a small, toy dinosaur inside—that my husband spent hours baking while I was on a work trip. (In all fairness, I asked him to make small cups, and he went all Jurassic Betty Crocker on me.)

Nature centers offer endless ways to explore natural wonders, and they often have excellent program opportunities. They are great places to strengthen your naturalistic intelligence (the eighth type of Howard Gardner's multiple intelligences) and dive into a new level of science learning.

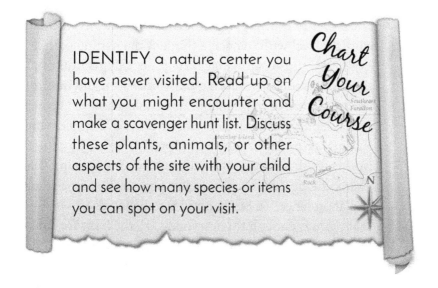

IDENTIFY a nature center you have never visited. Read up on what you might encounter and make a scavenger hunt list. Discuss these plants, animals, or other aspects of the site with your child and see how many species or items you can spot on your visit.

Chart Your Course

MEET MICHAEL

I ONCE TOOK part in a leadership retreat that was somewhat of a social experiment. A foundation sent twenty nonprofit leaders to a nature-based retreat center with no agenda other than to see what might organically happen. I gained some of my deepest, lifelong friendships from this process. Michael, a Native American man, brought an unparalleled strength, balance, and gentleness to our group.

It was clear that he had a deep reverence for nature and an appreciation for the interconnectedness of life. Over time, I have enjoyed watching him parent his son. I asked Michael to share some of his thoughts on science learning.

> When I think of feeling empowered to encourage or facilitate a child's learning, regardless of their knowledge and comfort level with science, I think of the natural path. In exploring and teaching science, especially to my son, I think of it more as exploring our connection and interrelatedness to all of the creation. As Haudenosaunee (People of the Longhouse), we are taught to do a Thanksgiving Address every day to show our appreciation for the natural world and all it provides for our health and well-being. The Thanksgiving Address puts us in a perspective of gratitude and abundance. To be thankful for all, but also to realize that there is enough for everybody. It's the basis for finding peace and living in harmony, while also recognizing the power and wonder of the natural world.
>
> A few days after my son Dawit was born, he was given an address that is said to our newborns. In it he was told that all of the creation is here for him—it is available for

him to tap into and use for his health and well-being. Then in the next verse, he was told that he is here for all of the creation and that he has the responsibility to ensure that it is taken care of and to be able to provide for our future generations.

We are also taught to think inter-generationally. With every action and decision we make, we must think of and ensure the well-being seven generations down the road. Just as we give thanks to those that came before us seven generations ago and did the same for us.

From an indigenous perspective, science itself is the process of discovery. We knew things worked for us, whether it was natural medicines, star knowledge, or understandings of nature and cycles. We just accepted it as gifts from creation, our creator, and our ancestors. We didn't have to prove it, so as science today now explores these connections and providing proof for the benefits of this ancient knowledge, it is proving what we already knew.

We didn't have to convince others, we just gave thanks and then shared the knowledge with others and our future generations. However, bridging the gap in awareness and understanding is what brings us together as humans and as generations.

As we spend time in nature, I encourage my son to look, experience, and observe. We are taught to reflect and give thanks for all the beautiful things, and I encourage him to do so as well. Whether I walk along the waters or hike in the woods or mountains, I choose to stop and then just be still. I can then use all my senses to take it all in. I would find a rock and feel it; I feel the breeze, hear it as it flows through the trees, listen to the birds, taste the air and smell the aroma of the plants and flowers. By being still you will see more as well—animals will appear, you'll see the smaller creatures like insects you would have missed if you rushed through the trail. Or likewise, gazing up at the stars at night and realizing you can see planets and stars with your naked eye that are enormous distances away.

When you engage all your senses, experience all the small things, and reflect, it helps you to realize the larger picture of interconnection through the universe, while also reflecting on how interrelated all of the creation and our generations are, you realize that we do live in a world of wonder. You can feel big and small at the same moment. It also helps to be thankful for all and continue appreciating the wonder and amazement that is surrounding us.

PARKS & TREASURE HUNTING

"When I grow up, I want to be a fox."

–Age 2½

NATURE MAKES SOME of its most dramatic appearances in National Parks. From coast to coast, there are more than fifty parks in the National Parks System. National and State Parks are incredible resources for learning about the geology and geography of an area. They are equipped with maps, knowledgeable staff members, and other resources. When visiting a park, stop into their visitor's center before you head out on your adventure (and after). You never know how serendipitous bits of information might influence or affect your experience. You may choose a different trail based on the ranger's suggestions, or you might learn about wildlife spotting that steers you in a new direction. You may also receive valuable safety tips about mud, erosion, and local wildlife.

Geocaching and *letterboxing* are fun ways to engage with parks, and they come with the added bonus of helping your family develop skills in geography and navigation. Geocaching is an activity that uses GPS to hide and seek caches around the world. You can look online for coordinates in your area or an area to which you are traveling. Once you arrive at the destination, there will (hopefully) be a cache with a small treasure inside (e.g., a keychain). Individuals typically leave something of equal or greater value, usually in the form of toys or trinkets, in the cache after locating it.

Letterboxing is another kind of outdoor treasure hunting that involves finding and seeking a box that has a stamp and log book. The seeker stamps their log book with the stamper in the letterbox and then uses their stamp to leave their mark in the letterbox's logbook. Some of the stamps are highly intricate and handcrafted.

What I love about these activities is that they remind us that the earth holds many secret treasures for us. Of course, it is fairly ironic that searching for a box is what reminds us (not the majestic waterfall it's hidden next to), but my motto is, "Whatever it takes!"

Chart Your Course

RESEARCH geocaching and letterboxing and see which one appeals to you or has the most offerings in your area. Enjoy the process of preparing to engage in these activities with your child, such as carving a letterbox stamp or selecting a cache item.

YOSEMITE

"Snow is nature's art."

— Age 5 ½

WHILE MY FAMILY and I have been to several National Parks, Yosemite National Park is at the very top of my list. From the moment we approached the Park entry for the first time, I was awestruck. The granite cliffs and domes and the luscious evergreens were everything naturalist John Muir had promised about America's first national park.

The informational books we checked out of the library just days before didn't do this valley justice. Nothing prepared me for the majesty of this place. The autumn colors—all shades of brown, gray, green, and yellow were both cool and warm.

We invited a friend from Paris who was visiting the States for Thanksgiving to join us for this trip. While in Yosemite, we also met another couple with a boy my son's age as we were playing checkers in the lounge. We all ended up hiking together (and by hike, I mean we walked about five hundred yards while the boys climbed on every single rock and log on the trail).

Mule deer casually cruised by us as we made our way to Lower Yosemite Falls. Along the path, we watched a bobcat hunting a squirrel. As I saw the little tufts of hair on his ear and his perfect prowling, I felt like sneaking in for a closer look but reminded myself that I was not watching a documentary. We all kept a healthy distance.

Our first true hike was to Mirror Lake. Along the way, we saw fresh evidence of a living animal we estimated could be anywhere between the size of a raccoon and a T-Rex. I reflected on reducing my need for risk-taking. (My mother will be happy to hear that I am working on this.)

Making hot chocolate upon arrival at the lake was completely worth carrying the supplies in my backpack. I've found the premise of receiving chocolate upon reaching a destination to be an effective focus factor for both my kid and myself. (Setting our packs down and staring up at Half Dome was another pretty great reward.)

Since we had brought an adult friend of ours along on the trip, the following day, we decided to divide and conquer. Having a spare adult meant my husband could have a hiking companion to go get a closer look at the famous El Capitan, which was a much more strenuous hike than my son could handle. It also gave my son and me a chance to check out the visitor center, the museum, and the Indian Village, and freely play in this extraordinary landscape (instead of me spouting motivational quotes to help him keep up his pace every couple of minutes).

I, however, did eventually need those motivational quotes as the two of us took a hike up a giant stone staircase that leads to Upper Yosemite Falls. We had a conversation about stamina while I followed his lead. We reached a plateau on the walk and looked at how far we had trekked. The sun would soon be setting, and moisture was building in the air. He decided it was time to head back. I treasure the moments when I get to catch of glimpse of his sense of judgment developing. He was right — it was time.

My husband and our friend returned to the cabin shortly after us, looking a little worse for wear. The sky had opened into a full rain, and the trail led them astray. Some strangers had taken pity on them and had driven them back to the lodge. As they unpacked their drenched maps and flashlights, we exchanged stories from our days. I was grateful to all be back together. (Especially when I saw they had salmon-flavored jerky in their backpacks.)

By that evening, a beautiful snow began to fall. We took the shuttle to a lodge hosting storytelling by an enormous fireplace. The Roosevelts crossed my mind — FDR for his fireside chats, and his fifth cousin, Teddy, for protecting these great lands decades earlier. With hot chocolates in hand, we listened to wonderful tales that captured the essence of Yosemite.

After storytelling, the four of us returned to our cabin and went to bed feeling physically, mentally, and emotionally satisfied.

On the morning of our departure, we woke to a winter wonderland. By noon, my son's hands were numb from throwing snowballs. While I had remembered to bring him a winter coat, he only had cloth gloves and no snow pants. (I had a hard time believing that it snows anywhere in California, so I was a little delusional in my packing.) I mentally updated the long "what I'll do next time I go into the woods" list that I keep in the back of my mind. I know we'll continue to return to this magical destination. Each time we come back, the landscape will have changed, and so will have we. In this way, we will never experience the same space in nature twice.

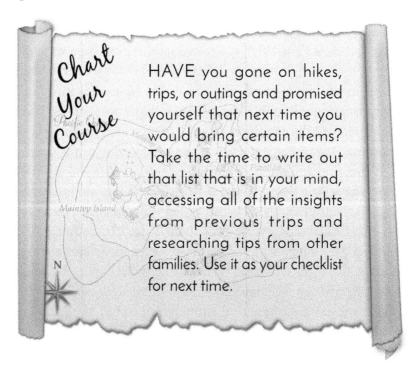

Chart Your Course

HAVE you gone on hikes, trips, or outings and promised yourself that next time you would bring certain items? Take the time to write out that list that is in your mind, accessing all of the insights from previous trips and researching tips from other families. Use it as your checklist for next time.

Natural Play Spaces and Adventure Playgrounds

"Mommy lay down and be a dirt pile.

May I can dig you?"

(well, at least he asked nicely)

—Age 2

THERE HAS BEEN a rising trend in creating natural play spaces, particularly those with loose parts. "Loose parts" is meant literally: parts and pieces, such as sticks, tree cookies (cross-sections of branches and trunks), and tires that children can play with and arrange however they wish. If we were to share this idea with our parents or grandparents, they might ask, "Isn't that just called playing outside?" For whatever it is worth, the pendulum has swung so far away from the natural state of play that we now seem to need a movement to recapture it.

One concept for natural play spaces is called an *adventure* playground. There's one in Ithaca, New York called The Anarchy Zone. Another one in Berkeley, California (officially called Adventure Playground) has child-built forts, boats, and towers. There are signs around the site that show the trade-in value of picking up nails and scraps from the Playground in exchange for materials and tool usage.

Adventure playgrounds are spaces where children are free to be the wild, discovering, exploring, muddy creatures they were born to be. They can exercise their imaginations by hammering and nailing climbing equipment together, digging in the dirt, working together, and adventuring.

There is plenty of research on the benefits of social, emotional, and cognitive development of play. Aside from the sheer confidence-building that designing their play equipment gives them, adventure playgrounds also provide a wonderful way for youth to build their STEM skills. When a child is estimating weight-bearing capabilities and hammering in support beams, they are developing these STEM skills in context, with the ultimate motivation: play!

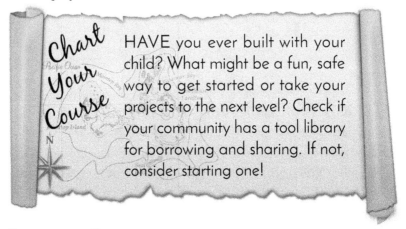

Chart Your Course

HAVE you ever built with your child? What might be a fun, safe way to get started or take your projects to the next level? Check if your community has a tool library for borrowing and sharing. If not, consider starting one!

SCULPTURE PARKS

"That's bizarre."

"What anyways does that mean?"

(uses fancy words, but does not always know meaning)

—Age 4 ½

MY FRIEND SIMON once told me about his father bringing him and his siblings to Europe. The kids all climbed on sculptures at a park—and were scolded for doing so by the individuals operating the site. This experience seeded the idea for his father to create a sculpture park, one where climbing and interacting with the sculptures was not just acceptable, but a vital part of the experience.

When we visit his family's property, Griffis Sculpture Park, my son climbs on larger-than-life caterpillars and peers out of bronze portholes that overlook the tree canopy (the result of the work that Simon's father initiated after returning from Europe). It makes me grateful for people who work to connect us with art, science, and the world around us. These subjects have enough "Do Not Touch" signs mentally hanging for the average person, so we can never have enough invitations encouraging us to climb.

It is realistic that some experiences have expectations for behavior and interactivity. When I saw pictures of a traveling exhibit that had come to town called *Architects of Air*, I was amazed at the incredible light and color in the images. It was set up in a large, open field at one of our favorite waterfront parks. As we came upon the exhibit, which looked like a large, multi-roomed blow-up castle, we were given an orientation that stated clearly that it was not a bounce house.

While inside, my husband and I worked hard to manage two five-year-old boys, my son and his buddy, who wanted to run through it and climb on the walls. Most of the visual triggers said "elaborate bounce house" to them. The ambient music and careful architecture did not seem to match their inner state. Nonetheless, we worked together to slow down, look, and listen. We sat in archways that looked like pods and listened to the way our voices echoed. We talked about why the exhibit was named *Architects of Air*. My winning suggestion to them was to crawl through the space, which seemed to help them slow down (by general laws of physics).

When we reached the end of the boys' patience level for silently creeping and crawling, my husband took them out to play. I remained in the space while they ran around outside, and I had my own experience. I saw new and different elements while walking through alone, observing the shadows, hues, and results of color and light dancing together. I saw angles and color mixing that I hadn't initially noticed before and took some beautiful pictures.

During a family or group outing, I often find a way to have a few minutes to roll solo. As much as I love to facilitate my child's learning and be with my family in general, I also like to have a few minutes alone with a piece of art, an interactive exhibit, or even a retail store (I love me some science *souvenearrings*). I happily return the favor and give my husband the same opportunity.

Breaking off in solitude or sub-groups (if and when possible) and then reconvening can be an excellent energy preserver and also allow individual group members to pursue some of their own interests. This split up can happen organically, for those who are comfortable with flexing with the moment, or it can be preplanned to aid in managing expectations or efficiency of logistics.

DO you know of a space where you *Chart Your Course* can interact with art (perhaps a sculpture in the park or by the water)? Visit this destination and then have a conversation with your child comparing and contrasting the experience with visiting a museum or place where you are not allowed to touch the displays. Look at the experiences from many angles – including how it felt, how you behaved in relation to the exhibit, and what details you remember about it. (The goal is not necessarily to identify which is *better*, but simply how these experiences differed.)

ECO-TOURISM, HAWAI'I

(hiking through a rainforest)

"Let's pretend we're on an expedition."

(OK, easy, because we are)

—Age 5

ON MY WAY back to the US from my internship in Australia, I managed to stretch my "layover" to six weeks on Maui, Hawai'i.

Experiencing nature, particularly salty nature, has always been my biggest pull toward science. When I open Jacques Cousteau's *The Ocean World*, a book from my childhood, I can still capture that feeling of infinite possibility and discovery.

I interned for Pacific Whale Foundation by the referral of a college professor named Paul who was, and still is, in a leadership role with the Foundation and its research. The six-week experience left such an incredible impression on me that I went back for a job six months later after I had graduated. I worked on the boats, serving as both crew and research interpreter. My job was to give whale watches and reef tours, and to clean up corn chips and Leona's semi-famous macaroni salad off the boat decks. (Have you ever seen the amazing expansion capabilities when corn chips absorb water? Science learning really *is* everywhere.) In many ways, it was a dolphin-loving college graduate's dream job.

During these eco-adventure whale watches, I saw pilot whales, humpbacks, spinner dolphins, Pacific white-sided dolphins, and bottlenose dolphins. One of my fondest memories is sitting on the very tip of the schooner's bow while false killer whales were bow riding. (I felt like Kate Winslet gone tropical.)

One sunny day in Hawai'i (which is basically every day), we were out on the water with over one hundred elementary school students. We were looking everywhere for whales, but to no avail. I knew I needed to get creative to keep the children engaged and their energy intact as they obsessed over lunch.

I had the microphone, and I performed a call and response chant. I said, "Whales, come up to breathe." And then the children repeated the phrase. I then said, "Come up to breach." No sooner had the children repeated the chant line for the whale to breach than a ninety-thousand-pound mother whale came flying out of the water next to the boat. The teachers, parents, and I looked at each other with tears in our eyes and our jaws on the deck. I have never taken the spontaneity of nature for granted since that day.

The whale proceeded to nudge her fifteen-foot calf alongside the boat. It was as if she was communicating, "See, this is what I was telling you about." One of the little boys then looked up at me and said, "Make 'em do something else!" I'm not sure I have ever felt as powerful as I did at that moment.

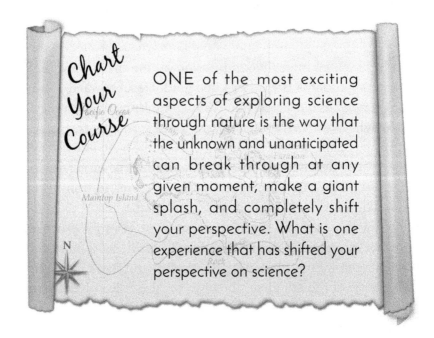

Chart Your Course

ONE of the most exciting aspects of exploring science through nature is the way that the unknown and unanticipated can break through at any given moment, make a giant splash, and completely shift your perspective. What is one experience that has shifted your perspective on science?

TRAIL OF CONFIDENCE

"When the sun comes up from
the bottom of the earth,
the moon just goes down past the
sun, so it doesn't get burnt."

—Age 4 ½

WHEN MY SON was a baby, I specifically taught him how to walk with the goal in mind of one day hiking with him into my favorite bamboo forest on Maui that leads to a waterfall. The trail is part of Haleakalā National Park, and stopping for banana bread, barbeque, and shave ice before the trailhead is a critical part of the journey.

As we approached the starting point of the hike, I wasn't sure as to whether or not his small legs would carry him through the four-mile trek. I felt certain it would be important to have "shiny carrots" along the way. Having hiked this path before, I knew there was a banyan tree, a bamboo forest, and some bridges on the way to the falls. It seemed to motivate my little guy to know what the next marker was along the path — as if it was a clue to a magical puzzle. Reaching these milestones seemed to give him the mental sugar he needed to keep on keeping on. At his request, we used Australian accents as we hiked along.

As the wind blew through the bamboo, playing nature's beautiful music, we connected to the floor in his playroom. I showed him a dried-out piece of bamboo that helped him understand how this material could be turned into flooring. We also used fallen pieces of bamboo as walking sticks and didgeridoos.

As always, it helped to have plenty of water and snacks to sustain us along the way and make rest stops more novel. It also contributed to thinking about the order in which we traveled. I noticed when my husband or I were in the lead, my son seemed downtrodden about keeping up. When we let him be in the lead, he was much more energized.

Hiking gave us the opportunity to talk about sure-footedness and safety, respect for the land, invasive species, and environmental and cultural connections (we sang head, shoulders, knees, and toes in Hawaiian along the way). It also gave me the chance to tell my son I trusted him as I surrendered to allowing him to choose the pukas (holes) where he placed his feet as he was climbing on the rocks. It is in these experiences that I know we are weaving relationship fibers that will last well into adulthood, and that he is gaining the confidence to interact with his environment.

Chart Your Course

YOU may or may not consider yourself the outdoorsy type. If you are not, think of what you might be willing to do to help ensure your child experiences the great outdoors. Hikes come in all shapes and sizes, so do your homework and choose the right hike for you. (If you need to get new, cool boots or an awesome backpack to motivate you, no one here is judging.)

If I had to pick one best way to advise others on engaging in science learning, it would hands down begin with stepping outside. Whether you are in Buffalo or Maui, I promise you that in most ways, it makes no difference to your child. So long as you, the sun, and the moon are in place, the whole world is at their fingertips to explore and make discoveries.

AT THE SHORELINE

"Type this: Cameras from scientists following mole crabs."

(asking me to go on YouTube following our beach outing)

—Age 5

WHEN I WAS tasked with writing the first membership newsletter for the Maui Ocean Center, I searched for the perfect name. I looked up "shoreline" in an online English-to-Hawaiian dictionary and found the word *Kahakai*—the edge where the water meets the sand. A shoreline is a dynamic place of exchange where the sea offers us her gifts and reveals some of her secrets. It also serves as a gallery for temporary collages comprised of seaweed, shells, and other salty treasures.

When I comb the beach on my own or with others, I look for evidence of what is going on beneath the waves. During one afternoon outing to a Pacific beach in Northern California, my son and I, along with some friends, raced to dig into the goopy sand each time the waves crashed and then rushed back out. We let the sand fall between our fingers and felt the tickle of mole crabs leaving our palms. These small crustaceans seem to have the same panic the waves do as they scurry to get back from whence they came.

Along with digging for mole crabs, we searched the shoreline for jellyfish washed ashore, mussel shells, kelp, and other bits representing the ocean's contents.

I'm oddly enraptured by seaweed, and I love to bring my seaweed field guide to the beach and try to identify various species. (Field guides set the stage for the ultimate game of matching, which can be fun for children and adults). In fact, as I type this, there is a plastic shopping bag with a giant piece of bull kelp on my patio. If I inhale closely enough to the nearest window, I can catch a faint whiff of it. (But why would I do that?) My son insisted on bringing it home from our beach visit with Grammy and Poppy. He played with that one piece for a good hour, digging holes to see if he could bury the tip and then keep it secure in the sand while he waved the base up and down. Each time, he dug a little deeper and packed the sand a little stronger. Unknowingly, he made discoveries about force, motion, and other science-based principles that serve as the building blocks for STEM learning. I feel almost certain I would have better understood sines and cosines had my math teacher used kelp.

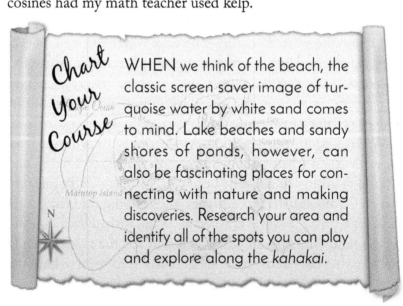

Chart Your Course

WHEN we think of the beach, the classic screen saver image of turquoise water by white sand comes to mind. Lake beaches and sandy shores of ponds, however, can also be fascinating places for connecting with nature and making discoveries. Research your area and identify all of the spots you can play and explore along the *kahakai*.

CASTLES AND TREASURE

"Mommy I love you."

("How much?")

"Six dollars."

—Age 1½

AMONG OUR HOURS of fun at the beach, one of our favorite sand activities is making drip castles with our hands. First, you need a beach with goopy, wet sand (Bodega Bay and Doran Beach in Northern California are perfect for it). Allow the sand to drip through your hands to build tall, skinny towers. When finished, drip castles appear to be made of thousands of small, intricately carved figures. (Warning: this is an internet image-search rabbit hole that will steal at least thirty minutes of your life.)

If you're less of a naturalist and more of an entrepreneur, I might have just the thing for you. We once brought my son and his friend to a beach that was loaded with a wide variety of rocks, logs, and bits of marine invertebrates that had washed ashore. We each set up our own small "shop" and sold our wares to one another. Rocks and mussels were our currency. My son sold fancier rocks with beautiful colors and designs; I sold empty crab claws, shells abandoned by their residents, bits of coralline algae, and other small treasures from the shore that could be used to make ocean fairy houses. My husband was selling organic cheese puffs—one for five rocks, which seemed like a good deal to the smaller merchants.

At one point I became a middleman, purchasing colored rocks from my son and delivering them to his friend's shop, where he was making natural face paint. He had attended Esalen in Big Sur, California and learned to wet and pound rocks to get the color off them. I ended up with a wonderful tribal face painting, which my husband had suggested I wash off prior to arriving at the barbeque place for dinner (I didn't). I suppose the sandstone did leave me looking a little jaundiced.

As I promote places like the beach for science learning, please know that I understand how these environments sometimes provide (annoying) challenges for families. I can quickly conjure an image of sand whipping in our faces and gulls dive bombing my perfectly-prepared picnic on a well-intended "lovely day at the beach." We do our best, but sometimes we end up giving or receiving a lesson in how to be flexible and adapt to situations rather than learning to identify sea life.

Chart Your Course

SAND can be an amazing medium. There are many fun forms of play sand on the market. If you have one or more types of play sand around, consider keeping it in a deep tub and making it an easy access play option. (Basically, bring it down from the top shelf where you put it after the birthday party).

Just as I suggest taking care of primary needs when arriving at a museum, this is also a general mantra for other places. We had set out to go tide pooling at the Pacific one morning, and my son almost immediately started asking to go home. We had only been there for five minutes, so I was disappointed and frustrated by his request—especially after the hour-long, winding drive to get there. (I may have unconsciously given him a deadpan look, complete with my head at a forty-five-degree angle—you know the one.)

When I found my loving patience (which I had apparently left back in the car), I checked in with him and discovered that he simply needed to use the restroom and was not thrilled with the idea of using the porta-potty on site. After resolving the restroom situation, he ended up tide pooling, completely in his element, for hours afterward. These environments can be intimidating for children, and we sometimes need to scale back, check in, and problem-solve to get the most out of an experience.

Chapter Twelve

Other Museums and Places for Science

("What does the coal car do?")

"It burns."

("And what does it give the train?")

"Allergies."

—Age 2 ½

In addition to some of the places we have discussed, such as science museums and aquariums, there are many other places and spaces for science learning. What other spots come to mind for you?

I can picture the exact shelves at our local library where the children's science books are located. When my son sits in front of those shelves, the universe is literally at his fingertips. Consider the power of combining some of your favorite science learning places, such as a visit to the zoo and a trip to the library to research primates, or a trip to the planetarium and a night sky viewing at a nature center. (Along with learning about science, you will also be employing the important creativity skill of making connections!)

Now, where shall we start?

PLANETARIUMS

"I wish that I could play with the moon."

("What would you play if you could?")

"I would do tricks with it. Like strunts.

You know, the Hot Wheels game where you do strunts?"

(aka stunts)

— Age 2 ½

PLANETARIUMS ARE DOMES on which images of celestial objects, such as planets and constellations, are projected from within. Some planetariums live inside of other buildings, while others look like giant inflatable igloos (sometimes transportable for museum outreach at schools, summer camps, and other places). Some universities even have planetariums (though not all of these are made available to the public).

Most planetariums have a live interpreter, a multimedia show, or a combination of the two. There are traveling shows specifically designed for planetariums, much like traveling exhibits at science museums. But whether you're experiencing a traveling show or a permanent one, you're likely to feel a sense of immersion. My imagination takes the lead when I sit in the theatre-style seating, the darkness pierced with shining stars. These facilities are so effective at connecting us with the cosmos.

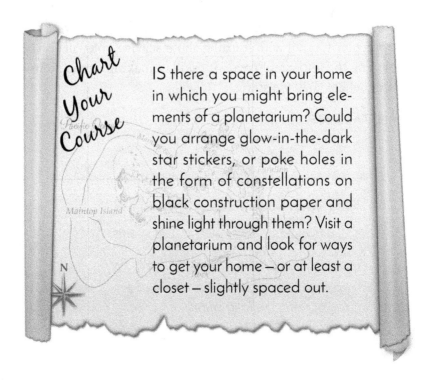

Chart Your Course

IS there a space in your home in which you might bring elements of a planetarium? Could you arrange glow-in-the-dark star stickers, or poke holes in the form of constellations on black construction paper and shine light through them? Visit a planetarium and look for ways to get your home — or at least a closet — slightly spaced out.

ARBORETUMS & BOTANICAL GARDENS

(his two wishes when blowing the dandelion seeds)

"I wish I could think.

I wish I could twinkle."

—Age 2½

AN ARBORETUM CAN be thought of as an outdoor museum of trees. It's a place where trees (and often plants and shrubs) are cultivated for preservation, conservation, scientific study, education, and ornamental purposes. A botanical garden is a place that is dedicated to the collection, cultivation, and display of plants.

The plants are typically labeled with their botanical names and are artistically arranged.

Arboretums and botanical gardens give insights into biology, ecology, conservation, and countless other science-based topics. Many of the individuals who work and volunteer in these places have a passion for their roles and for the environment. They typically love to share that passion with others and are willing to spend time helping you better understand what they do and what they know.

You might find yourself at an arboretum or botanical garden for a wedding or other event, but these settings have so much more to offer than beautiful backgrounds for photos. Consider visiting them for research on what types of plants to grow in your yard, or to help your child learn more about local plants and invasive species.

Once again, I encourage you to bring your sketch pads, pastels, and colored pencils. If you live where it gets chilly in the winter, sitting in a greenhouse drawing plants with your child might be just what the doctor ordered when the cold winds start to blow.

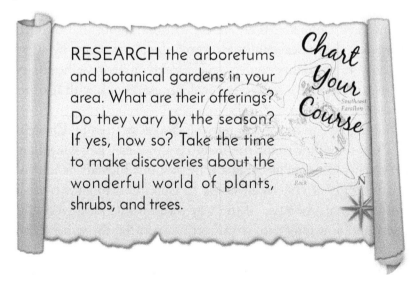

RESEARCH the arboretums and botanical gardens in your area. What are their offerings? Do they vary by the season? If yes, how so? Take the time to make discoveries about the wonderful world of plants, shrubs, and trees.

Chart Your Course

LIBRARIES

My son was confused as to why I
wanted to go to the library for a book
written by "*a blockhead monster.*"

(umm...Einstein, not Frankenstein)

— Age 3

PHYSICAL BOOKS HOLD a special power for me. When I pick one up that I've already read, I can often recall the way I felt during that particular phase of my life in a very visceral way. When I open the book *Flow* by Mihaly Csikszentmihalyi, for instance, I can feel myself in a blissful state riding in a youth hostel van in Australia.

While I tend to do most of my research online, I still take advantage of checking physical books out of the library. I once was writing a blog post on the relationship between creativity and science and came across an Albert Einstein quote that bridged this relationship beautifully. However, the quote varied by a few words from two online sources, so I decided on a trip to the library to seek the primary source—a real, physical book with texture, scent, and *accuracy*.

Setting out on a quest to retrieve a book written by Einstein in 1938 somehow made me feel like a modern-day Magellan. Maybe my excitement bar is a little low, but I loved the idea of orienting my afternoon around a treasure hunt to view typeset words, perhaps because of the way those words (and who said them, and how long ago) so perfectly supported the writing and thinking I was doing about science that day.

When I arrived at the Buffalo & Erie County Public Library with my son and inquired about the book, the *Evolution of Physics,*

I was asked to come back in ten minutes, as they had to retrieve it from the special stacks. (Tell me that the phrase "special stacks" doesn't make your heart skip a beat. I was living the stage that master educator E. Paul Torrance identified as Heightening Anticipation!) After a jaunt in the children's section, we returned for the goods. It was the faded navy blue that only old library books don—a color found nowhere else in nature.

That evening, after the busyness of the day subsided, I flipped through the pages, and there it was on page 95—the precise quote highlighting the fact that properly formulating a problem is often more essential than solving it.

It amazes me how this one individual contributed so much to our modern-day pursuit of understanding how the world works. Einstein's insights were profound and multidimensional, reflecting his habit of whole-brain thinking. Years from now, if I open the *Evolution of Physics*, I will remember how I felt visiting the library with my son on a snowy afternoon, passing on a love of science, curiosity, and smelly pages that take you on an adventure.

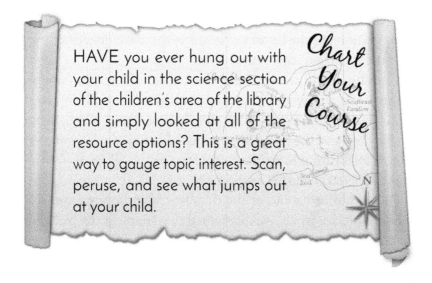

HAVE you ever hung out with your child in the science section of the children's area of the library and simply looked at all of the resource options? This is a great way to gauge topic interest. Scan, peruse, and see what jumps out at your child.

Chart Your Course

History Museums

"They only had black and white crayons in the 19-8's."

(my child's reasoning on the
appearance of old photos)

— Age 4 ½

MY SON USED to often refer to a period called "The Nineteen Eights." After some efforts to understand his thinking, I narrowed the timeframe to be after the dinosaurs, but before modern-day happenings. He typically referenced this particular period in history when he saw antique furniture or black-and-white photos. He informed me that the 1950s were in the 19-8s, so there's that.

Once, as we toured the Buffalo History Museum together, I was struck by how much science was part of the exhibits. I stared at the thick glass of a lighthouse lantern, admired the tools of a shoemaker, and imagined the well-crafted ships that made their way along the Erie Canal. Many individuals have devoted their lives to studying the history of science; there are dozens of ways that these two subjects intersect and overlap.

On our way down into the lower level of the museum, we picked up a scavenger hunt sheet and tried to find the list of items in the train diorama. We searched endlessly for the figure sunbathing and the barbershop model. Having the list gave us a lens to look through, similar to the way history gives us a lens to look at societal changes over time.

As we noticed some of the details in the diorama and read the interpretive labels, we discovered that many of the buildings depicted in the scene were still standing at the time of our visit. It occurred to me that organizing ourselves around the details in this scene could give us at least twenty field trips. We could compare changes, from infrastructure and renovations to variations in the natural landscape to people's clothing and accessories. The process of exploring ideas of this nature lends itself to learning about geography, ecology, culture, engineering, industry, and more. Imagine if we thought of our lives as one long field trip (bus and paper bag lunch not included).

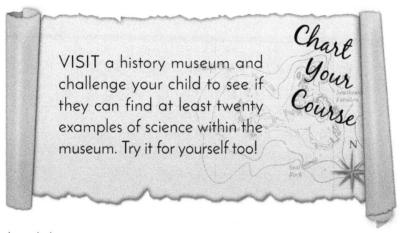

VISIT a history museum and challenge your child to see if they can find at least twenty examples of science within the museum. Try it for yourself too!

Chart Your Course

ART MUSEUMS

("What is pollution?")

"I dunno. Maybe it's art."

— Age 2 ½

LIKE HISTORY MUSEUMS, art museums offer another lens through which we can find science. I once saw an exhibit that explored how paints were made, highlighting the various regions of the globe where certain minerals existed and were used to create specific pigments. It was something I had never thought about prior to that moment. And that is often the magic of museum exhibits.

One evening at a free family night at the Albright-Knox Art Museum in Buffalo, the hands-on activity for kids was based on the work of Lucas Samaras, a photographer, painter, sculptor, and performance artist who is well-known for his use of mixed media.

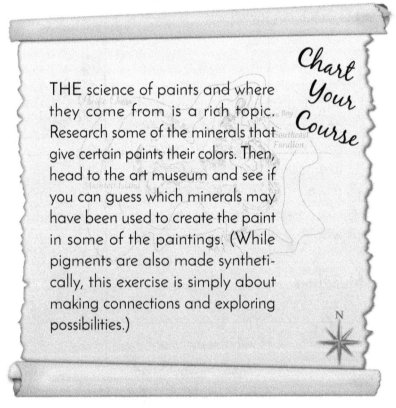

Chart Your Course

THE science of paints and where they come from is a rich topic. Research some of the minerals that give certain paints their colors. Then, head to the art museum and see if you can guess which minerals may have been used to create the paint in some of the paintings. (While pigments are also made synthetically, this exercise is simply about making connections and exploring possibilities.)

Visitors were given a piece of white construction paper to use as the base, a black sheet of construction paper to fold, cut, and place on top of the white sheet, scissors, pastels, and patterned tape. When my son began to glue a piece of paper to the very edge of his base, I had to consciously hold back from telling him that I thought it would easily fall off. I was surprised at how difficult it was for me to hang back. (I also had the overwhelming urge to add glue to every corner of each black piece of paper that he had cut out and placed on the first piece—but again, I held back.)

I have a high degree of comfort with messy, ambiguous, inquiry-based science experiments, but I realize I am slightly more inhibited when it comes to exploring art (which is hard for me to admit). I know some of the "right" things to do, but it still surprises me when these feelings of guidance and control creep up.

I was glad that I didn't offer any technical advice about not gluing to the edge of the construction paper page, especially when my four-year-old son proclaimed that *that* was the dumping bed that had been lifted by the pistons of his monster dump truck, complete with a green cab. I would have gotten in the way of the expression of the two very most important features of his piece: the truck bed and the building of his self-confidence.

ANYWHERE AND EVERYWHERE

"Siphine"

(where my son says we are going
to listen to the orchestra)

— Age 7

WHILE PLACES LIKE science museums, science centers, aquariums, zoos, and maker-type spaces readily lend themselves to science learning, I hope you can see how virtually any space or place can serve as a platform. It truly is about the learner and their curiosity, interests, and sense of wonder. When you are more mindful of your child's science learning experiences, you may be surprised by the places that begin to look like laboratories and workshops. And the most surprising place is often your very own home. We will explore this fantastic science learning platform in chapter 14. (Remember the stage of TIM this represents? *Heightening Anticipation...*)

Chart Your Course

NOW that you have thought a little more deeply about science learning platforms, what is one other unique space you have either accessed or can think of that might serve as a place for science learning? Plan to head there next time with a new set of eyes.

Chapter Thirteen

The Science of Making

*"When you're older you may be
like Thomas Edison if you practice
making stuff when you're younger."*

—Age 7½

When I heard a commercial for a famous company referring to people who like to do projects as "makers," I realized the once-somewhat-underground "maker movement" was now mainstream. If it's your first time seeing the term *maker*, think DIY meets STEAM-based community building. People who would not describe themselves as scientists, technologists, or designers are trying out mysterious equipment and expressing their creativity in new ways—from making vinyl wall stickers and light-up backpacks to launching entrepreneurial ventures.

In an address President Obama gave to the National Academies of Science, he urged us to find creative ways to engage young people in science, encouraging them to make, build, and invent—to be the makers of things and not just consumers.[32]

Adults and children across the nation have answered this maker call to action.

There are thousands of dynamic spaces and places around the country—in garages, workshops, museums, warehouses, and everywhere in between—where makers can gather and use resources, get training, garner inspiration, and collaborate. The success of maker-type spaces is often as much (if not more) about the climate created and cultivated within the space as it is about the physical design and tools that are available.

MAKER MOVEMENT

"*Freezing cold latte, a cappatino, and coffee with booth – that's just the kind of sugar we have.*"

(my barista making coffee on the bathtub ledge)

— Age 3 ½

THE CONCEPT OF "making" long predates community-based workshops with 3D printers. There is a rich legacy of inventors, innovators, and other "makers" that were the earthquake that caused the tsunami that is now known as the maker movement.

I happen to currently live in an area (the San Francisco Bay Area) that pulses with the lifeblood of the maker movement. During his kindergarten school year, my son and I marched in our town's famous Butter and Eggs Day Parade, which boasted the motto, "City of Makers." Fellow parents, students, teachers, and faculty from his school paraded behind a flatbed truck carrying a giant metal Ferris wheel sculpture, donning red shirts that read, "We are Makers." The metal sculpture was soldered by the students of the school, under the direction of the maker instructor—one of only four women ironworkers to work on the Golden Gate Bridge. The wheel won awards at the 2016 Maker Faire.

If you have ever heard of (or attended) a Maker Faire, these events were launched under the direction of Dale Dougherty, the founder, president, and CEO of Maker Media, Inc. I can remember when I purchased my first few copies of *Make:* magazine from a cart outside of a used bookstore in Boston. While I did not plan on making an automatic cat feeder out of a VCR (at least not at that particular moment in time), I knew I wanted to connect to the people who did. Eventually, my career path led me to the very heart of creativity, innovation, and making.

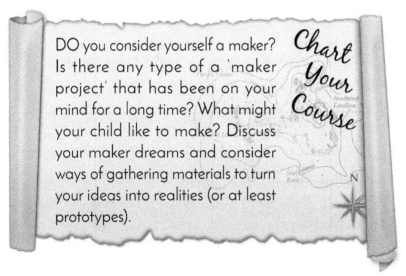

DO you consider yourself a maker? Is there any type of a 'maker project' that has been on your mind for a long time? What might your child like to make? Discuss your maker dreams and consider ways of gathering materials to turn your ideas into realities (or at least prototypes).

Chart Your Course

Dougherty launched *Make:* magazine in 2005 and created the Maker Faire, which first ran in San Francisco, in 2006. I have attended several Maker Faires around the country, and what I continuously find most energizing is the variety of people and interests. From techies operating robots to teens flying drones through stunt tracks, there is no shortage of fascinating folks carrying out hands-on projects; people who are thrilled to tell you their story.

There is a long, rich timeline of making that connects us to our ancestors' need for survival on this planet. While the current maker activity we see now is exciting, it is important to recognize the many individuals who have brought us to this maker place and time over the centuries.

MEET EDRYS

I ONCE VOLUNTEERED to facilitate a retreat for an initiative known as Emerging Philanthropists of Color. Through this event, I befriended a teacher, musician, and artist named Edrys who, I learned, took great pride in being a husband, father, and maker. I keep track of him on social media and find deep inspiration in his endeavors, including his latest involvement in an urban public art initiative called *The Freedom Wall*, which depicts portraits of twenty-eight notable civil rights leaders in American history, past and present. He shared the following:

> Without realizing it, I guess that our household shows many glimpses of STEAM in what we'd describe as a typical day for us.
>
> My wife, Alexa, is trained in the culinary arts, qualifying her as the best and most experienced person in our kitchen. There are a few things that I, along with our two sons, can prepare for personal consumption from time to time, but there is a clear distinction between preparing food and cooking meals! The process of planning recipes and discovering new methods with which to create edible delights, whether savory entrees or sweet desserts, involves lots of math, technology, and science.
>
> Alexa often includes our boys in her culinary experimentations in the kitchen, putting them to work, which also may help them be self-sufficient young men who can feed themselves in the future. Whether for a family

of four or for larger numbers (like catering, for example), measuring is crucial when cooking. From tablespoons to teaspoons, to dry or wet measuring cups, portions for ingredients may be an essential component of successful cooking. Although basic, the mathematical skill necessary for measuring and calculating fractions and whole numbers is regularly used in the kitchen. Whether our children are adding pinches, half cups, or quarts of any ingredient or setting the timer clock, mathematics is being applied.

The frequency with which I've involved our boys in my jewelry studio hasn't been steady, but as they age and mature, I hope to bring them into the fold more often. The same challenges and hazards that exist for them in the kitchen are present in the studio, but I feel it's a great deal more dangerous in consequences if an error or dropped focus occurs in the studio. The tools for cooking are sharp, but the sharp tools used for jewelry are powered. The oven gets hot, but the torch used in the lab is a flame exposed to temperatures of twelve hundred degrees, again, upping the chances for more serious injury.

The few times that they have created jewelry, they've looked over my shoulder to see how annealing works. Annealing is applying an open flame from a torch onto the metal to soften it, permitting the craftsman to bend, twist, and manipulate it into a new shape or form. The molecules in a solid are packed and arranged in a way that makes the metal hard or rigid, but the heat makes those particles move around, somewhat changing the composition of the metal, making it more pliable. If fired for a longer time, it will enter the stage of becoming a liquid form or molten.

The heated metal can become blackened from the interaction with the flame. The dark-like substance is carbon, which is a by-product of oxidation. Oxidation often occurs during this annealing process. When the metal is quenched in water, it cools and stops the heating process. The dark-colored substance or carbon can be removed with a handheld power sanding tool or chemically extracted with a mixture of water and a dry acid compound which will eat away at the carbon. When the metal is removed from either the acid mixture or plain water, it is still workable for hammering or bending or rolling through a mill, but soon it will return to its previous state of rigidness.

My wife and I in our respective trades are delighted to expose our children to experiences that have such significant underlying relevancies to math, science, and tech.

I wasn't aware that we were using STEAM to such a large extent in our home, but I'm happy for the enlightenment after being challenged to identify it.

STARTING TO MAKE

"I have pins and nails.
That's how stiff my foot was."
(aka pins and needles)

— Age 7 ½

MY FRIEND'S SON was about to turn eight, and I overheard him saying that he wanted a multi-tool. I went to the hardware store to see if I could get him one that did not have a knife as part of it. I could not easily find one that was knife-free, but I was set on equipping him to build and make.

The task ended up being more challenging than I had imagined at the outset. In the end, it required assistance from a half-dozen employees, just to get a young builder started. Having designed so many hands-on building projects in my professional world, I felt like I should have been more knowledgeable about something as simple as a starter kit for a beginning builder or maker. As I looked up and down the aisles, I asked myself what advice I would give to someone else in the same scenario. I would tell them to work backward from what they know and to start asking questions.

The first items I asked questions about were hammers. After receiving some helpful tips, I chose a lightweight one with a wooden handle. I was advised to wrap the upper part of the handle with electrical tape for when it accidentally slips and hits the nail (which I was assured would happen).

The second item I went to find were the nails, but I was advised to select my wood first. I was hoping to find pieces of wood bundled in the same way cedar shims are, but this did not seem to exist. I had to buy a couple of two-by-fours and then have them cut into pieces. I randomly asked for six- and twelve-inch pieces. (I later found out at the register that the cuts were twenty-five cents each, so see if you can do this part at home.)

Once I had my hammer and wood, I went back for nails—long enough to hold two of my board pieces together, but not so long that they would go through. Seeing the green coloration that came off the nails, I added a pair of gloves to the kit. The inside tip on gloves for this purpose is to get ones that do not have a rubber palm so that the builder can feel the nail through them.

I chose a simple red toolbox, stickered the top with my friend's son's name in vinyl letters, and placed the other items inside. I wrapped the box and hoped that one day he might look back on this gift as the spark that got him building.

While I could have bought this young friend a ready-to-assemble kit, like a birdhouse, I wanted to equip him to go beyond someone else's blueprints. I wanted him to have endless possibilities—which is exactly what tools accomplish.

The main employee who helped me throughout my shopping process was a carpenter with over twenty-five years of experience who lit up at the possibility of helping a young person engage in his first building projects. He spoke about the hammer and nail options like a sous chef touring me through his kitchen. We cruised the aisles, creating the perfect recipe.

As you consider ways of helping your child build their twenty-first-century skills, you'll find that the path is filled with uncertainty. You should know, however, that you cannot mess this up. Engage in conversation, tap into the people and resources around you, and don't be afraid to buy the wrong box of nails. The return trip to make a better choice, equipped with a clearer sense of what might work best, may give you and your child a deeper learning experience than having gotten it "right" on the first try.

Chart Your Course

WHAT experience does your child have with tools? Real or pretend? Consider working safely alongside them to use a screwdriver to change their own toy batteries. Add in safety goggles for extra flair and safety practice and awareness.

THE RIGHT ANGLE

"If you get earrings, we get donuts."

(my son bartering on behalf of himself and my husband)

—Age 7

YOU MAY HAVE heard the old adage that the only way to become a writer is to write. The same is true of becoming a maker — you must make. My husband, son, and I all consider ourselves makers (of different types).

It has long been my dream to have my own yurt (a round tent-like structure that was used as a dwelling by nomads). I have stayed in these structures at various campgrounds and parks and love the feeling of them. When I moved to California and saw the prices of real estate, my dream of living in a semi-permanent tent started looking like an even-more-appealing option (though my husband said he didn't want people breaking into our house with scissors).

My husband often says to me, "You think of it, I'll build it." We have worked well in these roles of idea generator and implementer. One day he announced that my yurt dreams were going to come true: he came home with a truckload of panels — many of which were triangles — and a bucket with a giant tube coming out of it. Apparently, someone in San Francisco was giving away the hexayurt kit they had created and used as temporary housing at Burning Man. Now, don't get me wrong, I am grateful for any realization of a dream, but this was nothing like those magical structures I had pinned online.

We attempted to move forward with assembling it in our backyard. Aside from the fact that it looked like a UFO had landed in my yard (and the fact that the metallic surfaces were burning our retinas), I don't think Archimedes himself could have assembled the precise and perfect angles this structure was requiring of us. (We probably just needed six more adult hands.)

Long story short, I do not have a yurt in my yard. I do, however, have a large stack of really cool boards that my son and his friends have made into dozens of different structures. They use the playset (which is only half set up in our backyard after being passed on to us from a friend) as the frame and build onto it. The freeplay with them has been amazing, and I am grateful that I allowed a dream to dissolve and provide the material for something else new and interesting (and best yet, open-ended!)

Many great inventions have been the result of finding a new use for an unintended material. As makers, we must keep an open mind to the evolution of our ideas and dreams. Deviating from the blueprints can sometimes result in more windows and doorways.

Chart Your Course

ARE there makers in your town or city? (I promise you, yes!) Are there maker spaces in your city? Find these people and places and consider connecting with them. If your search is unfruitful, perhaps your family will plant the maker seed for which your community has been longing.

Chapter Fourteen

Home as Your Laboratory

"Ma, are we playing sewing shop?"
(poor kid has never seen an
iron used in this house)

— Age 3 ½

Take a moment to think about your home as a laboratory. What type of lab is it when it's in its ideal state? Is it more of a sterile laboratory or a dynamic maker-type space? What does your child have access to on their own and what types of supplies and materials do they need to request? How and where do activities take place? No matter what your answers are, or what kind of ship (plane, train, or automobile) you run, there are many ways that your home can become a center of science to the degree that you desire.

This may mean taking baby steps for some, while others may be ready for a home transformation that screams, "Experiment Here!" Let's see what we can work out for you. We all know that when we push ourselves too far, too fast, it can swing the pendulum in the direction and be an unsustainable venture.

The key is to consider where you currently stand with your home being a venue for science learning and discovery, and to make some tweaks and enhancements that increase the odds for organic science engagement along the way.

HANDS-ON MATERIALS

*"I have to touch the Jell-O and
see if it's bouncy enough."*

(yes, please make sure)

– Age 5

WHEN MY SON was two years old, he smooshed a dough ball together, pressed his fingertips into it and said, "Here mama, I made you a heart." I stared at it in awe, as it did not look like the crafty heart shape with which I knew he was familiar. It looked like a real heart, complete with an inferior vena cava.

While the details of this particular object were serendipitous, it was an important reminder to me of the value of open-ended materials, materials whose possibilities are only limited by the imagination. This sentiment extends beyond young children. I have used clay and small foam pieces to create simple models of what would later turn into full-blown science museum exhibits. While this approach does not offer the precision of a computer design program, it does help to take ideas from the intuitive level and start to give them physical form.

This is the real spirit behind prototyping. Prototyping gives us the opportunity to react to, adapt, and build upon our ideas. It allows us to manipulate ideas into physical realities. It also gives others the chance to respond to, engage with, and collaborate around those ideas.

We all have seeds of artists, architects, engineers, and designers in us. Imagine if we gave ourselves more permission, time, and tools—at every age—to play with open-ended materials that give our ideas form.

CONSIDER how we might help *Chart Your Course* older children and teens continue to use materials like markers, blocks, and clay, in new ways that reflect their maturity, yet honor their need to shape and manipulate their ideas in physical form. The next time you have a gathering, and there are multiple ages involved, consider having these materials available and asking people, "If you could create anything in the world, what would it be?" Watch the creative ideas and fun ensue.

UPCYCLING

(after I asked him to put a box in the recycle bin)

"That's not very creative."

—Age 5

IF YOU BROWSE a high school or college science laboratory, there is some equipment present that costs hundreds or thousands of dollars. But science does not have to be, nor should it be an expensive endeavor. The inventor of the Hovercraft used vacuum tubes and tuna fish cans to design his first prototype.

So much of the packaging that finds its way into our homes can be upcycled before it is recycled. Upcycling is turning trash into treasure by giving it another use. Remember that soup can pencil holder you made back in second grade? Your teacher was way ahead of their time—a clear innovator.

Chart Your Course

CHECK your recycle bin right now and see if you have accidentally tossed aside some treasures. Set up a clean recyclables bin for future projects (complete with a cool, kid-made sign). Find, rinse, design, play, repeat.

Some food packages are so unique that they are begging to be upcycled into something new and useful. I once had purchased small pastry cups that came in plastic divider trays. I showed the trays to my son and was almost charging ahead with my ideas about what they could become when I remembered that facilitating creativity is a huge part of my professional career path. I paused and invited him to brainstorm some alternate uses of the trays.

We ended up with a rocket ship control panel, a paint palette, and a playdough muffin tray.

STORING MATERIALS

(my son explaining to me why he
can set the race track up)

"Since I have a littler life,

I can remember that easilier."

—Age 6

I HAVE SHELVES stacked with tubs of materials that we use for science play and learning—from gliders to spinning tops and poppers. I have these items in clear shoe-sized tubs so that they stay organized, are easy to see, and can be quickly pulled out and then tucked back away.

You can keep your materials out in the open, behind closed doors, in a particular room, or spread throughout your entire home. It's a personal decision. After spending a lot of time running up and down the stairs of my last home, I decided to move all of my supplies and materials for science play and arts and crafts to the first floor to ensure that they were easily accessible and could be a fluid part of everyday life. I noticed a big difference in how often these items were used after making this switch

I'm a big fan of plastic totes. It's an excellent idea to have a tote or two off to the side (like in a closet or the basement) where you can toss cool items that can be rescued from the recycle bin and used for creating, experimenting, and designing at a later date. Things like food trays, CDs, the red netting from clementines, and rinsed-out containers are the perfect items to gather. (The little plastic white spacers that come in the pizza boxes are particularly useful. When I was young, they served as the end tables in my doll house.) You will be amazed at what your child can do with these items when given a pair of safety scissors and a roll of tape.

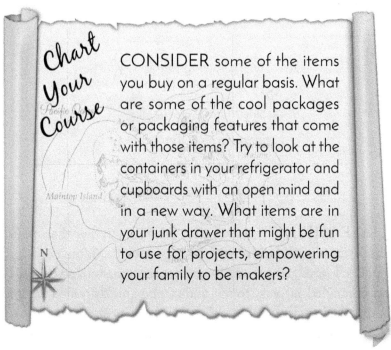

Chart Your Course

CONSIDER some of the items you buy on a regular basis. What are some of the cool packages or packaging features that come with those items? Try to look at the containers in your refrigerator and cupboards with an open mind and in a new way. What items are in your junk drawer that might be fun to use for projects, empowering your family to be makers?

In Our Totes

(me asking where anything is)
"Fortunately, I don't know."

—Age 6 ½

SOME OF THE toys and materials that we keep in totes for easy take out and put away include magnets (a mix of multiple sets, which are more fun to play with together), marble and gear machines, lab-type equipment (like funnels and test tubes), circuits, and nature items with magnifying glasses.

One of our best totes is our spy kit. In it, we have night vision goggles, rear-reflective glasses, a secret message pen, a play phone, a notebook, a pair of binoculars, amethyst, play coins, gloves, and a small treasure box. This is the result of combining random toys left over from birthday-present kits, novelty items from the bottom of the toy bin, and a few props. It's the first bin that one of my son's friends goes for when he comes over to play.

I cannot stress enough the ease, convenience, and novelty factor of having off-the-shelf items to grab and rotate. It integrates science into our lives in a much more accessible manner. Whether you're buying a little time to prep dinner or energizing a rainy Saturday afternoon, it's nice not to feel as though you're starting from scratch each time you want to suggest a little science play.

FIND five shoe boxes (or colllect/purchase clear plastic totes). Use them to make five science or creative play kits this week and label them. (Labeling is so therapeutic.) Place them in a spot that is easy for your child to access.

Chart Your Course

YOUR SCIENCE SPOTS

"Mama, is a corn cob pipe bad for you?"

—Age 5

FOR MY SON'S fourth Christmas, my husband and I made him a workbench. We used two-by-fours that we had lying around and purchased a sheet of pegboard, as well as a variety of small containers and organizers with hooks (to attach to the pegboard). Over time, this bench has proved to be all that we had hoped. When our child sits down at it, he knows that the sky is the limit.

Some of the objects that we have had at our workbench include real and pretend tools, a microscope, drawing utensils and stampers, notebooks, test tubes, eye droppers, a jar of marbles, magnets, washers, small electronics, and empty mint canisters filled with small items. Some of these objects have safety concerns, so it's imperative to know your child and your situation to decide what's appropriate and safe to keep at your workbench or station.

The possibilities for materials at the workbench are endless, and the available materials have changed, based on safety allowances and interest, as my son has aged. His plastic toy screwdriver has been replaced with a real one, and the decorative stickers have gotten slightly edgier.

One of our very favorite activities to engage in at this bench is Snap Circuits. When I managed a satellite science studio, I found that toddlers through adults were engaged by these circuits. They are the ultimate workbench toy, and there are many different adaptations of the kits: you can make a simple fan, a working radio, or an elaborate space sounds system, just to name a few projects. (A nice feature is that when one part breaks, you can replace it—the whole kit is not lost in vain.)

Having a designated spot or area for circuit parts or other activities is a physical invitation for exploring science. Friends of ours have a little nook in their kitchen that is primed with paper, drawing utensils, and a clothesline with small clothespins for hanging new pictures. The space begs you to draw and create. We can make the same opportunities to plug in and play science. Or better yet, we can create spaces where science and art have the opportunity to coexist.

The kitchen, in particular, lends itself very well to science. In addition to being a prime area where this subject naturally boils up, there are many easy resources for STEAM exploration, such as water, mixing bowls, containers, recyclables, basters, items from junk drawers, consumables (e.g., flour and sugar), and the surface of the refrigerator.

One day, my toddler niece was visiting, and we loaded the fridge with our magnetic tiles and shapes. We played with 2D and 3D structures, experimenting with color, weight, dimension, and form. It was a fun reminder that not all science activities take place on a horizontal surface.

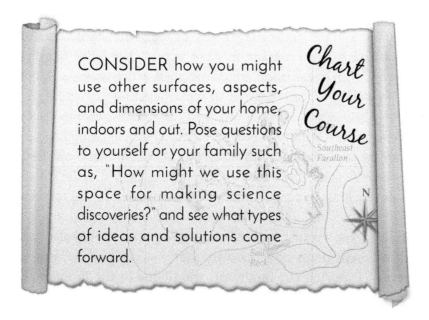

CONSIDER how you might use other surfaces, aspects, and dimensions of your home, indoors and out. Pose questions to yourself or your family such as, "How might we use this space for making science discoveries?" and see what types of ideas and solutions come forward.

Chart Your Course

On another occasion, my son and his friend were playing with a tote of magnetic toys outside and discovered how well the magnetic tiles stuck to the edges of the steel patio table. The tiles made a colorful perimeter around the table and turned it into a ring for small toys and other games. They were particularly fascinated with the pull of the smaller magnets and magnetic balls onto the table as they dropped them from varying heights. This was learning and discovery at its best—through play, pursuing answers to the questions that were forming each time a north and south pole met (or didn't).

Changing Indoor Spaces

"Mom, you go in the basement.
I'll wait up here on land."

— Age 3

ONE OF THE first science museum exhibit spaces for which I served as a project manager was a gallery that could take on the theme of any program. In this space, we had large, tree-like stations with sizeable leaf table tops, all of which were on casters (with locking wheels) for ease of movement and placement.

The gallery was a tabula rasa, and the stations were its pages. We had a wide variety of program themes, such as Structures and Patterns, and could set a diverse array of activities and materials at these stations. The other objects in the gallery, like the stream table—a long, rectangular table filled with small bits of recycled plastic "sand" and a recirculating water source, intended to teach about rivers, streams, and sediment transport— could also take on different items or accessories that would allow them to be part of featuring the programmatic theme of the moment. (I once facilitated a team-building session with real estate agents who were *way* into setting up villages of tiny plastic houses and changing the water flow in the table. Science learning can be fun for grown-ups, too!)

It was through my experience with this gallery that I understood the value of using flexible spaces that serve as a stage versus trying to find the perfect, detailed set design that fits every single performance. There is no complete set of science equipment that every child should have, nor an ideal way to arrange it. It's much more valuable to think about cultivating a flexible environment where tinkering, play, and experimentation are encouraged and accessible.

It's like my dining room table. I purchased it from the scratch and dent section of the furniture store, and over the years we've added to its imperfections with paint stains, scratches from LED prongs, and a few nicks from wood projects. It's nothing that a beautiful tablecloth can't hide. I have friends whose homes are so impeccable that you can't imagine that children actually live there. I also have friends whose homes look…well, the opposite. Be realistic about what your level of comfort is regarding how you take on science in your home. My advice is to check in with yourself and your family, and then set a comfortable stretch goal.

Museums often rotate their activity items and materials in a similar way in various program spaces and galleries. This practice aids in piquing visitor interest through novelty and communicates a sense of freshness that humans often look for in an experience. Our senses are re-engaged as we explore new materials in common spaces. This approach is usually preferable over having all items out at one time, which can create chaos and be overstimulating for children.

I have experimented with the classic trick of placing some of my son's birthday presents (toys) in the closet following his birthday party and reintroducing them one rainy Saturday at a time. This approach has allowed us to get to know one toy at a time and give it our full attention. (Note: This worked better when he was younger. He now keeps a mental spreadsheet as he opens his presents and ensures that they do not get shuffled away to the closet.)

When we give toys or materials their own space, we optimize their chance of being used. It's amazing to see how well children respond to furniture being moved around to form small zones for play. Sometimes toys and activity items that have received little to no attention from a child will take on a new life, just because they are placed in a defined area. Children often enjoy the novelty of refreshed parameters. (The most interested I ever saw my child in an old toy was when I placed it in a box labeled Garage Sale.)

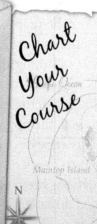

Chart Your Course

EXPERIMENT with placing a few objects (e.g. a pine cone, a leaf, and a fossil), along with crayons, magnifying glasses, colored pencils, and large index cards on a small folding table surrounded by small chairs. See what kind of an invitation it can be for exploration, sketching, discovery, and hands-on engagement.

ACCESS

"Just give me cardboard boxes and tape, and I can create really cool stuff."

—Age 7

AS I FINISHED up work one evening and came downstairs to join my husband and son, I realized that I had accidentally left an electronics project connected. My son told me he had noticed, and that he'd switched out the nine-volt battery I had left connected to a computer fan for one that was "cooled off." I was excited he used his safety knowledge and accomplished this on his own, not to mention that his fingers had seemingly strengthened overnight to be able to pry open those alligator clips (sometimes it's just the little things).

We don't always have to facilitate activities and explain how to use materials in order for our children to learn. Internal motivation and curiosity, combined with access to materials, is often a magic recipe for cultivating their interests.

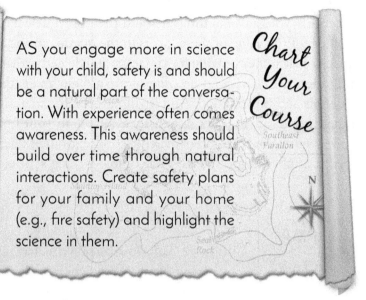

AS you engage more in science with your child, safety is and should be a natural part of the conversation. With experience often comes awareness. This awareness should build over time through natural interactions. Create safety plans for your family and your home (e.g., fire safety) and highlight the science in them.

SCIENCE IN A BOX

(my son as the two of us opened
the Sea Monkey package)

"Two scientists sitting together doing scientific things."

—Age 5

THERE ARE A wide variety of science toys and boxed science kits on the market. I have explored many of them and have seen an increase in both the quantity and quality of STEM toys lining the toy aisle shelves.

You may have noticed that some of the boxed science kits have beautiful graphics on the outside, but contain a dollar-fifty-worth of materials inside (e.g., straws, string, and coffee filters). These materials are often the items you might have in your kitchen cabinet and junk drawer and could pull together yourself. The question comes down to, "Will you?" The answer for myself is sometimes yes and sometimes no (and this is my life calling).

Much of the value of these kits is in the organized and intentional scenario they provide for you to sit and do certain activities and experiments, without needing to run around and gather the materials and information. And in all fairness, the materials are sometimes items that are not easily available in your home or grocery store. We have gotten incredible mileage out of the super-sized test tubes that came with our candy-making science kit.

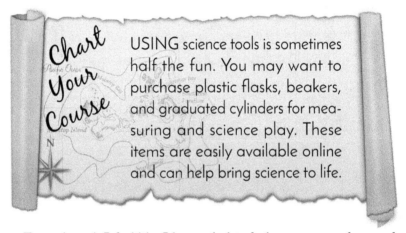

Chart Your Course

USING science tools is sometimes half the fun. You may want to purchase plastic flasks, beakers, and graduated cylinders for measuring and science play. These items are easily available online and can help bring science to life.

Even though I feel like I have a behind-the-scenes understanding of the value of the box contents, I continue to purchase and gift these kits and am enthusiastic to receive them, as they are a mindful placeholder for slipping science into our everyday lives. They remove some of the barriers that keep science learning from being a more prevalent part of our playtime.

A few ways to maximize the use of science kits is to take your time and look at every step as an opportunity to play and build STEAM skills. If an activity calls for one liter of water, let your child measure out and pour ten 100 mL cups of water. Not only is this a great way to expand on skill-building opportunities, but it also extends the experiment or activity. With some forms of whizz-bam-phenomenon science (where there might only be ten seconds of peak reward), this approach can be constructive in bringing more meaning to the overall experience.

SCIENCE IN A BAG

● ●

"I'm so ascited."

(his response to almost everything of interest)

—Age 4

I AM A working mother. At times, my work involves traveling. The first time I had to leave my son for a few days (he was around two years old), I put my blinders on. I looked away from toddlers on the plane; I stuck my nose in my book and laptop; I held my breath, and I melted when I finally returned home. I decided that I would try not to press the pause and numb button in future scenarios of this nature. I had an upcoming program I needed to attend in Texas, so I decided that I would face the separation head on, with trust, engagement, and creativity. For the most part (besides bawling when he handed me his payloader to hold and think of him) we all survived just fine. In fact, we've had many successful business trip separations since then. But nothing compares to the pangs of those first separations.

In preparation for our separation, I had put together several science discovery bags for my husband and son to explore while I was away. I used colorful lunch-size bags left over from a previous event and purchased no materials to make these kits. I looked through the toy, art, science, and activity bins and pulled various items that could fit in these bags and be given a second life by being isolated and highlighted. Sparkle glue pens, which were sitting at the bottom of the paint bin, now had a chance of being used when paired with a blank sheet of construction paper in a shiny green bag. I hid ten bags (two for each day that I would be away) around the house. I then wrote a clue card to where each bag was hidden, folded the cards, and placed them in another bag. My son could draw a card each day and have the joy of demystifying the clue, finding the bag, and doing the activity.

Most of the bag contents were very simple. One bag had eight table tennis balls. His challenge was to make and find targets to bounce them into. Other bags had art and drawing supplies, like playdough to make a snake city or a pencil and a lined tablet to practice writing his name. The most elaborate bag, which was hidden in the new uninstalled dishwasher, was a mini volcano experiment.

I prepped this activity by removing the top of a paper egg carton, flipping over the bottom egg tray, poking holes in the individual egg holders, and inserting several plastic flower tubes (the kind that hold a single rose when you buy it). It was the perfect test tube rack. Ask your florist if they have a few they are willing to share (and then support their business when possible). The corresponding activity bag included baking soda, vinegar, a tiny spoon, and a red and a black marker to color the individual egg compartments (mini volcanoes). A small amount of baking soda could be spooned into each tube and vinegar could be poured in to make the volcanoes explode.

When I returned home, the reality of the situation was that my husband had not needed or used most of the bags (though they did explode the mini volcanoes). They had their agenda filled with racing cars, visiting Poppy and Grammy, and playing outside (as well as the sometimes-laborious tasks of washing, dressing, eating, and sleeping). It was a worthwhile experiment, however, that—at minimum—allowed me to feel I could contribute to my child's days while I had to be away.

MIGHT you consider prepping a few simple experiments and keeping them in a bag for a sitter, a playdate, or just a rainy day? It is often easier to do this ahead of time than to try to create it in the moment of need. Ask any teachers in your life for advice on the value of prepping.

Chart Your Course

BACKYARD SCIENCE

Is it normal for a two-year-old to say *"dump truck"* in a dark, demonic, swearing tone when they don't want to put on their coat and leave somewhere?

(asking for a friend)

– Age 2

OUR PREVIOUS HOME was located in an urban setting, and we had limited yard space. It was important that my (then) two-year-old felt like he could run outside and have a special space to play, so we created a ten-by-twenty-foot play area next to our garage and filled it with pea gravel.

In designing the space, I tried to think of it as a flexible area that could grow and change with him over time. It could be used for exploration and learning activities by multiple ages and help other parents think of creative ways to use limited space to engage their child outdoors.

To maximize the vertical area of the space, we painted gutter pieces and created a ball run on the fence and built and hung a giant chalkboard on the garage. We added decorative features like a banner and three sails overhead.

One of the major changes we made after testing out the play area was removing the sandbox that was an initial key feature. I found that a lot of sand ended up being tracked into the house and that I was ushering him away from the area if we only had a few minutes before we had to leave in the car, or if I didn't want him to play in the damp sand. After removing the sandbox, however, I could tell that my son missed having a defined space within which he could play with his trucks and cars, so I ended up keeping and using the sandbox frame for this purpose. I also filled a small play table with sand, which appeased him, and found that to be much more manageable.

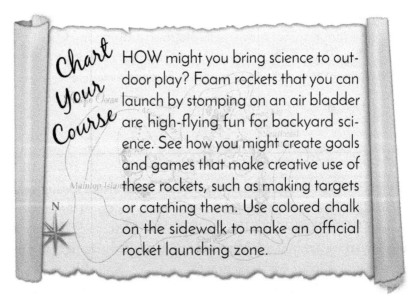

Chart Your Course HOW might you bring science to outdoor play? Foam rockets that you can launch by stomping on an air bladder are high-flying fun for backyard science. See how you might create goals and games that make creative use of these rockets, such as making targets or catching them. Use colored chalk on the sidewalk to make an official rocket launching zone.

MEET RICK

AS I WALKED my son to preschool each morning when he was younger, we often crossed paths with our British neighbor who is a professional photographer. We covered a lot of ground in our quick morning chats over the course of the year. We often spoke about his son. He had that glimmer in his eye when we chatted that silently communicated how seeing us brought him back to his days of having a young boy. He often spoke about his son's interest in computer science. Here is Rick's story:

"

My name is Richard, and I was born in a beautiful part of England. I was born in Colchester, Essex, England. My life was one of playing outside as much as possible; often myself and some friends would play in an area at the back of my house called the back fields. There was also a council dump there. This was an area in which old TVs, radios, and other mechanical items would be dropped. I used to collect mechanical and electrical items, take them home and, using my dad's tools, take them apart. This is one reason I grew up loving working on anything mechanical.

Sebastian, my son, was born on the third of May, 1988. As soon as he was old enough to sit, he showed interest in anything mechanical.

As a child, he was brought up with LEGO and Meccano (a series of bars and angle pieces that can be bolted together). I bought Sebastian his first set of building blocks once he was of an age where he would not put them in his mouth.

This and LEGO were his favorite toys to play with. My career when Sebastian was a baby was a service engineer. He came with me to work and loved to play with the tools. I remember he used to like the clinking sound two wrenches would make. As he got older, he showed an early interest in my computer. He would sit on my desk and loved to press the keyboard and see what happened on the screen. As he grew up, he was always trying to solve problems. If something would not fit or work, he wanted to know why. I realized he was mechanically minded and able to solve problems quickly. I knew he was working problems out logically.

He attended school, and although he did well in many subjects, his love was computers. He attended college for computer study and passed exams with flying colors. Once he left school, he started work with a computer repair shop; he was well known for his ability to solve spyware and virus problems on computers, often reinstalling software and cleaning computers to new. As of now, my son is still working in the computer repair field, solving the most problematic tasks. I am a firm believer that because my son was surrounded by mechanical situations, this encouraged him to become mechanically minded and able to solve problems logically.

Piece by Piece

(after telling my son about how interesting
it can be to take apart machines)

"What's a VCR?

Can you bring me home a radiator or something?"

— Age 5

SO MANY OF the engineers and inventors I have ever met have shared their experience of taking items apart as a child. This act seemed to be critical in leading them down pathways that allowed them to believe they had the skills to solve some of the world's greatest challenges, fill identified gaps, and pursue opportunities for invention and innovation.

I have spent hundreds of hours watching goggle-clad children learning to use screwdrivers and wire strippers as they have taken apart machines and upcycled their parts and pieces into new creations. The process of children seeing how an entire assembly of gears, magnets, and motors once brought them entertainment (e.g., when they functioned as a toy, radio, or computer) is revealing and powerful. Think about it: most children (and adults) do not understand how a smartphone works. Giving your child the opportunity to take apart old devices allows them to have a better understanding of how their everyday world is put together.

It's important to note that the art of taking devices apart has many safety concerns that come along with it. Capacitors can store charge, some devices have mercury in them, and many machines contain glass and sharp components. Research any item that you choose to take apart. If you deem it appropriate for your child, be sure to follow basic tool safety and always protect your eyes — this goes for all other kids and adults present, too.

My son and I once took apart a broken microscope. He loved pulling out and cutting the wires. He had the immediate notion of saving all of the pieces to make something new. It is possible to upcycle the parts of machines, putting them together in new ways for invention prototypes. Sometimes items from these machines can even be re-powered. Computer fans and motors are rewarding in this sense.

Check your basement or the appliance section at your local thrift store and see what you can come up with. Sometimes the most basic mechanical devices can be the most rewarding.

Chart Your Course

CHOOSE a broken toy to take apart and look inside. Be sure your child and you wear proper eye cover and use tools safely. Make predictions about what you will find beforehand and compare it to what you actually find.

Chapter Fifteen

Everyday Science

(when I showed my son a crocus
coming out of ground)

"Ohhh, I get it... that's where
frogs come from!!!!"

(looks up at tree branch and says...)

"Hey, bud.

Get it??"

—Age 5

Though it is sometimes camouflaged in tasks and activities that we take for granted or perform on autopilot, our days and lives are filled with science: from the way our bodies feel in the morning to the lever and wedge we use to butter our toast (yep, a butter knife), to the complex systems within the automobiles that transport us from here to there. As we look more closely at these experiences, we allow ourselves to be more opportunistic and playful with science within them. This mindfulness, in turn, can serve as a reminder to take the time to dig into some of the whys and hows of what's happening around us.

It is important to remember that weaving science into your everyday family life does not need to feel like an extra step on your already-too-long "To Do" list. It doesn't need to feel flashcard-like. If it feels a little forced or somewhat academic at first, be patient with yourself. It will likely come more naturally the more you practice. The key is that everyone (including you) is pursuing their questions and curiosities in an authentic manner.

MAKING TIME FOR MOMENTS

(hands behind head, leaning back)

"So, Mom, what's it going?"

—Age 2½

ONE EVENING (WHEN my son was a toddler, and there still seemed to be fifty-two hours before bedtime), we were running all of our toy cars and trucks over flattened pieces of playdough to see what types of tire tracks each vehicle made. We enjoyed making predictions and putting our theories to the test.

It's often these simple moments of play that make a great plat-form for science-based conversation and learning. We compared and contrasted textures and wheel-width imprints, and gave our opinions about which tracks were our favorite. At one point, I made imprints of several of the tires and asked my son to match their vehicle. He loved guessing, and I watched first-hand how answering built his confidence (even ones he got on the last try).

I was also thinking about how similar this type of play is, in many ways, to laboratory and field work in science. In an elaborate science experiment, it wouldn't be uncommon to take a material and see how various other materials affect it. Before experimenting, predictions would be made.

Our vehicle track-making activity somehow evolved into us being "insplorers" (aka explorers) looking for dinosaurs that ultimately played a game of dreidel at the living room table. You never know where the play will take you ten minutes or ten years from now.

> WHAT is one activity your child engages in that lends itself to testing variables? Ask them questions that help them compare and contrast their observations.
>
> *Chart Your Course*

BETTER ANSWER, ANY BODY?

(looking into my mouth with a flashlight)

"What's that nipple doing back there?"

— Age 3

A GREAT DEAL of a parent's time is spent teaching their child how to care for themselves and their bodies. There's the teeth brushing, the hair combing, dressing, using the potty, washing one's hands after using said potty, eating healthy foods, and the list goes on. The questions that come along with this process of learning self-caretaking can be interesting. Allow me to share one of my less-than-epic responses to this process of discovery.

My son was in the bathtub and asked me what certain body parts were for. I may or may not have told him that that is where his body stores the seeds of life. I was going for accurate biology, though I regretted my answer when he asked a week later if another aspect of his body was a rocket ship for the seeds of life. I headed to Amazon, confident that there were people more skilled on this topic than me and that we would all benefit from their experience and knowledge. While I encourage integrating a variety of disciplines of science into everyday life and conversation, I assumed that astronomy was not meant to be part of this discussion.

Biology, anatomy, and health are excellent gateways to science discovery. Visits to the doctor can serve as incredible platforms for science learning. From looking at the charts hanging in the waiting room to giving your child the chance to ask questions about their body in the examining room, a sick or well visit is a prime opportunity to explore the medical and health sciences. Encourage your child to observe the supplies and tools within the doctor's office and to think about all the people who have been involved in creating the innovations surrounding them.

Doctors and dentists often have models they use to help explain various body parts and functions. A wellness visit is a perfect time for body learning. Helping your child take advantage of these types of opportunities to learn about their bodies also helps build their self-esteem and empowers them as their body's primary caretaker.

Many children play with plastic doctor kits, giving their stuffed giraffes lots of shots. You can help up their game by adding in some real materials (e.g., gauze, adhesive bandages, a real stethoscope, and tongue depressors), and integrating books, posters, and online resources. Ask your doctor or dentist if they have any extra (and safe and appropriate) items they may be willing to share. Many practitioners would be honored to take part in helping groom the next generation of medical and health science workers.

And who knows—you may turn a place of potential intimidation for your child into a community resource they associate with discovery and learning.

WHEN is your next pediatrician appointment? Talk to your child about what they wonder about their bodies and/or being a doctor. Encourage them to ask these questions during their next visit.

Chart Your Course

PLAYING WITH SCIENCE

"There are setherval volcanoes in South America."

(aka several)

—Age 5 ½

WEAVING SCIENCE INTO playtime is one of the easiest ways to integrate more science into your child's life and your parent-child interactions.

Sometimes a pumpkin spice latte is just enough to activate my inner playmate, fueling hours of tower building, car racing, and puzzle making. Other times, I need to dig deep and use a catalyst that costs less than $4.95 a cup. My primary strategy is to select an activity that is as engaging for me as it is for my child. My entertainment bar is low, so this is not a complicated task, but it does occasionally require creativity.

I once tapped into my fond, salty memories of the Southampton College marine laboratory, to build a mini marine science station for the train city that we had assembled on the living room rug. As my then three-year-old was using the words "marine research laboratory," I wondered if I should order his pocket protector right at that moment or wait (perhaps have it monogrammed for his kindergarten graduation).

The train pulled up to the dock and dropped the passengers at the ferry, which took them to the research boat at the marine station. There were fish deliveries and visitors back and forth between the dock and the station all day. According to my son, all the trains came and went at two o'clock (but he also said that he weighed twenty dollars—his details were often sketchy in those preschool years). And what would a marine research laboratory be without an aqua-blue tornado tube bottle for background immersion?

Imaginative play involving the building of worlds, cities, and scenes lends itself well to highlighting STEM careers and content in context. The more that science is a naturally integrated part of your child's daily life and play, the more the notion of "not liking" science becomes an irrelevant future decision-making point. (Beats drum.)

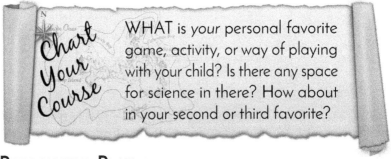

Chart Your Course

WHAT is your personal favorite game, activity, or way of playing with your child? Is there any space for science in there? How about in your second or third favorite?

PORPOISEFUL PLAY

"Pretend that I'm your kid."

(OK, easy, you are my kid.)

—Age 2 ½

I HAVE ANOTHER marine science playing confession. I say confession because I find my internal engagement level to be embarrassingly high for this activity.

My bookshelf is filled with whale, dolphin, coral reef, and general sea life books. These books represent various phases of my interest in the ocean, ranging from a yellow-paged (from aging) Cousteau book to the spinner dolphin book I tried to memorize to be a competent naturalist on eco-tourism boats in Hawai'i. When I pick up the spinner dolphin book, I remember the emotions that filled me before launching into a professional career I had only played in my room just years before.

There is a game I used to play with my younger sister, and now play with my son, that I like to call "whale watch reservationist." I realize exactly how nerdy this sounds, but this is a free world, where some people play dolls and blocks, and others play whale watch reservationist. It's kind of like playing office, but with a sea life spin. Calls come in, and you have to write the tourists' names (or practice writing the first letter of their name after sounding it out) and what time they want to go whale watching. You tell them about what other types of sea life you have been seeing while out on the boats and look up pictures and information in ocean books. It is critical to play ocean or whale sounds in the background for added ambience.

When we play this game, we sometimes draw and sketch animals that we "saw that day" on the research boats. I once brought things to the next level by spraying a beach-scented spray in the room we were playing. (The phrase "taking it too far" popped up in my mind at least once.)

In this one (admittedly obscure) game, we can weave together writing, reading, music, art, marine science, and more. As we are reading and researching, I inevitably pick up informative tidbits about marine life and hone my drawing skills as I attempt to sketch scientific illustrations of squid. When we play games that have real-world context, we give children (and ourselves) the opportunity to practice real-life skills.

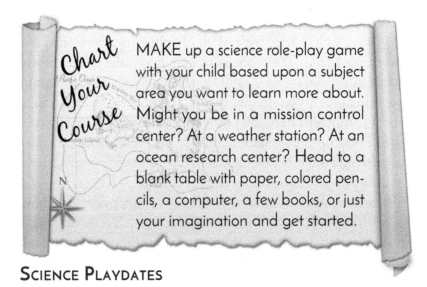

Chart Your Course MAKE up a science role-play game with your child based upon a subject area you want to learn more about. Might you be in a mission control center? At a weather station? At an ocean research center? Head to a blank table with paper, colored pencils, a computer, a few books, or just your imagination and get started.

SCIENCE PLAYDATES

"The F-22 is the most sussificated fighter plane."

(aka sophisticated)

— Age 6

IF YOU ARE reading this and thinking, "This woman is a little too into her whale games," (a) you are likely right, and (b) this doesn't have to be your thing. Weaving science into play does not mean that you have to be a key playmate. You can create opportunities for your child and one or more siblings or friends to explore science together. This can be as simple as placing a few materials at a table (like containers of colored water, eye droppers, and ice cube trays) and allowing them to explore on their own or to facilitate an activity or experiment.

One stormy day, my son's friend came to our house to play. Somewhere in between Thomas being rotated on the turntable and the second handful of goldfish being consumed, a bolt of thunder echoed through the house. When I saw the surprised look on the boys' faces, I pulled one of my science experiment books off the shelf, and we read a little bit about what causes thunder and lightning.

Unable to resist the pull of exploring electrons, I grabbed tissue paper, scissors, and balloons. I had the boys cut small bits of the paper so that they could each rub a blown-up balloon on their hair and see the power of static electricity as the balloons then attracted the pieces of paper.

As the boys worked hard to build up a charge, I remembered that a humid, rainy day does not provide the best conditions for static electricity. Aside from the somewhat anti-climactic results, there was still an excitement about exploring the science behind what we were visibly and audibly experiencing. (It's no surprise that there is a growing body of research that supports the power of play, discovery, and learning in context.)

This experiment lent itself well to talking about how things don't always work out perfectly in testing, and how there are many different factors (variables) that can affect what happens (results).

Hands-on science activities open the doorway to the ongoing dialogue about how the world works. We will try this exercise again on a cold, dry day and then compare our results. This will most likely lead to more questions and more investigations.

GIVE your next playdate a science twist. Look at materials or toys you have available at home, check online, or search through books, and see if you can pick one simple way of playing with science.

Chart Your Course

MEET DIEGO

MY FRIEND AND colleague Diego is the President and founder of Idemax, a creativity and innovation consulting firm, as well as an entrepreneur who lives in Santiago, Chile. We met through the International Center for Studies in Creativity and share a common passion for tinkering and making. Diego focuses a lot of his attention on play and play research. I asked him to please share his insights on the relationship between play, creativity, and science. Here is what he has to offer:

> Play is a core behavior to human beings of all ages not only because it provides pleasure and fun but because it is a primary mechanism for learning and growth. From a biological perspective, play behavior is the mechanism by which humans, dolphins, reptiles, birds (and other animals) explore and adapt to the challenges imposed by the environment, social context, and each species' developmental cycle. Therefore, it is no wonder why infants and children are so prone to play. It is not only because they want to have fun, or because of the absence of adult-like responsibilities, but mainly because childhood is an extreme period of exploration, self-expression, adaptation, and learning.
>
> Play is the natural way of engaging the challenge of "knowing" the world. In this line of thought, when we understand science as a structured discipline (method) for getting to know the world, it is natural to hold science and play as two very close constructs. However, it is not uncommon in educational settings, work environments, and the public to observe how play and science are regarded as opposites. On one hand, play is relegated

to childish, frivolous, unproductive, loose time behavior whereas science is equated to adult, serious, and productive work. Probably the gap between play and science pivots on structure vs. unstructured dynamics that apparently govern each discipline.

When we think about play, immediately we are driven to an unstructured space of fun, freedom and open divergent (infinite) possibilities. When we think about science, we imagine a precisely-defined space, with a structured process, logical sequences, a controlled environment, and a very specific array of possible convergent results. Both imageries are wrong. Play is far more structured than it appears; the fun factor that is at the heart of play is an emergent condition of the structure, rules, and boundaries (explicit and implicit) that govern the play space. On the other hand, science is far more chaotic, erratic, and prone to randomness than the structured process depicts. This is not to say that scientists are not rigorous in their endeavors, but that many of the questions, challenges, and mysteries of the universe dwell more in the domain of uncertainty rather than on predictable space.

Thus, it is not surprising that many scientific discoveries in history are not the product of a discovery plan that turned out exactly as predicted but rather of serendipity, flukes, and mistakes that reveal new, unexpected solutions and possibilities. In saying so, we need to understand that play and science have much more in common than we normally think they do. At the core of both phenomena we find an intense drive to discover, explore, experiment, and create new possibilities and knowledge; both give us intense pleasure and a sense of reward and accomplishment. At a deeper level, science and play fuel one another constantly in one big journey of discovery and creativity. As we face twenty-first-century challenges at local and global scales, we need to make a great effort of placing play and science back together in education, work, and public policy, to harvest the full potential of our adaptive nature to face the problems of today and mold a prosperous reality for tomorrow.

No Passports Necessary

(things my kid teaches me on the way home from school)

"*Buddha. He was a guy.*"

(pause)

"*He was meditational.*"

— Age 6 ½

HAVING WORKED IN multiple science museum environments, I have experienced the incredible connection between science, nature, and culture. Whether it is making Native American corn husk dolls, African gourd rattles, or models of geoglyphs (designs on the ground made of stones), there are boundless opportunities to use natural materials to create projects that explore these connections.

One of my favorite personal experiences of science and nature meeting culture occurred on a snowy day in February when we turned our snow-banked yard into the Himalayas. We had received what I'm sure was our millionth pounding of snow that winter and were all feeling stir crazy. I either needed to make my yard into the Himalayas or buy a plane ticket and head to the Bahamas. The latter wasn't really a practical option. And since the plow service had been barreling up our driveway all winter, pushing snow against the fence and creating a compact mountain range, making the Himalayas was the only reasonable choice.

We set up a tent on one of the snow mounds, complete with sleeping bags. We also created and hung Tibetan prayer flags (child-crafted from construction paper) around the deck. I made hot chocolate and filled thermoses, while my husband downloaded music filled with handbells and cymbals (lovingly rolling his eyes all the while, I'm sure). Last, but not least, we hid over one hundred gold coins in the snow throughout our yard.

We invited our neighborhood friends over and asked them to each bring a shovel and bucket. Upon arrival, the expedition crew members were given a bandana and a map. I drew the basic layout of our yard, and my son enjoyed making random X's all over them to mark where the coins were located. Most of the children wanted their bandana tied around their arm. I noticed what a strong sense of camaraderie this simple act seemed to give them.

We began the experience with an orientation on the deck. Expedition crew members sat on sleeping bags, drank their cups of hot chocolate, and looked at a map of the Himalayas in an atlas I had on hand. We spoke about this region of the world, and they received their mission to find as many gold coins as possible. There was only one collection bucket for the coins to go in, so we worked cooperatively (versus competitively) to collect all of the coins.

One young girl had to go home early for a nap. I later knew the excavation was a complete win when her mom impersonated her screaming, "I want to go back to the Himalayas!!!" This confirmed the experience as an immersion success.

We continued to find the coins well into the late spring, long after the snow had melted.

OPEN an atlas with your child. Flip through the pages. Find a country that piques your child's interest. Search for music from that country, and play it while you create something from there (e.g., a food or a form of art).

MIXING MATERIALS

("What was the best thing you've ever done?")

"Ate bugs.

Unrolled the whole toilet paper."

—Age 3

WHILE I LOVE labeled containers with homogeneous materials in them (e.g., cars or action figures only), I know very well that allowing them to mix often leads to fun, creative play. Mixing toys and materials makes some parents cringe, while others can't imagine that this is not the norm. If you are on team *cringers*, experiment with combining two different toy sets (like magnets and small figures) for future play. If all of the toys in your house are mixed, consider experimenting with a few selective combinations.

A simple act, like giving a child a large piece of butcher paper and crayons, can give one of these tubs of mixed toys new life. I once covered the dining room table with butcher paper as my son was about to play with ocean action figures. He drew a dock and a marina, and I drew an ocean scene. The marine research vessel drove along the wavy waters and collected samples of seaweed (green playdough). There is a magic in combining more definitive materials (like a plastic boat) with open-ended materials that can be manipulated (the dough and coloring scenes). Not only does it increase the chances of engagement (including time spent playing), but it also offers greater use of dimension.

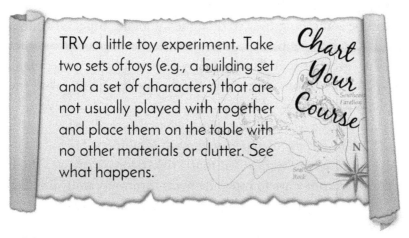

TRY a little toy experiment. Take two sets of toys (e.g., a building set and a set of characters) that are not usually played with together and place them on the table with no other materials or clutter. See what happens.

Chart Your Course

Many great scientists and inventors have combined more than one idea to create a new product, object, or system. Helping our children play with a combination of materials plants seeds around the value of mixing, matching, combining, and synthesizing. (Please know this advice is coming from a mother who used to move the wooden milk from the play kitchen cupboard into the play kitchen refrigerator. Just because.)

MATH AROUND THE HOUSE

"They are just calling it quadrillion
until they find another name."

— Age 6

IN CHAPTER 8, you heard from my friend Chip, who I met through our *Math Momentum* Project. It was during this project that I discovered you could play with math.

If you want to give people's science inhibitions a run for their money, start asking them about their feelings around math. It will likely not take you long to come upon someone ready to tell you, "I'm bad at math." They'll say this with a definitive certainty, and it will be something they've thought for a long time. Of course, you'll also find people who express with the same certainty that they're "great at math" or that they love it. Like science, many people's perceptions come from their early experiences with the topic as a subject in school.

In the *Math Momentum* project, we authentically played with math, and I felt my own personal math inhibitions begin to dissolve and my willingness for math risk-taking increase. There are so many fun ways to integrate math into your family life, and building math skills is a huge (and important) part of science and day-to-day life. I was ill-prepared for the pre-calculus class I showed up to in my first semester of marine science. (I'm not sure if I thought I was going to go whale watching all semester or what, but there was definitely a skills gap for me at that time).

The Lawrence Hall of Science at UC Berkeley has an incredible array of books that are part of their GEMS series (Great Explorations in Math and Science) which offer fun ways of playing with math. I've used their *Family Math* book to make a Family Math night involving games with tokens, play money, puzzles, bubbles (I always squeeze in bubbles), and more. (Bonus: If you're looking to make up for how few rolls of wrapping paper you sold for your school, this could be your rocket ship to being the star of the PTA.)

Some of the ways we play with math at home is through estimating and then counting to see how close we are; playing store with money; considering scale as we build with clay, action figures, and boxes; keeping data on a clipboard as we race cars; measuring while cooking and baking; playing with tangrams; and putting a

CD in the microwave to discover fractals (well, we only did this once, and it was super interesting, but overall a dangerous idea).

Looking at patterns in nature is also a powerful way of seeing math in the world. Watch a few YouTube videos or read up on the Fibonacci Sequence (a number sequence where every number after the first two is the sum of two preceding numbers), and then look for examples in nature such as pinecones, pineapples, and sunflowers.

Using non-standard units of measurement, such as a finger, forearm, or a piece of paper, is another compelling way of weaving math into everyday life. It sends the message that math can be accessed at any moment—even when we don't have pencils, graph paper, and fancy calculators on hand. Help your child see

Chart Your Course

TAKE a tour of your own home and see if you can find the math. Discover math in the angles of your walls, the use of measurement (e.g., hanging pictures), money in a change jar, a scale, weights on bottles, and distance between furniture. Do this alongside your child — do not feel like you need to go around and collect the answers ahead of time. See where they lead you. (And know that that this can be an ongoing activity — it's not a one-time "test.")

that math exists beyond their homework sheets and is an amazing part of their daily lives.

SCIENCE IN THE TUB

. . . .

"Is there a plug in my butt

so that water doesn't go into my body?"

(deep thoughts from the bathtub)

—Age 3

SOME OF THE best entryways to weaving science into daily family life come from our everyday tasks and routines. Aside from the summer months when I occasionally try to write off pool, sprinkler, and hose time as ample cleansing, bath time is a prime spot for science.

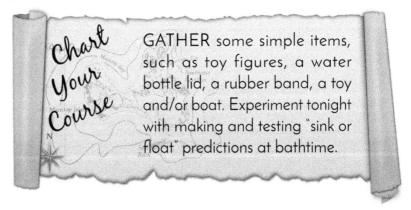

Chart Your Course

GATHER some simple items, such as toy figures, a water bottle lid, a rubber band, a toy and/or boat. Experiment tonight with making and testing "sink or float" predictions at bathtime.

Some of the ways we have tapped (see what I did there) into science in the tub have been: using submersible LEDs, playing with toy submarines and other boats, bath-safe color tablets, conducting bubble explorations, making sink and float predictions, and wave making (yeah, I know). One big secret about your bathtub is that it isn't only for bathing. Plunk your youngin' in a dry tub with other activities and experiments and be one step closer to cleaning up afterward!

Out to Dinner Science

(pointing out all the fun things my son got to play because he finished his dinner in a timely manner, asking him if this makes sense)

"When I was four, that didn't make sense

...but now it does."

—Age 5

THERE I WAS, on a Valentine's Day double date with our friends in a restaurant. The ambience was perfect, the food delicious, and the conversation runneth over. The children were safe and sound. Under the table. With a tablet. We had moved away from family and friends and had not established a trusted sitter, so this seemed like the next best idea.

I regularly challenge myself, however, to avoid pressing the easy button of technology and instead give a chance for building relevant social skills, like not standing on the bench seat in the restaurant, gnawing on ketchup packets (my husband has almost completely stopped doing this).

During one restaurant outing, when my son was a toddler, the refined couple next to us looked like they wished we would retreat to the nearest pizza joint, I looked around the table and realized I had a small science laboratory at my hands.

We began our lab investigations by turning ourselves upside down. We accomplished this by looking at our reflections on the backs of our spoons. We then practiced transferring water from a cup to a plate, using a coffee stir stick as a pipette (this skill may

CHALLENGE yourself to try one of these ideas when you are out to dinner. Also, consider placing a few science-themed toys in a bag that can easily be brought to a restaurant (e.g., a calculator, polished gems for sorting, a small kaleidoscope, or a balancing bird). Check out the small toys at your neighborhood toy store.

come in handy in the lab someday when there are budget cuts). Next, we experimented with melting the ice from our drinks using the salt. Lastly, we compared dissolving sugar in cold water versus hot tea water.

I accomplished my mission of not ruining others' fancy dates and killed (I mean spent) twenty minutes engaged in a meaningful exchange until our lasagna arrived.

ADAPTING TOYS AND ACTIVITIES

(hears commercial on radio)

"The people who do the commercials try to get you to do it, but we don't, right Ma?"

—Age 4 ½

THERE ARE MANY ways to take your child's favorite toys and activities and put a small twist on them to encourage science exploration and skill building. It's amazing the difference that subtle tweaks can make. We have a lot of different balls around the house—from table tennis balls to super bouncy balls and poppers from birthday party loot bags—that lend themselves well to science play. We keep them in a large, clear tub that we can easily grab off the shelf.

We often use these balls along with cups, containers, buckets, and baskets to make up our own games (complete with ever-changing rules). Through playful exploration, we make discoveries about force, angle, momentum, trajectory, and other science concepts. We don't always geek out and call these elements out individually, but I know that these experiences lay down information that becomes part of my child's (and my own) understanding of the way the world works.

If your child loves to use stampers or stickers, try making a chart to keep data on items or activities in your home. Maybe track the new foods that are tried, or each family member's vote on their favorite cereal. Many scientists spend a lot of time collecting data, and it's never too early to start enjoying the process. By giving children positive first exposures to these types of activities and behaviors, we increase their familiarity when they come along as tasks at school.

If your child enjoys playing with cars, how might you help them design racing experiments? Might you have them make predictions as they race along the track? Might you engage their engineering design skills by encouraging them to change the height of the track and see how it affects the results? It's important for children to generate and pursue their own questions and ideas for play, but simple prompts on occasion can add to their library of possibilities.

THERE is something magical for children about clipboards. If you have one in the closet, dig it out, put some paper on it, add a pencil, and set it somewhere easily available. You can also make your own by layering cardboard sheets together and attaching a giant binder clip to the top.

SCIENCE IN YOUR AREA

(when asked how the bread from the farm share tasted...)

"B-I-O-M-G"

(the modern-day version of "B-I-N-G-O")

—Age 6 ½

WHILE THERE ARE dozens of ways to conduct science at home, exploring your neighborhood and region offers boundless opportunities for science learning.

I had quite an intense transition in my late twenties when I moved back home to Buffalo, New York from Maui, Hawai'i. These locations are only slightly different. One of the unexpected benefits, however, was that sometimes places that make you work harder to uncover their beauty (in this case, Buffalo) often bear a deeper sense of reward when you find it—and you will find it. The history and ecology of upstate New York is incredible.

While playing with my son less than ten miles from our Buffalo home on a beach along Lake Erie, I connected to a time over 350 million years ago. I found a brachiopod, a two-shelled marine animal that looks like a small, hard ancient clam (though they are very different). These creatures were common in the warm waters that covered Western New York and much of the world during a period known as the Devonian.

As I came upon that brachiopod, my imagination was piqued, and I was drawn in. (I had the same excited searching feeling that I once had in the middle of a Dollar Store in Canada when I realized it was the eighty-eight-cent store based on the exchange rate.) I looked back down on the sand and found a second and third brachiopod and then a piece of fossilized coral. I started sorting through piles of small shells and rocks to see what else was there.

I think about how this feeling drives so many scientists, inventors, and explorers. It is not only the pursuit of the unknown but the search for the unknown that seems to be within one's reach. It is the notion that at any moment, at any place, something can be discovered.

Later that summer, when it was time to identify the take-home loot for my son's fourth birthday party, I knew exactly what we would give out. He and I returned to this beach and gathered fossils for his friends that we placed in small burlap bags, along with the directions to get to the site.

What types of trees and plants are native to your area? What is your soil comprised of? There are many different clues that we can decipher to gain a deeper understanding of a place. We are constantly taking in data about our surroundings and making decisions. We decide to avoid planting certain shrubs that "never seemed to take" or flowers that dried out too fast in the full sun. We are part of the ongoing narrative of our region. How will you help shape the story?

Chart Your Course RESEARCH what your area was like one hundred years ago, ten thousand years ago, and 250 million years ago. Tap into your local museums for their knowledge. Compare and contrast then and now with your child. Not only is this an interesting exercise, it is valuable data for deepening your sense of place.

SCHOOL SCIENCE PROJECTS

("Why is your shirt all wet?")

"The water wanted to dance and then it just fell out of my mouth."

(beware of the local dancing water)

—Age 3 ½

WHEN I WAS in elementary school, I loved participating in the annual school science fair held in the *cafegymitorium* (the room in our small school that served as our cafeteria, gymnasium, and auditorium). One of my projects was focused on agronomy—the study of producing and using plants for a variety of purposes—from food, fuel, and fiber to land reclamation.

I can still picture my rust-orange kitchen counter lined with cups of soil. I had planted a bean sprout in each cup and every morning I "watered" the sprouts with a different liquid. I used water, milk, coffee, and laundry detergent. I compared and contrasted how the various liquids affected the seed sprouting and plant growth. I remember being pleasantly surprised at how well the coffee did.

My kitchen was my laboratory, and I learned to make observations, be perceptive, and record data on a daily basis. If children are fortunate enough to experience hands-on science activities at a young age, they often experience fast rewards (like exploding a volcano or quick-growing polymer snow). Conducting experiments that take two weeks to unfold is a wonderful way to help our children develop and exercise patience and persistence, and learn to compare controls and variables.

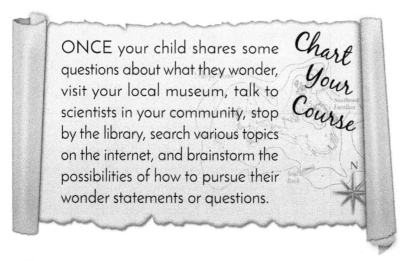

ONCE your child shares some questions about what they wonder, visit your local museum, talk to scientists in your community, stop by the library, search various topics on the internet, and brainstorm the possibilities of how to pursue their wonder statements or questions.

Chart Your Course

There are many ways to go about identifying and developing science projects. I cannot say that I was genuinely interested in agronomy at the time I conducted this experiment—I had probably never heard that word before. It's more likely that I flipped through a school science projects book and jumped to quick closure, picking one of the first ones I found.

Helping your child select a science fair topic is a wonderful chance to tap into their natural curiosities and interests. Spend time asking them what they've always wondered and what types of questions they have about the world around them. Encourage them to dream big. Above all, encourage them to keep open while gathering and considering ideas, and to then be deliberate when selecting one.

Meet Jennifer

I WAS ON a flight from San Francisco to Washington, D.C. and struck up a conversation with the woman sitting in my row. We spoke about our careers, interests, and families. When she heard that my work was in science, she shared a bit about her son and his science project. Jennifer's story demonstrates the diverse and inclusive power of science.

> When my son Ozzie was two and a half years old, we received two confirming diagnoses that he was on the Autism Spectrum. I was pregnant at the time with our second son, and I had no idea what the diagnosis even meant. My husband and I were scared and dove headfirst into an endless amount of reading and research. We had no idea if Ozzie would be a part of the "neurotypical world" (referring to those not affected by a developmental disorder, particularly autism) or if his invisible disability would have him living in a world of his own.
>
> Then our second son, Calvin, was born, and he brought with him all the opposite symptoms of his brother—exceeding the expectations of that neurotypical world and excelling in language and emotional intelligence far beyond his age. He would be the catalyst helping Ozzie advance further in his speech and serve as Ozzie's own personal translator (even for us as his parents).
>
> *Merriam-Webster's Dictionary* defines Autism Spectrum

Disorder as "any group of development disorders marked by impairments in the ability to communicate and interact socially and by the presence of repetitive behaviors or restricted interests..." This definition does not work for our family, as we do not consider our son to be "impaired."

Ozzie went on to be the first child under three years old to be approved for more than forty hours of Applied Behavior Analysis (ABA) therapy in our county under the supervision of a team of local therapists. For the last five-plus years, our home and his school have welcomed speech therapists, physical therapists, and behavior therapists to help Ozzie reach his highest potential. The *best* part is that he has responded incredibly well, without any medication, and is socially engaged with his peer group. He is verbal and has been mainstreamed this entire time, keeping up with his peers and assisted minimally by a full-time aide at school.

Slowly but surely, my husband and I were brought back into the neurotypical world to participate in "regular life." Life was no longer becoming about protecting and helping Ozzie, but allowing him to explore and be his own person. Multiple years of silent car rides home were now filled with random commentary of observations. We occasionally dismissed some of this commentary, but we came to realize that Ozzie had an incredible memory and amazing attention to detail. He was able to quickly observe and recognize patterns that the average person would just dismiss.

For the last several years, Ozzie has spent his time memorizing all of the routes we travel, the roadways we go on, the exit numbers on the highway, and even the directions of the arrows that lead you off the road. Yes, lo and behold, if you look at every freeway exit, it is assigned an actual exit number. Ozzie even knows when they skip a number.

This type of behavior for people on the spectrum is known as a perseverative interest. I *now* like to call it *science*.

Merriam-Webster defines *science* as, "a system of knowledge covering general truths or the operation of general laws especially as obtained and tested through scientific method." Ozzie had discovered "the science behind the designs of the highways and freeway systems," and he was choosing to make it the topic of his first-grade science project.

Admittedly, I was befuddled as to how this was going to work and if people would find the topic odd or not interesting. We worked on the project together as a family. Ozzie decided that it was imperative that he draw his favorite exit and discuss why he liked it so much. We read to him the history behind the freeway and highway system. Then we found data on its design, features, and purpose.

What we came to discover is that so much of what we see in our day-to-day lives is filled with science. The human mind's attention to detail is astounding, and Ozzie's observations have woken us to all of the effort that people put into the everyday things that we take for granted. Science is everywhere and in everything. One person's passion can be the catalyst to great change and this new interest can convert a common subject matter into perhaps finding a new purpose.

Ozzie has also made us see the human element behind the subtle details of life. He has inspired me personally to see that there is no limit to the interests that evoke our passions. He has shown me that, on a daily basis, we are constantly recording data in our minds, creating hypotheses, and testing things out. And we do this so that we can grow, discover, and gain new insights from those places, people, and objects we believe we already know so well.

As for Ozzie's first science fair project...it was a

complete success! He never ceases to amaze me and has taught me to never stop observing the details of the world, exploring my own potential, and looking for new truths.

"

ME, YOU, & THE TUBE

(responding to a man who says he is from Wales)

"My mom
LOOOOOVVVVEEEEESSSSS whales!!!"

—Age 6

OUR FAMILY IS not always out on dramatic hikes, wiring circuits, or having life-changing conversations. Sometimes we are in our pajamas at an inappropriate hour, watching television and eating salt and vinegar chips. (I fully believe this time together can be just as meaningful as playing with wooden toys while eating organic apples.)

In September 2015, we tuned into PBS, along with thousands of others, to watch *Big Blue Live*, a partially-live documentary from Monterey Bay, California. While I thoroughly enjoyed seeing the live head slaps of humpback whales, the feeding behaviors of sea otters, and the discovery of a random, floating squid eyeball, I think what I loved the most was the collective science-based experience that I knew we were having with others.

Many people associate science with quietly working alone, poring over a microscope for hours in silence while wearing a sterile lab coat. However, as we've discussed, science can also be messy, loud, colorful, and collaborative.

During Big Blue Live, I joined the Twitterverse in making nerdy science jokes ("I'm sitting on the edge of my reef"), exchanging inspirational quotes about conservation, and reacting to the animals that the research boats and helicopters were coming across — (finally) including a blue whale! Not only was I sharing this experience with my family, I was also enjoying it with strangers with a common interest. The sense of community that is built by having a shared science experience such as this provides a rich network for exchange and learning. (A side message that I hope you are reading here is that you can be a slacker in your pajamas, eating chips, and still engage in meaningful science learning.)

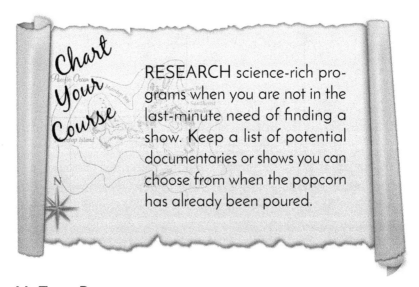

Chart Your Course

RESEARCH science-rich programs when you are not in the last-minute need of finding a show. Keep a list of potential documentaries or shows you can choose from when the popcorn has already been poured.

HI-TECH PARENTING

"FU-Fos and Aliens."

(aka UFOs)

— Age 3

MY FAMILY WAS flying from New York to California, so I loaded our airplane bags with travel activities. My son was at the end of his toddler phase and no longer nursing, so I felt that I had lost 90 percent of my superpowers on an airplane. We spent the first two hours of the flight reading books, looking at magazines, filling in a sticker book, eating apples and cookies, and storytelling about Mars, comets, and UFOs using a vinyl space scene. And then there were still two and a half hours left before landing. My husband brought out the tablet and showed my son an app he had downloaded that required him to sort garbage and recycling icons. I cringed at this, as I wanted to steer clear of relying on tech for entertainment, but I also welcomed the opportunity to relax for a few minutes.

There is an inner woodland fairy in me that only wants my child to play with puppet gnomes and hand-carved pull toys for a very long time. But there is this other part of me that is excited to watch him navigate the skill-building involved with technology. As my son dragged various icons into the compost, recycling, and garbage bins, it was obvious that he was building his spatial skills as he was moving puzzle pieces in place onto the payloader.

The National Association for the Education of Young Children is an excellent resource for research on topics like technology and young children. Parents face ever-expanding digital decisions as their children (and the world of technology) grow. With these choices and decisions come opportunities for setting boundaries and building self-management techniques.

A piece of tech research that concerns me most is that youth are spending so much time engaged with technology that many are not developing the appropriate empathy skills that are built when engaged in face-to-face conversation. In natural conversation there is downtime, and this downtime is imperative to developing empathy. This factor continues to be one of my main reasons for having parameters around technology in my child's life.

I will continue to cringe and be simultaneously delighted as I help my child navigate the world of technology and digital media. I will continue to ground him in this reality while he is exposed to virtual reality. And I will continue to select turning a doorknob to go outside over a power button to stay in and zone out. But I will also be the one to show him how to integrate technology into his life without hanging an alluring "do not touch" sign over it.

In our family, we talk about the process of brain development, and I tell my child that one of my most important jobs is to make sure that his brain has the opportunity to grow in the best ways possible. This concrete, biology-based reasoning goes further with him, in relation to placing parameters around tech, than "because I said so." We have made it to age seven with no game systems in the house, but he is allowed to play non-violent games occasionally at a friend's house or arcade. I can tell that there are going to be a lot of discussions and decisions around this topic in the coming years.

Chart Your Course

SPEND some time researching technology usage and children. Get informed. Talk to others about their approaches. Think about what your gut tells you. Get clear for yourself on your feelings and any other adults' feelings in the home. Clarify your stance and parameters with your child.

Whatever pathways your family takes with technology, I offer the following advice: (1) make safety a priority, (2) set parameters and limits that are well-informed, (3) have conversations with your child about the pluses and minuses of engaging with technology, and (4) protect your family's unplugged time and natural state of being as much as possible.

SCIENCE, EVERY DAY?

(son staring off into space, looking serious)

("Honey, is everything OK?")

"Yeh. When you're not talking,

sometimes it leaves a face."

—Age 4

PERHAPS THE TITLE of this chapter made you think, "Seriously, you want me to do science every day?" And to that, I would say, "No." I don't want you to *do* science; I want you to recognize and embrace it. (I actually want you to *be* science, but I'm trying not to scare you based on promises I made earlier in the book.)

As we recognize the science that exists in our everyday lives (along with opportunities for science learning), we open ourselves

TAKE stock of where you are at with this juicy conversation we are having. What are three realistic takeaways that you have picked up thus far and plan on applying?

Chart Your Course

up for making deeper and richer connections with the world.

What I desperately want to offer you—more than activities and experiments (as you can easily find these online)—is a guarantee that the most important tool in your toolbox is your mindset.

Chapter Sixteen

The Perfect Time for Science

(on the Bunny in relation to Claus...)
*"He lives in a spring place
that's real far away.*
That's why they never see each other."

—Age 5

Seasons, holidays, natural occurrences, and other markers of time lend themselves well to considering science opportunities for your family. Whether it is the science of fire in the candles you light or in the food you prepare that is connected to certain family holiday traditions, it is always the perfect time to celebrate science.

As we were headed into the grocery store in late February, a Jewish family was running a *hamantasch*-making station outside of the store, in honor of the upcoming celebration of Purim. Hamantaschen are triangle-shaped treats made of flour, egg, salt, and sugar and filled with poppy or other pastes and sweets. (We have touched on the fact that baking is wonderful exposure to science, but I would like to add that every single ingredient and its role in a recipe is its very own science treasure chest. Table salt, or sodium chloride, for instance, is made up of tiny cubes tightly bound together, and impacts the fermentation rate of yeast.)

While I was tempted to rush by in order to quickly grab our groceries and get back home to finish the laundry, I challenged myself to slow down and make time to honor this family's offering and take in a lesson in their religion and culture.

Not only did my son enjoy rolling the dough and placing in his fillings, we had a rich, Purim-inspired conversation with the family running the station about the fact that not all special happenings and occurrences are necessarily flashy and showy. We returned home and continued our mundane Sunday afternoon tasks of laundry (which, as it so happens, also involves lots of fun science) and cooking with enhanced gratitude and mindfulness. My son baked the hamantaschen for our dessert, and they were delicious for so many reasons.

SCIENCE IS ALWAYS IN SEASON

"May I have some more apple powder?"

(aka cider)

−Age 3

SCIENCE LEARNING AND food go hand in hand. I love maple syrup season when we can make a connection between our breakfast pancakes and the cycles of nature. It always brings me great pride to take my child to the sources of his and our food. On a crisp fall day in Western New York, we used to drive to the country to see the maple trees being tapped, ride in horse-drawn carriages through the sugar maple trees, eat maple donuts, and drink maple coffee (yes, it is as good as it sounds).

In summers past, we have worked together with our neighbors to can cucumbers and beets that we can enjoy throughout the year. The simple art of canning is loaded with science, including vacuum sealing and atmospheric pressure, acidity, and temperature change.

Growing food and herbs is another great way to bring areas of science, such as agriculture and ecology, into your family's life. The process of planting seeds, watching them sprout, comparing and contrasting growth, looking at variables (like temperature, water, and sunlight), and enjoying the results for health and wellness is a wonderful way to explore science and its personal implications in our lives—one season at a time.

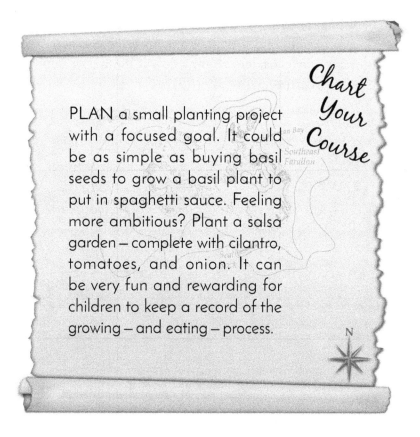

Chart Your Course

PLAN a small planting project with a focused goal. It could be as simple as buying basil seeds to grow a basil plant to put in spaghetti sauce. Feeling more ambitious? Plant a salsa garden – complete with cilantro, tomatoes, and onion. It can be very fun and rewarding for children to keep a record of the growing – and eating – process.

SPRING SCIENCE

"'Tend you're an ant and I'll be a person
that just spilled some lemonade."

—Age 4 ½

IT WAS SPRING break week, and the neighborhood kids were looking for some fun. Slime and goo are the low-hanging fruit of hands-on science, so I brought out the glue and Borax and made pink, baby blue, and light green spring-themed goo. I have found that it's easy to put holiday twists on many science experiments (pink slime can be considered bunny taffy if the Easter bunny is part of your festivities).

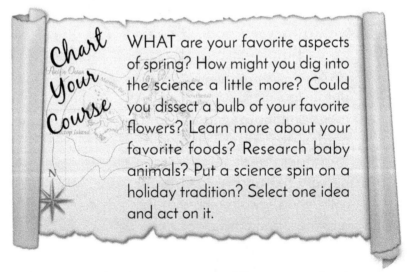

Chart Your Course

WHAT are your favorite aspects of spring? How might you dig into the science a little more? Could you dissect a bulb of your favorite flowers? Learn more about your favorite foods? Research baby animals? Put a science spin on a holiday tradition? Select one idea and act on it.

A few days after Easter, my son and I were in our local cooperative market. We had bumped into an artist friend named Michael and had a quick chat. We parted ways and soon came upon a sample taste station that had *matzos*. My son tried a piece. Since he is a *carbohydratarian*, he enjoyed it. I tracked down Michael, who I knew was Jewish, and asked him to come over to the station and tell us about matzos.

He gave a simple but meaningful explanation that combined science, culture, religion, nutrition, and more. I knew a few things about matzos, but I knew Michael was a better primary source for this information. Never underestimate the power of the human resources surrounding you.

SPOOKY SCIENCE

● ●

"What do ghosts call balloons?"

"Boo-loons."

— Age 7

● ●

HALLOWEEN IS ONE big invitation for science fun. Whether you're putting dry ice in your spooky punch, designing elaborate mechanized props, or making glow-in-the-dark decorations, there are many ways to play with science if you and your family partake in this holiday.

Science careers lend themselves well to inspiring costumes. As we researched and put together my son's paleontologist costume at age four, he learned about some of the tools that a paleontologist uses and the process of digging and finding a bone and safely bringing it to a museum (placing a plaster cast around it).

At Halloween age five, he was an underwater worker, inspired by one of his LEGO Ocean Explorer guys. Since conceiving my child and discovering Pinterest, I have been waiting for an excuse to cover two-liter soda bottles with aluminum foil and turn them into scuba tanks. I also saw this as a chance to capitalize on my child's interests and explore underwater STEM career options (underwater archaeology, anyone?). After all, pretending and role-playing isn't just for Halloween.

I once again used up the aluminum foil tape that my husband purchases for house-related projects (you should have seen the perfect rockets it made) and then can *somehow* never find. It was the perfect material to cover the 2L soda bottles scuba tanks and make a belt on the zip-up suit. (I suggest adding a grown-up following behind the scuba tanks, with a bubble gun for special effects. Grown-up sold separately.)

Chart Your Course

ROLE-PLAYING various careers and characters gives children the opportunity to try on and immerse themselves in those roles. Identify opportunities to allow for this to happen. (We gave an astronaut suit to my son's friend in preschool and he only removed it to bathe over a course of several weeks.)

Beyond providing insight into various scientific careers, Halloween also highlights many fascinating animals, such as spiders and bats. It is a perfect time of year to go beyond how they are portrayed in decorations and learn more about the important roles these animals play in the ecosystem.

My favorite autumnal nature center program invites children to walk along wooded paths and collect items for a witch apprentice's brew. They stop at various stations, including one with rehabilitated owls, and make nature-based discoveries. It is a wonderful way to have fun with a holiday that can often portray scary imagery for children (and adults). I like to stick to corn mazes and hayrides, and steer clear of the haunted houses at this time of the year.

'TIS THE SEASON FOR SCIENCE

("Santa is coming tomorrow night!")

"And he'll get off the chair?"

("Yes honey, he will get off the chair.")

—Age 2

ONE DRIZZLY SUNDAY afternoon, we found ourselves at our local science museum chatting with the college students who were facilitating a balloon rocket zip line. Aside from the fact that my two-year-old learned to say Newton (ashamed we hadn't already covered this at home), I also connected with a young woman who was well on her way to a STEM career. She told me she was studying mechanical engineering because it was the field of both of her parents. They encouraged her to pursue the field since she excelled in math and science. When I asked her if she went to work with her parents when she was younger, she said that her mom stopped being an engineer when she was born, and her dad worked at a high-security site where the family could only visit once.

This young woman's replies triggered a deluge of thoughts in my mind. It made me curious as to what percentage of youth who choose STEM careers are influenced by one or more parents or family members who have walked that path. I wondered if her mother ever stopped *feeling like* or *being* an engineer simply because she had left the workforce. I also thought what a shame it was to have had two parents in the field that she chose to base her life's work upon, yet not have had very much exposure to the engineering work environment. STEM workers have an amazing opportunity to expose potential future workers to their respective fields and work environments.

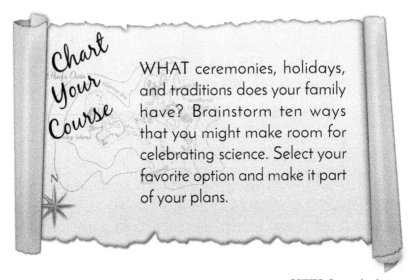

Chart Your Course

WHAT ceremonies, holidays, and traditions does your family have? Brainstorm ten ways that you might make room for celebrating science. Select your favorite option and make it part of your plans.

In addition to gaining these insights about STEM workplaces, talking to the student facilitators made me realize that I needed a balloon rocket zip line in my living room. Since we celebrate Christmas and had just put up our tree, I thought this would be the ideal vertical post for one side of the zip line. When we got home, we tied one end of a long piece of cotton string to the top of the tree, slid a straw onto the string, tied the other end of the string to the back of a chair, grabbed a balloon and a balloon pump (a must for repeat testing), taped the balloon onto the straw, and experimented with our new zip line "rocket-sleigh." This playful investigation is an excellent way to introduce the concept of testing variables, which we did by trying out a variety of balloon types, where the tape is placed, the incline of the string, and more.

Our finishing touch was printing out a picture of Santa and attaching him towards the top of the tree, awaiting his sleigh. Use your imagination with making characters out of the launcher and the target—maybe an elf receiving a present or a reindeer waiting for an apple? The possibilities are endless.

Remember to take down your experiment string at the end of the fun, in case someone (especially you) tries to sneak a Christmas cookie in the middle of the night. (You're welcome.)

REAL-TIME EVENTS

"If I had to wear a bra,

I would use it as sunglasses."

(#thingstoconsider)

—Age 5

I'M SO INTERESTED in real-time-science events that I chose my wedding date based upon the Venus Transit. Venus was visibly crossing the sun's path, so I had stayed overnight at the science museum (where I managed the public programs) to be able to watch it happen first thing in the morning. Witnessing this event on the day of my wedding with my husband-to-be, my family, and dozens of community members at six o'clock in the morning on the museum rooftop is something I will remember forever.

These experiences allow us to bask in the majestic awe of our planet and the time in which we live—whether we're watching a live nature documentary or shuttle launch, or congregating with others on a museum rooftop to watch the day or night sky. We gather and collectively celebrate our sense of wonder. When we give ourselves the time and space to marvel, exchange ideas, ask questions, and explore our curiosity, we acknowledge ourselves as part of something bigger, and we acknowledge science as part of ourselves.

Chart Your Course

IS there a science and nature-based event that your family might take advantage of viewing this year? An eclipse? A meteor shower? A salmon run? A bird migration? Nature's patterns —though some are subject to change — often give us the opportunity to plan ahead.

NATURAL OCCURRENCE SPRINGBOARDS

My son makes me play a game that goes like this...

"I'm thinking of something that's made out of molecules...."

And then I have to guess.

The answer has been dirt more than once.

You play by listing everything in the universe that you can think of that is a solid, gas, liquid, or plasma and he just says, "No." "No." "No." "No."

It's super fun. Try it at your dinner table tonight.

— Age 5 and on

AS HURRICANE SANDY made its way through the Caribbean and Eastern Seaboard of the United States in October 2012, my son was hearing tidbits of news coming in from the Weather Channel on TV. He was immediately intrigued.

While the science behind hurricanes is fascinating, there is an underlying sensitivity to the multiple ways in which extreme weather affects the lives of those in its path. General news exposure may sometimes not be parents' preference for helping their children explore and understand current weather events.

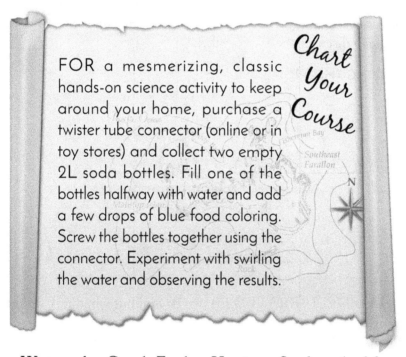

FOR a mesmerizing, classic hands-on science activity to keep around your home, purchase a twister tube connector (online or in toy stores) and collect two empty 2L soda bottles. Fill one of the bottles halfway with water and add a few drops of blue food coloring. Screw the bottles together using the connector. Experiment with swirling the water and observing the results.

Chart Your Course

We turned to Google Earth as Hurricane Sandy evolved from Tropical Depression formed to the north of Curacao (near Aruba), stopped by Jamaica as a Category 1 hurricane, visited Cuba as a Category 2, and then dropped back down to a 1 as she swung by the Bahamas and traveled up the East Coast.

To explore the phenomenon, we made a clear glass of hot tea, removed the tea bag, and stirred the water in a counterclockwise direction to represent the eye of a hurricane. It was a great chance to discuss the directions of clockwise and counterclockwise, as these concepts serve as a foundation for later exploring more complicated concepts, such as the Coriolis Effect—an effect caused by the rotation of the earth.

Topics such as hurricanes, cyclones, and extreme weather allow us to speak to children about the many ways that science has broad impacts on people's day-to-day lives. As you are trying to raise an informed and compassionate human, it is important to remember that you do not have to have all the information down pat before heading into the storm of a science topic with them. You can discover the eye together.

SEIZING THE MOMENT

"How many anchors big is the sun?"

("What do you mean, honey?")

"Like some people say ten anchors big."

(oh, acres)

—Age 6

I HAD DELIBERATED for two days about whether I would go to an event hosted by our local Astronomical Association at the beach. The event was centered on viewing the super moon lunar eclipse, which I knew meant keeping my son up way past his bedtime. The truth is, I struggle with routines in general. I have a preference for spontaneity that I have had to learn to manage as a parent. I have seen firsthand how rhythm and routine benefit my child. I still, however, like to throw all of that out the window once in a while (or once a week) in the name of science.

Sometimes I make what I call a good, bad decision. These types of decisions are motivated by wanting to do something enriching, in exchange for rest and other healthy habits. I find that science and adventure are typically the driving forces.

On the morning of the eclipse, we watched a few YouTube "e-clips" that explained what was going to happen. I was surprised at the effectiveness of viewing those models as I listened to my son explain to my mother how the moon revolves around the earth and the earth revolves around the sun later that day. This simple interaction swayed me from heading home for a proper bath and bedtime to heading to the beach for the evening. As I pulled up to a lawn full of telescopes—from an eight-inch refractor to computer-controlled reflector scopes—I knew that I had made the right choice.

My son looked into a variety of telescopes with wonder and amazement. We watched and listened to small presentations given by the Astronomy Association members that seemed to be a mix of science, poetry, and art. Most importantly, we sat on a blanket eating donuts, drinking cider, and watching the eclipse.

I thoroughly enjoyed listening to my offspring explain to the astronomers how the sun follows him everywhere he goes. We left in the middle of the eclipse, to ensure that said offspring was not a complete wreck for school the following morning.

As I drove down my city street, with my son asleep in his car seat, I saw an unusual amount of people standing in front of their houses and in the road. It brought me great joy to see so many people engaged with this science-based event. I thought about what might have been different about this occurrence than other natural phenomena. Was it the news coverage, was it the ease of looking up and seeing the change with the naked eye, was it the way social media promoted it through their event tagging? Whatever the reason(s), it is very powerful when we all stop what we're doing and collectively engage in a science-based experience together.

The next time this will happen I'll be of the age to get free coffee at certain local restaurants, so I seized the moment.

CHECK for astronomy events in your local area, including basic stargazing. Make a plan to attend with your family. Invite another family along and plan to bring a picnic (complete with astro snacks) and some books on the topic.

Accessing the Universe

∞∞∞∞∞∞∞∞∞∞∞∞∞∞∞∞∞∞∞∞∞∞∞∞∞∞∞∞∞∞∞∞∞∞∞∞

"Which one is bigger, my love or Saturn's dust?

Compared to my love,

Saturn is the smallest dust."

—Age 5 ½

∞∞∞∞∞∞∞∞∞∞∞∞∞∞∞∞∞∞∞∞∞∞∞∞∞∞∞∞∞∞∞∞∞∞∞∞

ON ANOTHER ASTRO-RELATED occasion, I picked my son up from school and drove to a fossil dig site that had telescopes set up to view the Transit of Mercury. As we drove onto the site, it was like landing on the moon—a wide open, rocky surface colored in various shades of gray. I realized how challenging it would be to have my son excited about looking at a dot through a telescope when, for only three dollars more, he could dig for ancient fossils. I was on my lunch hour from work, so I coaxed him into settling for planetary viewing until we had more time to return to dig at a later date.

When I looked into the first reflective scope, I felt that connection to my old friend, the Sun. I was amazed at how much smaller Mercury appeared compared to Venus, which I had watched transit in 2004 and 2012. The phrase "Mercury is the smallest planet," a sentiment I must have read a thousand times since grade school, was suddenly backed up by a personal experience with the planet.

Chart Your Course

CONSIDER purchasing or obtaining a telescope. Unfortunately (but possibly fortunate for you), this is an item in many people's closets, attics, and basements. Ask around and see if someone wants to pass theirs onto you or sell it at a low cost. There are also apps you can download to look at the night sky through a tablet. In addition, the moon can be seen through binoculars. Find one way to begin connecting with the night sky.

We live in a time when exploring and connecting with the universe is at our fingertips. We can view jaw-dropping images from the Hubble Space Telescope online, but there is no comparison to placing our eye at the end of a long tube and personally witnessing bits and pieces of the night sky with our own eyes.

Every time we use technology to access an experience, we are connecting ourselves to the lineage of STEM innovators that have afforded us the opportunity to do so. As we watched this particular planet (which whips around the sun four times faster than the earth) cross the face of our Solar System's star, we were connected to Galileo, Newton, and the other individuals who have made sky viewing possible.

As my son compared his views between the various telescopes on site, I thought about how far we have come with viewing technology and how lucky we are to benefit from those advances. When we give our children access to exploring the world in which they are a significant speck, we invite them to not only reach for the stars but to also believe those stars are within their grasp.

Chapter Seventeen

Birthday Science

*(informing my son that his
birthday was coming up)*
"Oh and I will be a new person?"

—Age 3

One of the most popular programs we ran at the satellite studio I mentioned in chapter 6 was birthday parties. We took every part of a classic birthday party and brought out the science. We made our own decorations by blowing up balloons with the gas produced by the combination of baking soda and vinegar, and, of course, we made our own ice cream.

It's hard for me to contemplate designing a fun birthday party without including at least some science. My son's seventh birthday was centered around battling robots as the core activity, surrounded by more open-ended activities, like designing tracks for wind-up robots, and robot-making with craft supplies and recyclables.

There are many ways to lean on science for party assistance. Here are some ideas to put in your birthday cooker.

SCIENCE FAIR BIRTHDAY PARTY

"Ma, it's your birthday.
You should let myself do whatever I want."
(loving, selfless son)

— Age 3 ½

PER OUR USUAL planning process, my son's mind changed several times about what he wanted as the theme for his fifth birthday party. At one point, he requested a shark-eating-a-mermaid cake, which led to a dangerous animals theme, which eventually led to a science fair birthday (I will admit to some prompting) featuring dangerous animals activities.

When I commit to something of this nature, I look for engaging activity opportunities in the set-up process. I figure there are elements that need to happen (or that I want to happen), so I may as well get the most bang for my buck in providing an activity and checking a task off of my list.

One of the first preparatory projects was to make banners. After all, what's a science fair without banners? My friend had recently dropped off a giant roll of banner-type paper from a printing press that was closing, making materials for this project easy to check off the list. (Watch for opportunities in your area of businesses closing — the treasures are endless.)

I wrote the names of the different activity stations on the banner paper in giant bubble letters using a permanent marker, and then my son painted the insides of the letters.

Whether at home or in a science museum gallery, it has always amazed me the way that signage brings an experience to life, frames the activities, and creates boundaries that make everything seem more official and engaging.

While our signage served as the majority of our decorations, we also filled mason jars with water and food coloring and placed them along the railing of the deck. They looked beautiful as the sun shined through them. We also placed balloons all around, inside and out. (Helpful tip: do not wait until eleven o'clock the night before the party to try to get the balloons at the grocery store. Your five-year-old will end up with burgundy and taupe balloons.)

We set up stations that featured a variety of themes: bubbles, volcanoes, slime and discovery, laboratory, racing, fossils and dig excavation, circuits, making, snake throwing, and walking the snake plank.

BUBBLES

BUBBLES ARE MY number one science go-to. They are one of those lenses through which you can teach all aspects of STEAM and people of all ages can be thoroughly engaged for hours. After experimenting with a lot of different bubble recipes, I found that blue Dawn dishwashing liquid seems to work best for bubble making. Throw in some off-the-shelf bubble solution and add glycerin if you want to be a serious bubble-ologist. For my son's party, we used an old water/sand play table (which had long ago had its legs sawn off) and set it on top of a table. We filled it with dishwashing liquid and water and threw in our bubble wands and a variety of other bubble-making materials such as CDs, rubber bands, and spatulas. Essentially, anything with holes or openings in it—like the weaving on lacrosse nets and tennis rackets—makes a great bubble wand!

VOLCANO STATION

I CANNOT RESIST the awe-factor of dry ice. I brought a cooler to the local dry ice supplier, signed my life away on a waiver, and brought it home to include in the science fun.

As always, safety is an important consideration in science play. I made sure to use gloves to unwrap the dry ice, and I kept it in an open cooler. We crinkled and wrapped brown craft paper around the cooler to form a volcano, painted red lava running down the side, and poured hot water over the dry ice. I prepped the activity for this station by drilling holes in the bottom of three-ounce paper cups to serve as the mini volcanoes when turned upside down. Children had the opportunity to color a cup and tape it down over a plastic shot-size glass full of baking soda, then pour vinegar into their volcano to make it explode. This station was a huge hit (minus the bees that were attracted to it).

SLIME & DISCOVERY STATION

THESE TOPICS AREN'T usually combined in nature, but there are only so many cousin helpers to go around at a five-year-old's birthday party. This station was armed with glue, Borax, hot water in a thermos, food coloring, cold water, and bowls, with spoons on one end of the table and natural objects and magnifying glasses on the other. We began the party with one batch of slime already made. This was a good call, as there was some experimenting with getting it just right. The supplies were there to make additional batches throughout the party. Some form of slime is the essential low-hanging fruit for any science party. There are so many recipe directions online—from glitter and confetti slime to making your goo glow in the dark—so get creative!

On the Discovery side of things, we used objects that I try to keep a healthy stash of for just such an occasion: shells, rocks, paper wasp nests, gems and minerals, leaves, and other materials. I have used these objects for general discovery, sketching, and facilitating workshops. I love to ask people to select one object from a basket that represents a thought, feeling, or experience in response to a meaningful question. Objects are a wonderful bridge for allowing us to tell stories—hence why they line the halls of museums and galleries.

LABORATORY STATION

FOR OUR LABORATORY station, we pulled together some beakers and test tubes from random toy science kits we had either received as presents or purchased, ice cube trays, funnels, cups, and bowls of various sizes. We filled them with colored water (using food coloring). You will be amazed that children need almost no direction when it comes to approaching test tubes, containers, and colored water. The condiment-style containers with lids that are sold in the paper plate aisle are wonderful for this. We also added some aprons and goggles to this station, as engaging in chemistry is much more fun in official lab gear.

RACING

WE DRAGGED OUR toy racetrack out of the house and set it up on some interconnecting foam tiles in our yard. We retrieved these tiles from a sales booth at a convention center—always upcycling! In a similar way that signage defines spaces, floor boundaries can also help in creating special areas that focus children's attention.

FOSSIL & DIG EXCAVATION

REMEMBER THAT PLAY area we set up in our concrete urban yard? Over time, it became quite the excavation site. Each time we went to that fossil-rich beach along Lake Erie (the same location where I gathered my son's birthday party loot), we brought home fossils and threw them amidst the pea gravel. Unable to resist the pure joy of fossil hunting for his upcoming party, we made one more stop at this beach to load up our play zone with fresh coral fossils from 250 million years ago. Although dinosaur fossils are not found in New York State, I got over my scientific accuracy and loaded the play zone for this station with plastic dinosaurs and Jurassic palm trees. This felt as grave a sin as when we play with plastic penguins (Antarctica) and polar bears (Arctic) at the same time, but it was worth the inaccuracy.

CIRCUITS

MY FAVORITE ACTIVITY at the party was the Circuit Station that featured wooden blocks with basic electronic components, such as DC motors, computer fans, alarms, light bulbs, and battery power packs. These components can all be connected using alligator clips to make working circuits. The time my husband and I spent sawing, hammering, soldering, and gluing was well worth the investment (as the blocks lasted long after the party). If you're looking to try this out yourself, The Exploratorium (the museum of science, art, and human perception in San Francisco, California) has easy-to-follow instructions to make your own circuit blocks.

Most children's museums, particularly those with maker-type spaces, feature these blocks or something close. They allow young children the opportunity to make a circuit without requiring the fine motor skills to hook alligator clips onto the ends of fine wires (as they can clip onto a copper nail to which the electronic component is soldered).

THINK & MAKE STATION

NO SCIENCE FAIR is complete without designing prototypes of new products and inventions. My aunt dressed up as Mad-uhm Scientist, complete with pocket protectors and glasses to hand out to the kids, a glass drinking bird, and an instant camera. She ran this station equipped with graph paper and pencils for sketching ideas, lots of recyclables, and vibrantly-colored tape. The pictures were a huge hit and made an instant party favor! This is actually a great activity to help you feel old, as most of the children had never seen this technology.

SNAKE STATION

A FEW DAYS before the party, we upcycled (garbage picked) two-step aerobics platforms that were the perfect structures to place a two-by-six board across, with a blue tarp underneath covered in snakes. Children had to walk over the rubber cobra snakes (thank you 75 percent off end-of-summer drugstore sale). We also placed a wading pool on a tarp and set up a masking tape line approximately three feet away as the standing spot for tossing the rubber snakes into the pool.

LOOK through the various ideas from our party. Choose one to use or adapt it to suit your family's interests or available materials. When children play, they are learning. Give them fun experiences with science content and help them form a base to which later formal learning can stick.

Chart Your Course

MAKING YOUR OWN SCIENCE KITS

"They can learn new stuff that they probably didn't even know.

And they can have fun with it and then they want to do it again."

(why my son likes giving science kits as birthday presents)

— Age 7½

ONE OF MY favorite ways to share science with friends is through the gifting of experiences. Experiences are multi-layered presents. There is the fun of opening the present, the excitement of having the experience, and then the joy of reflecting on the memories of that experience. This process may lead to deepening interests and other points of inspiration.

I have had many conversations with parents who tell me they would love to do more science at home, but that it essentially feels like too much work. There's the finding of an activity, the gathering of materials, learning the basics behind it, facilitating the activity, and the dreaded cleaning up. I really do get it. And this is why I love giving science experiments in a box as birthday presents. It removes some of these obstacles and takes parents and children straight into the quality-time-together part.

One example of a birthday kit that I often put together includes a plastic tote filled with baking soda, vinegar, balloons, a plastic funnel, a plastic spoon, empty plastic water bottles, and directions for making blow-up balloons that put a twist on the classic volcano experiment. I also add kid goggles, a paper apron for safety and extra flair, and a bendy figure to serve as the birthday guy—excited to have a balloon blown up for him.

The directions involve pouring vinegar into a plastic bottle, funneling baking soda into an uninflated balloon, placing the balloon mouth on the bottle mouth *without allowing the baking soda to fall into the bottle*, counting backward from ten to one, dumping the baking soda from the balloon into the bottle of vinegar, and then watching as the balloon blows up, and your child lights up. (Note: The experiment still works if you don't count backward from ten to one. You could also yodel for ten seconds, rearrange your silverware, or recite the Pledge of Allegiance.)

This experiment also works great as an activity during a birthday party. Sadly enough, I remember once purchasing and guzzling waters at the science studio I was managing, so that I could have the bottles in time to facilitate the experiment. Sometimes drinking on the job is simply what it takes to be successful in science education.

Chart Your Course

IT can be easier to prepare a kit for someone else than it is to do for yourself (I find making salad to be like this, as well). Do you have a child's birthday coming up? Consider looking for an interesting experiment online. Print out the directions, gather and prep the materials (e.g., cut the string, count out the straws), and place them in a bin, tub, box, or bag. Then sit back and plan on being a big hit at the next party.

SCIENCE BY THE KIT

"Mom, with gum, do I swallow
the sweet flavor that comes off of it?"
(me successfully having kept gum at bay)

— Age 6

I HAVE SEVERAL science-based kits on my son's top shelf that have been given to him as birthday and holiday gifts. I am saving them for a rainy day, or for when I have an energy burst to read the directions or an absurdly high surge of patience (still waiting for the latter).

I do this for a living, and I experience the intimidation factor with some of these kits that have varying expectations around your time, intellect, and energy. Having pushed myself past these barriers at various times, I can tell you that it is often very worthwhile. I typically end up building my own self-eSTEAM as much as, if not more than (at times), my child does.

The kits range in topics—from making gum and candy to soda science to robots that draw. One helpful tip is that many packages make it easy to take the materials out and put them back with little to no visible change or harm to the packaging. It may be useful to explore the materials and directions solo before working together with your child. Pouring yourself a cup of tea and getting a handle on the activities after your child has gone to bed is not cheating—it's planning.

While I am an advocate of learning together, I'm also a fan of parents staying sane and families having positive experiences with science. I have had that moment one or a million times when I was trying to read the directions of a kit and little hands were grabbing all the pieces and knocking them on the floor. It doesn't always work out well.

On the contrary, I have also watched an adult build something while the child stared at the ceiling and got next to nothing out of the experience. My main point is to assess the challenge at hand. Consider the available time, energy, patience, and interest levels of all involved, including the all-important readiness factor, and decide what type of recon, if any, might be helpful.

TEST out one of these kits or use *Chart Your Course* them as inspiration to make your own. It is likely that you have one of these toys in a box on the shelf, unopened or unpursued. Remember that it's OK to feel your way through the dark and just give it a try. If it's not going well, there may be a resource on the toy company's website or demos of other children or families using it on You-Tube. It can also happen over several sittings, so just open the can of worms (i.e., the box) and get started.

N

GIFTS THAT KEEP ON GIVING

(on this half birthday, he wants to know...)
"Do I talk differently?
I've gotten wiser."

—Age 5 ½

IN ADDITION TO creating experiment kits as presents, the following are other science-rich ideas that I have used for gift-giving:

- A microscope with treasures collected from nature and/or around the house (explore standard and digital microscopes)
- Tickets or a membership to a science-based place (e.g., the local science museum, science center, or fossil dig site)
- Gift certificate for a science-based camp, workshop, or other program
- Lab coat embroidered with the child's name
- Tools to turn cardboard and other recyclables into treasures and structures (e.g., plastic clips and hinges, straw connectors)
- A set of homemade (sanded) wooden blocks
- Outdoor adventure coupons ("This certificate entitles you to one hike, insect hunt, and picnic at a secret spot in the woods!")
- Scientific room makeover (e.g., astronomy theme, complete with glow-in-the-dark stars, astro blanket, and constellation projector)
- Any structure-building toys with a certificate to invite two friends over to take over the living room for a day and build a giant city
- Date with a scientist (connect with an engineer or other STEM professional in your community and set up an opportunity for an older child to shadow)
- Materials to make your own instruments, along with a world music playlist
- Indoor paleontology dig site (fill a tub or baby pool with rice or other material and bury "fossils" or animal models, then make an "identification key" by taking photos of the buried objects)
- Set up an aquarium or terrarium and then give a small gift certificate for obtaining the plants and fish. (Check that you are only supporting responsible collecting practices.)
- Adventure pack (backpack, binoculars, magnifying glass, field guides, snacks, and of course—a compass!)

- Certificate for a creepy crawly date night (gummy snake candy, a bug game, and insect-themed movie)
- A laboratory or tinkering studio set up in the basement or other nook—complete with a cool sign (e.g., "Enter Mia's Laboratory at Your Own Risk!") and bins filled with materials like CDs, string, magnets, recyclables, and alligator clips

Chart Your Course

CHOOSE one of these and make a plan. We all have good intentions about ideas we come across. Remember that cool artsy table you saw at the festival and said, "Oh, I can totally make that." Well, did you? (No? OK good, because it is not advisable to copy other artists. It is, however, advisable to get inspired and put that inspiration into action.) Unless we commit to small action steps, good intentions stay just that.

Chapter Eighteen

Setting Sail

*(asking my son if he had any advice
for the parents reading "our" book)*
*"Build and create your mind.
And make new discoveries."*

—Age 5

When you consider any skill set with which you feel proficient, there are likely hundreds of hours of practice behind it. And there are very likely many layers and dimensions to it. Facilitating science learning is no exception. It requires an investment in resources — namely practice and time.

Every time I facilitate a weeklong science program, I have the same feeling on the last day. I always hope that, like the caterpillar, the end of the week is the beginning of a new stage for each child.

I hope that they will go home and observe the tree on their street more closely, or see new possibilities for their cereal boxes and yogurt containers. I hope they will be inspired to want to fix their toys and find new uses for them. I hope they will leave with more questions than when they arrived. Above all, I hope they will feel empowered to pursue their curiosities, taking full advantage of the science resources available to them.

THE STRUGGLE IS PART OF THE ADVENTURE

"It's like OK to struggle, but just try your hardest.

*Because the only way you can do
it is trying your hardest."*

—Age 7

AS YOU HELP your child extend their experiences, be kind to and patient with yourself. It is very likely that the individuals you see as the experts around you are struggling to figure out the best ways to share science as well. It is an ongoing and ever-evolving process.

I was involved in a museum project to design content for mobile app tours that allow science museum visitors to remotely trek through galleries under certain themes and pathways. I find this work rich and gratifying, as it allows for both creative and critical thinking in the design process.

I also find it challenging from the standpoint of being required to put on the science generalist hat—needing to know a little about everything. It's a common hat to wear when designing programs or exhibits for informal learning situations. This week, the theme is dinosaurs, the week after that it is astronomy, and after that, a deep dive into biodiversity. Each topic is a slippery slope of fascinating content, ever-changing facts and figures, and thousands of exceptions to every rule.

It doesn't matter how many classes I take, podcasts I listen to, or behind-the-scenes tours I go on. I know that I will never scratch the surface of being a "science expert." This statement used to reflect a lack of science confidence for me. Now, it reflects an empowered enthusiasm about my potential for growth and lifelong learning.

When I tackle a science challenge, such as designing an app or a new curriculum, I obsess on the authenticity and accuracy of the information I'm assembling. I regularly need to make a deep, dark, lonely dive into an information abyss to crank out something useful that spares others of the journey I had to take to understand it. My grueling process is often represented in one fool-proof sentence on a label next to an artifact, or a question on a trivia quiz, mocking me with its simplicity. And yet, I enthusiastically go back for more. Pilot testing an app, a tour, or a program I have designed is its own incredible reward.

As I was writing energy-related questions for this one particular museum audio tour, I was struggling to capture some of the specifics involved in using the Niagara River to generate hydroelectricity, as well as the overall layout and relationship between Lake Erie and Lake Ontario. My confusion led me (and my family in tow) to the New York Power Authority's Niagara Power Vista, with a fantastic view of the Niagara gorge.

I spent the evening following our visit wrestling with the language I wanted to use in one trivia question before finally arriving at wording I felt good about. I'm sure no one thought twice about what was behind that question as they viewed it on their smartphone. They most likely selected answer "C" and moved on to the next question. I, however, will continue to think about the experience I had with my family, the majestic views from the observation deck, and the deeper understanding I have of the mighty Niagara.

The process that I went through, and that I go through on a regular basis, is similar to that of engineers. Behind so many of the simple buttons that we press every day are likely thousands of hours of tinkering, testing, failing, re-soldering, and tweaking to arrive at an elegant solution. Most of our children (and most of us adults, for that matter) have used a computer, but have never seen the inner workings. A well-designed piece of technology allows the user to complete their task without having to think about the parts and pieces behind it. Nonetheless, we should all be aware that there *is* a process. And it can be fascinating to discover the behind-the-scenes details.

As you identify some of the science questions that arise for your family, consider the adventures you might go on to seek the answers. While I could have searched the internet a little more or watched a YouTube video (or ten) to find my missing information, it was much more impactful to look at dioramas and speak to individuals who spend their days researching and interpreting this area, all while taking in the breathtaking view.

> *Chart Your Course*
>
> MANY science museums, science centers, aquariums, and zoos have visit enhancement opportunities. Consider renting an audio guide or testing out another form of a guided tour. Keep an eye out for other interactive tech opportunities.

GETTING STARTED

"I don't have to pee.
This is just a special kick that I do."
(#everyparentknows)

—Age 3

AS YOU ASSIMILATE your thoughts about integrating more science learning into everyday family life, consider some of the following questions:

- What are some of your local science-based resources?
- Who are the people you know, or would like to know, who have content knowledge and a passion for science?
- What are some of your child's natural interests that lend themselves well to science learning?
- What are *you* curious about and what do *you* wonder about?
- What thoughts, feelings, opinions, and attitudes about science has your child already formed?
- What are your family's favorite ways to play? Are there opportunities to weave in science?
- How does your family spend time together? Do you have a family movie night? If so, might you consider watching a science-based documentary or film together and then talking about it? (Maybe make science-themed cookies for an extra twist!)
- Have you made a field trip bucket list? Where are places you might visit to find out more about science content? Science careers? Scientific thinking?
- Do you know other families that might have more science in their everyday lives that can spend time sharing ideas they naturally integrate? Is there a family you might inspire?
- Might you have a thirty-days-of-science marathon, where you tinker, investigate, or experiment for ten to fifteen minutes a day and see what comes of it?

Just like kicking off a new workout or exercise routine, to get started, you must simply elect to get started. It sounds simple enough, but we all know it can be challenging to make the first move. Of course, when you really think about it, there is no first move in this scenario, as you have already been facilitating science learning, even if just by default. There is only one way to go on this elevator, and it is up.

Have fun exploring options. Follow your child's interests, and your own. Be open, vulnerable, and patient with the process. Use an experimental approach that models the true spirit of science as you test out the variables and possibilities. Remember that this is not a track meet — there are no trophies at the end. There are, however, infinite rewards along the way.

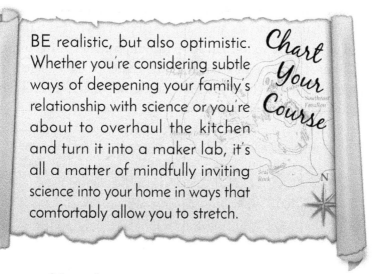

BE realistic, but also optimistic. *Chart Your Course* Whether you're considering subtle ways of deepening your family's relationship with science or you're about to overhaul the kitchen and turn it into a maker lab, it's all a matter of mindfully inviting science into your home in ways that comfortably allow you to stretch.

TRACKING YOUR JOURNEY

"Grammy, put your glasses on so I can see you."

—Age 3

CAN YOU THINK back on a notebook, folder, sketch pad, or diary from your childhood that you used to record your words, designs, pictures, and ideas? What did scribbling your thoughts into it make you feel? What do you use now, as an adult?

I believe I will always have the need to put pen to paper. I can think back on so many journals and notebooks that had special meaning to me at various points of my life. My earliest journaling took place in a pink and powder blue diary during the second grade. Each page started the same way: "Dear diary, today was a great day." Every single day of second grade was apparently "great!" (This diary doubled as a nutrition log, as I tallied how many evenings we had pizza and chicken wings—a true Buffalo, NY childhood.)

I also have an oversized notebook from a different part of my life, with stitch binding and thin, lined paper, which I purchased from a glass case in a small shop in Bali, Indonesia. Each time I pick it up, I'm brought straight to the center of the village where I purchased it. All these years later, the notebook cover still seems to have a faint smell of incense.

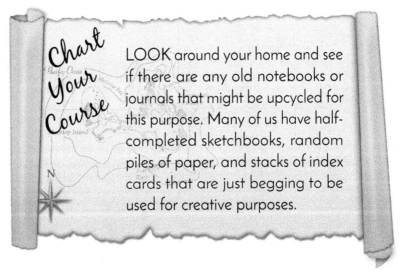

Chart Your Course

LOOK around your home and see if there are any old notebooks or journals that might be upcycled for this purpose. Many of us have half-completed sketchbooks, random piles of paper, and stacks of index cards that are just begging to be used for creative purposes.

Consider keeping a notebook for your family's science adventures. It can be used in a variety of ways, from recording data to sketching ideas to pasting in photos—it's yours to decide. Not only will this make an excellent memory book, but it will also help your child build skills in writing, sketching, self-expression, documentation, and reflection.

I also urge you to explore the possibilities that exist for designing your own journal or journal cover. There are online tutorials and public workshops to help you through the process. Selecting the paper and images for the front cover of your notebook can be a fun, artistic endeavor. It is a fabulous STEAM-based activity (hello, Arts integration!) and an excellent way to have older children work with younger ones. If you want to take it a step further, you can even make the paper for the journal yourself. (Pro tip: do not use your grandmother's old-fashioned milkshake blender that is/was a family heirloom.)

FORMAL AND INFORMAL LEARNING

(reporting out on his first day of kindergarten)

"It was a million fun."

(he asked me if he had...)

"...infinity courage and beyond."

—Age 5

I MUST REITERATE that Free-Choice Learning can take place in any setting, including formal education spaces. While museum-type settings lend themselves more to learners pursuing their interests in a very personalized manner, many classrooms around the country integrate and experiment with ways that children can shape their own learning pathways.

We see moments of this through inquiry-based, Project-Based Learning and Problem-Based Learning that has made its way into many classrooms. These approaches have the shared aim of empowering the learner to build their self-esteem and skills by tapping into their internal motivation, interests, problem-solving capabilities, and curiosities.

Schools can be creative and inspiring places for science learning. I have seen many classrooms, school gardens, laboratories, resource centers, and maker spaces that serve as vibrant learning environments for engaging with science.

Museum and school partnerships are also critical to student success in the twenty-first century. The work that has been conducted by the Center for Informal Learning in Schools, an NSF-funded partnership between the Exploratorium in San Francisco and King's College, London, is a shining example of how museums and formal education institutions can partner to engage and affect children in their lives in and out of school.

Chart Your Course

AFTER finding out a little more about your school's vision for science learning, consider specific ways of helping bring that vision to life or enhance it. Some specific ideas for this include science-themed activities at school family nights, science fairs, outreach-based science programs visiting your child's school, afterschool and summer science camps and programs, coordinating community scientists for career shadowing opportunities, and preparing hands-on activities for class.

Enrichment Programs

"I don't really use my imagination.
My brain just tells my hands what to
do, and I build something."

— Age 6

MANY OUT-OF-SCHOOL TIME programs exist for your child to deepen their relationship with science. Giving them the opportunity to be a part of these types of programs empowers their interests and allows them to build community with other children who may have similar interests. These clubs often allow children who may not work together during the school day to socialize while learning.

Enrichment programs also give families who choose to home-school, unschool, or use other methodologies access to resources

Chart Your Course

WHILE there are many clubs and programs your child can partake in for enrichment, there are also informal ways of accomplishing this. You can work with other parents to form an activity co-op and schedule playdates (e.g., the first Sunday of the month) where you rotate providing a special activity for the children (it could even be just for a small part of the playtime).

and platforms for social learning experiences. I have stayed in close touch with many homeschool families whose children engaged in science programs with me when they were younger. These learning-based relationships are powerful for the instructor and the participants.

In addition, the lens of science serves as an excellent platform for developing skills in other subjects and areas, such as reading, writing, and research. The exciting appeal, hook, and magnetism of science activities provide a gateway to enriched learning.

PLANNING FOR SPONTANEITY

(me: pulls random emergency
object out of backpack)

*"That's right, Mommy,
'cause you're always impaired."*

(yeah, something like that)

— Age 3½

WHILE I AM clearly a fan of engaging in enrichment activities, I am equally a fan of unstructured downtime. I enjoy leaving a little space for the muses to sneak in, for incubation to occur, and to invite the best creativity primer—boredom.

Unstructured time also allows for spontaneity. I love to set out with no plans and see where life takes me. One evening, while my son and I were waiting for my husband to finish a work trip and meet up with us, we headed out along Embarcadero (the eastern waterfront and roadway of the Port of San Francisco, along the Bay). During our stroll, we came upon an amazing, lit-up sculpture in front of the Exploratorium. I didn't recognize its structure at first glance (though I am a little disappointed in myself for that).

The sculpture was of a buckyball — a sphere-shaped fullerene molecule, with the formula C_{60}, that was discovered in the mid-1980s.[33] The particle was named after architect Buckminster Fuller, paying homage to his infamous geodesic domes. Buckyballs, which comprise carbon atoms arranged in a cage-like structure with a soccer ball pattern of pentagons and hexagons, naturally occur in interstellar dust and geological formations. There are a wide variety of uses being explored for the potential of buckyballs, including their role in composites to strengthen the material and modes of transportation for cancer-fighting drugs.

A man was programming the changing lights on the sculpture as we approached. We stopped to watch the lights and, lo and behold, it was the artist of the sculpture himself (called Leo) working on its programming. Leo was happy to allow us to enter the gate to chat with him and inspect the sculpture more closely. I felt like we'd stumbled upon Richard Burton backstage as he was practicing his lines for Camelot. Leo pointed out the aluminum center of his sculpture and explained the overall structure. My mind went back to a children's program I had designed, where the kids went home with plastic balls and sticks they could put together to make buckyball models.

In the same spirit as Buckminster Fuller, Leo seemed happy that we were so fond of his creation. We came to learn that he had another light-based installation just down the street from where we were living at the time in Buffalo.

The reflection of the ball-shaped structure in the water below was captivating with its bioluminescent appearance. My son told Leo that his sculpture was the best he had ever seen. For me, this experience validated the way that life seems to unfold and present magical opportunities when we don't have a set agenda and we keep open to its offerings. I also find that the more our science radar is up, the more likely we are to take advantage of these types of moments.

WHEN was the last time you set out to a new city, area, or neighborhood simply to explore and spend time together? We schedule so many of our outings around concrete plans that it can be very rewarding to simply keep open.

SENSE OF PLACE

(when asked what makes California great...)

"It has lots of resources."

(I'm sure the visitor's bureau would like this answer)

– Age 6 ½

THE TRIP TO Maui that I mentioned in chapter 11, where we hiked to my favorite waterfall, prompted a long-contemplated move to California. California seemed to be a happy medium between Buffalo and Maui—access to two places near and dear to my heart and located next to the Pacific Ocean. Based on a combination of proximities (to my housemates from Maui who now live in California with their families, to the redwoods, to the Pacific, and to the multicultural offerings of San Francisco city life) as well as our desire for a family-oriented town, we chose the North Bay town of Petaluma as our launch pad.

I often gauge how I feel about a town based on its cafés and shops. And when we first visited Petaluma, I fell for Copperfield's bookstore. While there, we came across the book *Neighborhood Sharks: Hunting with the Great Whites of California's Farallon Islands* in the children's section.

I was particularly impressed with the realistic illustrations. When I read the inside sleeve of the book, I learned that the illustrator, Katherine Roy, traveled to the Farallon Islands several times, in order to capture the essence and the details of the Great Whites that return to the Farallones (Spanish for "sea cliffs") each September.

I bought this book online when we were still in Buffalo, preparing for our move to Petaluma. Every time I was scared to leap into the next phase of our life, I would look at the book as a symbol of living a life of calculated risk-taking, and I would muster up some mojo to keep moving forward. I didn't realize how much this overall process would take my breath away—sometimes making space in my chest for the sadness that naturally comes with change, other times from exhaling in relief that the leap was just as worthwhile as it seemed in my imagination.

Two months after our move, the day finally arrived to see the chalky brown illustrations of the Farallones come to life from the pages of the shark book. The trip began at 8 a.m., and by 8:37 a.m., my husband was giving me the "why did I agree to this?" look. The two o'clock dock return was a long way away. As we traversed the fifty-eight-degree Pacific Ocean, I was in my full glory. Two-thirds of the boat—including my husband and son—did not seem to share my sentiments as we navigated the chop and swells. I made small talk with another passenger and used, "I think my family hates me" as my conversation starter.

It takes two and a half hours to get to the Farallones from San Francisco—quite the commitment. Jacques Cousteau referred to these islands as the Blue Serengeti of the California Coast. The waters of the Greater Farallones support a diverse array of life, including many threatened and endangered species.

I was happy to have brought a couple of new items in my backpack for my son, in order to throw some novelty into the long ride out. The travel dry-erase board was a big win, as well as the pack of clay. I ripped a large piece of clay off one of the sticks and gave it to a woman who subtly mentioned she was terrified. She was very grateful and used it throughout the entire expedition. She also mentioned that she was comforted by people in vests and hats (yep, that was us) because she said it looked like we knew what we were doing. (I see where she's coming from on this one.)

When we were approximately seven miles off the coast of the Farallones, we had a magnificent viewing of two separate humpback whales, one of which was repeatedly head lunging and breaching. It was National Geographic-style, and I don't have one single picture for posterity. The waves and spray were so heavy on the ride that I left my phone in the cabin. My husband was on "keep your eyes on the horizon" duty near the back of the boat, and I was primarily focused on keeping our kid from going overboard. While a part of me is disappointed that I couldn't capture the moment, I have to say that it was enjoyable to focus on having the experience versus documenting it. (Plus, I did return to shore with our child, so mission accomplished.)

As we approached the Farallones, we watched three sea lions swimming through the water, and I was amazed at how much they looked like dolphins as they surfaced and resubmerged. I realized that I'd primarily seen them basking on docks and cliffs and piers, and rarely swimming at their top speed in their natural habitat. We also saw gulls, cormorants, pelicans, terns, murres, and shearwaters. I thought about the Great White sharks (*Carcharodon carcharias*) that were likely lurking around the nearby rocky shores. I was hoping to get a glimpse of one, but the sea lions, I'm sure, were hoping otherwise.

Going on this adventure strengthened my sense of place in California. It gave me the context that I needed to allow myself to more fully relax into my new ecosystem (yes, it is highly odd that sharks make me relax). As we explore our surroundings and our relationship with our environment, we have the opportunity to see where we fit in, what roles we might play, and how we might be inspired and shaped by the world around us.

WHAT opportunities exist that *Chart* might help you connect more *Your* deeply with the treasures of the *Course* place where you live? Are there sites you have always meant to visit? Is there a town historian you have always meant to speak to? Is there an old growth forest within driving range? There are many opportunities to reinvigorate ourselves and our passion for the place we live. Gaining new insights is one sure way to do so.

MEET RAHWA

WHEN I THINK of people in my life who inspire me to facilitate science learning for reasons that go beyond the fact that I immensely enjoy it, I think of my friend Rahwa. She is the executive director of a community organization fighting to make affordable housing, as well as a transition to clean energy, a reality. Here are her thoughts on why we need to be thinking about science and the environment:

"We are made of the earth, not just part of the earth. I am a human being first and foremost. I am also a mother, a black woman, Eritrean—a child of mother Africa, and a social justice activist.

When we are born, I believe that we are all scientists. We are all connected and part of the earth. My work as a community activist—the beautiful struggle—strongly equates to the lack of balance with mother nature, with each other, with the natural world.

So many of the solutions to the challenges we face lie in bringing back balance. The move away from our extractive practices, extractive of people and planet, is the move back toward our natural state of being… back to our humanity.

Mother nature will provide for all of our essential needs—food, shelter, beauty, and imagination. But we have to give back to her too. We must earn our keep in the home she provides by minimizing and putting back what we take in some form. It is a reciprocal relationship based on respect, mutual benefit, and love.

The answers to the challenges facing the planet and its people lie within each of us. They reflect a reconciliation, an equalization, and a balance of all things that are natural—the ebb and flow between natural, organic beings.

PUTTING IT ALL TOGETHER

· ·

(sitting across from me putting
a building set together)

"I did what I couldn't."

(so, get out there, folks, and do what you couldn't!)

— Age 6 ½

· ·

IT IS IN the layering of science experiences and connection-making that genuine and deep science learning takes place. It's not enough for our children to have science experiences only at home or only at school. The power is in the collective value of all of their experiences combined.

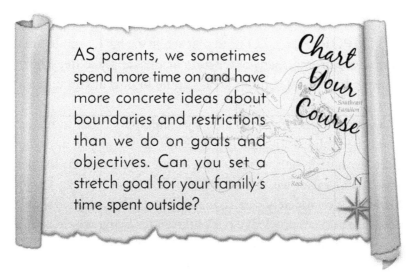

AS parents, we sometimes spend more time on and have more concrete ideas about boundaries and restrictions than we do on goals and objectives. Can you set a stretch goal for your family's time spent outside?

Chart Your Course

Sometimes the addition of layers is organic, while at other times it may be more intentional. You cannot go wrong in your endeavors to explore ways of weaving science into your family life. There are no accidental red buttons to hit.

Be a humble co-investigator alongside your child and see and explore the world through their eyes. We have touched on many ways of how you might go about this, but getting outside in the natural world should be at the very top of this list. There is a growing body of research that comes to the same conclusion: children need to spend time in nature in order to support their healthy development and well-being. (Ironically enough, there are many designers and programmers currently working on digital media and video games whose objective is to get kids back outside.)

BEYOND SCIENCE

. . . .

(finds a quarter, hands it to café cashier, and says,)

"Here's a safety tip."

— Age 4 ½

. . . .

IT'S IMPORTANT TO note that while we have been focused on science learning, many other content areas apply to free-choice learning. In fact, all content areas can be looked at through this lens.

You might take some of these tips and apply them to history or another subject area. Remember, it's all about you and your child having the opportunity to follow your natural curiosities. This doesn't mean we, as parents, should just sit back and enjoy the ride in a completely passive manner (*as if*). It means we should recognize and acknowledge our children for being whole people with natural interests and curiosities. It's about understanding the light inside of them and bringing them to caves where they can use that light to illuminate some of their own discoveries.

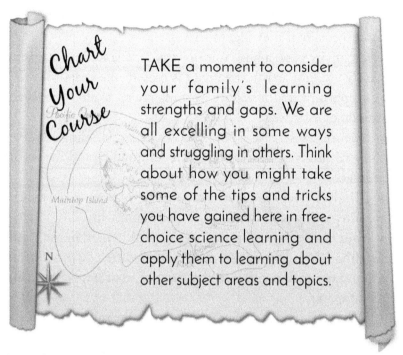

Chart Your Course

TAKE a moment to consider your family's learning strengths and gaps. We are all excelling in some ways and struggling in others. Think about how you might take some of the tips and tricks you have gained here in free-choice science learning and apply them to learning about other subject areas and topics.

IN A (PEANUT-FREE) NUTSHELL

"Mama, you don't need to give me Benadryl,

because it's just called the Peanuts movie."

(#sunbutterfamily)

— Age 5

THERE ARE A few points I'm desperate for you to have taken away from our time together:

- This is within your reach. *Really.*
- Science, in its purest and truest form, is accessible — to every person, not just an elite group that knows a lot of fancy words

and has million-dollar microscopes (though they're invited, too, especially if they like to share).

• Creativity plays a huge role in weaving science into everyday family life, and artistic creativity is merely one face of it.

• Opportunities for science learning are all around you, every minute of every day.

• Science can serve as a powerful vehicle for building relationships within your own family, your community, and the world at large.

• Mindset, language, conversation, and play are rocket ships for integrating science into your daily family life.

• Your immediate surroundings (your kitchen, home, yard, neighborhood...) make the perfect laboratories; further extend, expand upon, and enhance the learning that happens within those spaces.

• We can be (and *are*, whether we choose the role or not) facilitators of learning of all subject areas for our children, regardless of our attitudes, knowledge, and experiences with each of them.

• There are science-oriented places pining for you to go to and use them. They want to share their passion, wonder, resources, and mission with you. They simply need you to show up, sign up, or look up.

• Be open. Be vulnerable. Be flexible. Be curious. And be tolerant of risk-taking, ambiguity, failure, and maybe even some (brace yourself) *mental* and *physical* messiness.

AN INVITATION

"*Every day, my rocketship that loves you,*
goes even farther."

— Age 5 ½

THANK YOU FOR allowing me to share both my professional and family-based science learning journey with you. It has simultaneously been a public and a private path for me and, as you see by now, has shaped my daily life.

I don't have any idea where any of this is leading. But there is one thing I know for certain—I am having a wonderful time exploring life and investigating the world in a whole new way with my child. I also know we have only just begun to scratch the surface of our science learning adventures. I'm excited to dig deeper and go further in this pursuit, and to continue to build a community around de-shaming the quest for gaining science knowledge. I hope you feel validated and empowered to serve as your child's facilitator of science learning, no matter where your starting place lies; and that you embrace this challenge with enthusiasm.

I believe that unless we feel that science is something we have access to—something that is within our reach—we will see it as "the other." And at this important moment in time, we need to see it *in* and *for* and *as* each other.

I propose that we do more than love our kids to the moon and back. Let's love them deep into outer space and far below the ocean surface by helping them see and feel and know what is possible.

Remember the main requirement to be a scientist that was highlighted by Jacques Cousteau? It was curiosity. My family and I invite you to join us in pursuing your curiosity by taking advantage of the incredible opportunity to use...

WONDER AS YOUR COMPASS.

NOTES

Introduction

1. Alison Gopnik, "What Kids Need Most Isn't Parenting—It's Parents." Big Think video, 6:10, September 2016, https://bigthink.com/videos/alison-gopnik-on-parenting-and-what-kids-need-most.

2. Brené Brown, *Daring Greatly: How the Courage to Be Vulnerable Transforms the Way We Live, Love, Parent, and Lead* (New York: Penguin Random House, 2015), 15.

3. Jess M. Brallier, *Who Was Albert Einstein?* (New York: Grosset & Dunlap, 2002), 10.

4. Ronald W. Clark, *Einstein: The Life and Times* (New York: Avon Books, 1971), 28-29.

Chapter 1

5. John H. Falk and Lynn D. Dierking, *Learning from Museums: Visitor Experiences and the Making of Meaning* (Lanham, MD: AltaMira Press, 2000), 13.

Chapter 2

6. John H. Falk, "An Identity-Centered Approach to Understanding Museum Learning," Curator 49, no. 2, (2006), 151-66, http://thenhier.ca/en/content/falk-john-h-"-identity-centered-approach-understanding-museum-learning"-curator-2006.html.

7. Andrea Stone, "'Shark Lady' Eugenie Clark, Famed Marine Biologist, Has Died," *National Geographic*, February 25, 2015, http://

news.nationalgeographic.com/2015/02/150225-eugenie-clark-shark
-lady-marine-biologist-obituary-science/.

8. *Merriam-Webster*, s.v. "scientist (n.)," https://www.merriam
-webster.com/dictionary/scientist.

9. Scott B. Kaufman, Jerome L. Singer, and Dorothy G.
Singer, "The Need for Pretend Play in Child Development,"
Blog post in *Psychology Today*, March 6, 2012, https://www
.psychologytoday.com/us/blog/beautiful-minds/201203/the-need
-pretend-play-in-child-development#_=_.

10. Dale McCreedy and Lynn D. Dierking, *Cascading Influences:
Long-term Impacts of Informal STEM Experiences for Girls*, (Philadelphia,
PA: The Franklin Institute, March 2013), 1-44, https://www.fi.edu
/sites/default/files/cascading-influences.pdf.

11. John H. Falk, "Contextualizing Falk's Identity-Related Visitor
Motivation Model," *Visitor Studies* 14, no. 2 (2011), 141-157.

CHAPTER 3

12. Helen S. Hadani, PhD and Elizabeth Rood, EdD, "The Roots
of STEM Success: Changing Early Learning Experiences to Build
Lifelong Thinking Skills," (Sausalito, CA: *Center for Childhood Creativity*,
2018) 1, http://centerforchildhoodcreativity.org/wp-content/uploads
/sites/2/2018/02/CCC_The_Roots_of_STEM_Early_Learning.pdf.

13. "Nainoa Thompson," Interview by Jodi Wilmott, Filmed
December 11, 2013, in Honolulu, HI, *Talk Story* series video 1:12:55,
https://www.youtube.com/watch?v=7EpX8N2Ju7I.

14. Lilian G. Katz, "Distinctions Between Self-Esteem and Narcissism: Implications for Practice," (Urbana, IL: ERIC Clearinghouse
on Elementary and Early Childhood Education, 1993), 23-34, https://
files.eric.ed.gov/fulltext/ED363452.pdf.

15. Po Bronson, "How Not to Talk to Your Kids: The Inverse
Power of Praise," *New York*, August 3, 2007, http://nymag.com/news
/features/27840/.

16. Tim Brown, "Design Thinking," *Harvard Business Review*, June 2008, https://hbr.org/2008/06/design-thinking.

CHAPTER 4

17. Teresa M. Amabile, "Motivating Creativity in Organizations: On Doing What You Love and Loving What You Do," *California Management Review* 40, no.1 (Fall 1997), 40.

18. Scott B. Kaufman, "The Real Neuroscience of Creativity," Blog post in *Scientific American*, August 19, 2013, https://blogs.scientificamerican.com/beautiful-minds/the-real-neuroscience-of-creativity/.

19. Giovanni E. Corazza, "Potential Originality and Effectiveness: The Dynamic Definition of Creativity," *Creativity Research Journal* 28, no.3 (2016), 258-267, https://www.tandfonline.com/doi/full/10.1080/10400419.2016.1195627.

20. IBM, "IBM 2010 Global CEO Survey: Creativity Selected as Most Crucial Factor for Future Success," news release, May 18, 2010, https://www-03.ibm.com/press/us/en/pressrelease/31670.wss.

21. Po Bronson and Ashley Merryman, "The Creativity Crisis," Newsweek, July 10, 2010, http://www.newsweek.com/creativity-crisis-74665.

22. E. Paul Torrance and H. Tammy Safter, *Making the Creative Leap Beyond...* (Buffalo, NY: Creative Education Foundation Press, 1999), x-xi.

23. Jayme M. Cellitioci, "Utilizing Science Enrichment Programs as a Vehicle for Encouraging Meaningful Family Conversation and Creativity Skill Development," (Unpublished master's project, SUNY Buffalo State, International Center for Studies in Creativity, Buffalo, NY, 2005).

CHAPTER 5

24. Mihaly Csikszentmihalyi and Kim Hermanson, "Intrinsic Motivation in Museums: Why Does One Want to Learn?" In J. H. Falk & L. D. Dierking (eds.), *Public Institutions in Personal Learning: Establishing a Research Agenda*, (Arlington, VA: American Alliance of Museums 1995), 67-75.

25. Edward O. Wilson, "My Wish: Build the Encyclopedia of Life," Filmed March, 2007 in Monterey, CA, TED video, 22:21, https://www.ted.com/talks/e_o_wilson_on_saving_life_on_earth.

26. John H. Falk and Lynn D. Dierking, "The 95 Percent Solution: School is Not Where Most Americans Learn Most of Their Science," *American Scientist* 98, no. 6 (2010), 486-493.

27. Susan M. Keller-Mathers, "Creative Teaching," In B. A. Kerr (Ed.), *Encyclopedia of Giftedness, Creativity, and Talent*, (Thousand Oaks, CA: SAGE Publications, Inc., 2009), 197, https://books.google.com/books?id=_qPpCgAAQBAJ&pg=PA199&dq=susan+keller-mathers+encyclopedia+of+giftedness+torrance+incubation+model&hl=en&sa=X&ved=0ahUKEwi06en3zfXbAhVIR6wKHYTjAtEQ6AEIJzAA#v=onepage&q=susan%20keller-mathers%20encyclopedia%20of%20giftedness%20torrance%20incubation%20model&f=false.

CHAPTER 6

28. John D. Bransford, Ann L. Brown, and Rodney R. Cocking (eds.), "How People Learn: Brain, Mind, Experience, and School," (Washington, DC: National Academy Press, 2000), 44-45, https://www.desu.edu/sites/flagship/files/document/16/how_people_learn_book.pdf.

CHAPTER 7

29. John H. Falk and Mark D. Needham, "Measuring the Impact of a Science Center on Its Community," *Journal of Research in Science Teaching* 48, no.1 (2011), 1-12.

CHAPTER 10

30. Wallace J. Nichols, *Blue Mind: The Surprising Science That Shows How Being Near, In, On, or Under Water Can Make You Happier, Healthier, More Connected, and Better at What You Do* (New York: Little, Brown and Company, 2014).
31. World Economic Forum. "The Future of Jobs: Employment, Skills, and Workforce Strategy for the Fourth Industrial Revolution," *World Economic Forum*, January 2016, 1, http://www3.weforum.org/docs/WEF_FOJ_Executive_Summary_Jobs.pdf.

CHAPTER 13

32. National Academy of Sciences, 2013. "President Obama Stresses Importance of Science and Technology to the Nation's Future." Video filmed April 29, 2013 in Washington, DC, 23:08, https://vimeo.com/65081399.

CHAPTER 18

33. Earl Boysen and Nancy C. Muir, "What is a buckyball C60?" Nanotechnology for Dummies (2nd ed.), (Hoboken, NJ: Wiley Publishing, Inc., 2011), excerpt http://www.understandingnano.com/what-is-buckyball-c60.html.

Bibliography

Amabile, Teresa M. "Motivating Creativity in Organizations: On Doing What You Love and Loving What You Do." *California Management Review 40*, no.1, Fall 1997.

Boysen, Earl and Nancy C. Muir. "What is a buckyball C60?" Excerpted from *Nanotechnology for Dummies,* 2nd ed. Hoboken, NJ: Wiley Publishing, Inc., 2011. http://www.understandingnano.com/what -is-buckyball-c60.html.

Brallier, Jess M. *Who Was Albert Einstein?* New York: Grosset & Dunlap, 2002.

Bronson, Po. "How Not to Talk to Your Kids: The Inverse Power of Praise." *New York*. August 3, 2007. http://nymag.com/news /features/27840/.

Bronson, Po and Ashley Merryman. "The Creativity Crisis." *Newsweek.* July 10, 2010. http://www.newsweek.com/creativity-crisis-74665.

Brown, Brené. *Daring Greatly: How the Courage to Be Vulnerable Transforms the Way We Live, Love, Parent, and Lead.* New York: Random House, 2015.

Brown, Tim. "Design Thinking." *Harvard Business Review.* June 2008. https://hbr.org/2008/06/design-thinking.

Cellitioci, Jayme M. "Utilizing Science Enrichment Programs as a Vehicle for Encouraging Meaningful Family Conversation and

Creativity Skill Development." (Unpublished master's project, SUNY Buffalo State, International Center for Studies in Creativity, Buffalo, NY, 2005).

Clark, Ronald W. Einstein: *The Life and Times*. New York: Avon Books, 1971.

Corazza, Giovanni E. "Potential Originality and Effectiveness: The Dynamic Definition of Creativity." *Creativity Research Journal* 28, no. 3, (2016). https://www.tandfonline.com/doi/full/10.1080/10400419.2016.1195627.

Csikszentmihalyi, Mihaly and Kim Hermanson. "Intrinsic Motivation in Museums: Why Does One Want to Learn?" In John H. Falk and Lynn D. Dierking, eds. *Public Institutions in Personal Learning: Establishing a Research Agenda*. Arlington, VA: American Alliance of Museums (1995).

Falk, John H. "An Identity-Centered Approach to Understanding Museum Learning," *Curator* 49, no. 2, 2006. http://thenhier.ca/en/content/falk-john-h-"-identity-centered-approach-understanding-museum-learning"-curator-2006.html.

Falk, John H. "Contextualizing Falk's Identity-Related Visitor Motivation Model." *Visitor Studies* 14, no. 2 (2011).

Falk, John H. and Lynn D. Dierking. *Learning from Museums: Visitor Experiences and the Making of Meaning*. Lanham, MD: AltaMira Press, 2000.

Falk, John H. and Lynn D. Dierking. "The 95 Percent Solution: School is Not Where Most Americans Learn Most of Their Science." *American Scientist* 98, no. 6 (2010).

Falk, John H. and Mark D. Needham. "Measuring the Impact of a Science Center on Its Community." *Journal of Research in Science Teaching* 48, no. 1 (2011).

Gopnik, Alison. "What Kids Need Most Isn't Parenting—It's Parents." *Big Think* video, 6:10. September 2016. https://bigthink.com /videos/alison-gopnik-on-parenting-and-what-kids-need-most.

Hadani, Helen, S., PhD and Elizabeth Rood, EdD. "The Roots of STEM Success: Changing Early Learning Experiences to Build Lifelong Thinking Skills." Sausalito, CA: *Center for Childhood Creativity*, 2018. http://centerforchildhoodcreativity.org/wp-content /uploads/sites/2/2018/02/CCC_The_Roots_of_STEM_Early _Learning.pdf.

IBM. "IBM 2010 Global CEO Survey: Creativity Selected as Most Crucial Factor for Future Success." May 18, 2010. http://www .ibm.com/ceostudy.

Katz, Lilian G. "Distinctions Between Self-Esteem and Narcissism: Implications for Practice." Urbana, IL: ERIC Clearinghouse on Elementary and Early Childhood Education, 1993. https://files .eric.ed.gov/fulltext/ED363452.pdf.

Kaufman, Scott B., Jerome L. Singer, and Dorothy G. Singer. "The Need for Pretend Play in Child Development." Blog post in *Psychology Today*. March 6, 2012. https://www .psychologytoday.com/us/blog/beautiful-minds/201203 /the-need-pretend-play-in-child-development#_=_.

Kaufman, Scott B. "The Real Neuroscience of Creativity." Blog post in *Scientific American*. August 19, 2013. https://blogs.scientificamerican .com/beautiful-minds/the-real-neuroscience-of-creativity/.

Keller-Mathers, Susan M. "Creative Teaching" In B. A. Kerr (Ed.), *Encyclopedia of Giftedness, Creativity, and Talent.* Thousand Oaks, CA: SAGE Publications, Inc. (2009). https://books.google.com /books?id=_qPpCgAAQBAJ&pg=PA199&dq=susan+keller -mathers+encyclopedia+of+giftedness+torrance+incubation +model&hl=en&sa=X&ved=0ahUKEwi06en3zfXbAhVIR6 wKHYTjAtEQ6AEIJzAA#v=onepage&q=susan%20keller -mathers%20encyclopedia%20of%20giftedness%20torrance%20 incubation%20model&f=false.

McCreedy, Dale and Lynn D. Dierking. *Cascading Influences: Long-term Impacts of Informal STEM Experiences for Girls.* Philadelphia, PA: The Franklin Institute, March 2013. https://www.fi.edu/sites /default/files/cascading-influences.pdf.

National Research Council. 2000. *How People Learn: Brain, Mind, Experience, and School: Expanded Edition.* Washington, DC: The National Academies Press. https://doi.org/10.17226/9853.

Nichols, Wallace J. *Blue Mind: The Surprising Science That Shows How Being Near, In, On, or Under Water Can Make You Happier, Healthier, More Connected, and Better at What You Do.* New York, NY: Little, Brown and Company, 2014.

Obama, Barack H. "President Obama Stresses Importance of Science and Technology to the Nation's Future." Filmed April 29, 2013, in Washington, DC. National Academies video, 23:08. Remarks at 18:40. https://vimeo.com/65081399.

Stone, Andrea. "'Shark Lady' Eugenie Clark, Famed Marine Biologist, Has Died." *National Geographic*, February 25, 2015. http://news .nationalgeographic.com/2015/02/150225-eugenie-clark-shark -lady-marine-biologist-obituary-science/.

Thompson, Nainoa. "Nainoa Thompson – Talk Story [Full Video]." Video filmed December 11, 2013 in Honolulu, HI. "Talk Story" series. 1:12:55. https://www.youtube.co/watch?v=7EpX8N2Ju7I

Torrance, E. Paul and H. Tammy Safter. *Making the Creative Leap Beyond...* Buffalo, NY: Creative Education Foundation Press, 1999.

Wilson, Edward O. "My Wish: Build the Encyclopedia of Life." Filmed March 2007 in Monterey, CA. TED video, 22:21. https://www.ted.com/talks/e_o_wilson_on_saving_life_on_earth.

World Economic Forum. "The Future of Jobs: Employment, Skills, and Workforce Strategy for the Fourth Industrial Revolution." *World Economic Forum.* January 2016. http://www3.weforum.org/docs/WEF_FOJ_Executive_Summary_Jobs.pdf.

Thank You For Reading!

Please leave a helpful review on
Amazon letting me know what
you thought of the book.

Also, I treasure feedback and need your
input to make future editions stronger.

We are all learning and growing,
so please drop me a line at
info@jaymecellitioci.com if you see anything
that needs editing, updating, or attention.

THANK YOU SO MUCH

About the Author

JAYME CELLITIOCI, MS, a native of Buffalo, NY, lives with her husband and son in Northern California for easy access to the ocean, redwoods, and a dynamic mix of city and country life. She is a Creativity and Innovation Strategist for a national nonprofit organization and is dedicated to helping children and adults harness the power of STEAM (Science, Technology, Engineering, the Arts, and Mathematics) in their everyday lives.

An extra special thank you to my mother,
AnnMarie, for always encouraging
me to chart my own course.

CPSIA information can be obtained
at www.ICGtesting.com
Printed in the USA
FFHW01n1309280918
48620954-52565FF

9 780999 745908